COUNTDOWN

American Jews and God's Plan for Redemption

Rabbi Elie Mischel

Israel365

For sales inquiries, contact store@israel365.com

Cover by Yehudit Weingarten

ISBN: 979-8-9884403-5-2 (hardcover)

ISBN: 979-8-9884403-2-1 (paperback)

First Edition 2026

www.israel365.com

For Noa and Modi Kiel

who showed me, long before I understood it, what it means to give your life to the Jewish people.

Contents

Preface

On a Shabbat morning in late winter of 2026, Jews across Israel were reading God's command to destroy Amalek when Israeli Air Force jets crossed into Iranian airspace. By the time the morning prayers were over, Ayatollah Khamenei was dead. Days before Purim—the holiday celebrating the salvation of Jews in ancient Persia and the downfall of Haman—the modern Jewish state killed a modern Haman and launched a war to bring down the most viciously antisemitic regime on earth.

But at the very moment when Israelis are reliving the bumpy but glorious ending of the Book of Esther, American Jews are living its frightening beginning: the comfortable exile that is proving far more precarious than it seemed, as modern Hamans find their way into the mainstream of American life.

We are living in biblical times—and not in the way people mean when they toss that phrase around to add drama to a news cycle.

Rabbi Yehuda Leon Ashkenazi, perhaps the most innovative biblical scholar of the twentieth century, argued that the Hebrew Bible is not only a collection of inspiring stories about remarkable individuals, nor the historical foundation story of the Jewish people, nor a sourcebook of moral lessons. It is something far more radical than any of that.

As Rabbi Ashkenazi wrote, those who reduce the Torah to ethical instruction "completely ignore the prophetic dimension of the Torah—a dimension that is expressed precisely in the stories of the Patriarchs. The Torah is, first and foremost, a revelation of the wisdom connected to the identity of Israel and to what will happen to it over the course of Jewish history."[1]

The Torah is the spiritual DNA of the people of Israel—the key to our identity, who we are and why we exist. It is also our blueprint: the map of our entire history, from Abraham to the end of days, told in advance. Esau and Laban and Haman are not colorful ancient villains. They represent distinct types of enemies and rivals—each with his own motivation, ideology, and method. Each of them, in his own way, forces the Jewish people to become who we are meant to be. The Torah describes them in precise detail so that we will understand them, and know how to respond, when they appear again and again throughout our history.

In exile, scattered across the world and living as a minority under the rule of others, most of the Torah became remote from daily life. The stories were still studied, but what practical meaning did the tale of David slaying Goliath hold for a Jew in a Ukrainian shtetl who needed to keep his head down, pay his taxes, and avoid the attention of the local nobleman? Many of the laws were even more disconnected: the elaborate Temple service, the rules of war, the laws governing kings and courts and international relations—none of it was applicable or had any bearing on how a Jew actually lived in exile.

And so we learned to read the Bible differently. Our sages mined it for personal guidance, ethical instruction, and hidden spiritual meaning—readings that sustained Jewish life through two thousand years in the diaspora. For that we owe them an enormous debt. But this left us, as Rabbi Ashkenazi never tired of saying, partially blind. We lost the ability to read the Torah as God intended: as prophecy disguised as history, as the map of a nation's entire journey told in advance, and most importantly, as the key to understanding who we are and what is happening to us right now.

Rabbi Ashkenazi never let his students forget the cost of this blindness. "In the previous generation, the generation of the Holocaust, people did not know how to respond in time. Does our generation know how to respond? Are there not Esau, Laban, Ishmael, and Amalek around us today? Does the Torah not have what to teach us about this?"[2]

In this book, I try to read the Torah the way Rabbi Ashkenazi taught—placing the text in conversation with the unfolding events of history, and asking what happens when you bring the two together. I make no claim to his depth or originality. But his influence has shaped every page of what follows. Whether he would approve of my application of his method is not something I can know. I can only pray he would not be too disappointed.

I spent the first forty years of my life in America. I know American Jewish life from the inside—its warmth, its generosity, its extraordinary achievements. Five years ago, I moved with my family to Israel. Today I live in Judea, in the hills where King David grew up, a few miles from where our foremother Rachel is buried.

The distance has clarified things. I am from America but I am no longer of America, and that position—between the world I came from and the land I came to—is the position from which this book was written. I am not a critic writing from outside. I am someone who left, which is a different thing entirely. And what I have seen, from here, I cannot keep to myself.

This book is written for American Jews, a community I love and am genuinely worried about. When I criticize, it is not from disdain—it is the criticism of someone who sees people he loves drifting, in slow motion, toward a cliff. I write as a brother, not a judge.

I like to be liked. A reader of my articles might be forgiven for thinking I enjoy controversy, but the truth is that I don't particularly enjoy angering people through my writing. And yet the Levite blood running through my veins compels me to say what others will not.

Levites were designated to serve in the Temple, to sing and play instruments. But we are also the tribe that answered Moses' call — "Whoever is for the Lord, come to me!" — and stood at his side during the sin of the Golden Calf. Rashi emphasizes that the Levites "did not recognize their brothers" when they fought their fellow Israelites to end the sin of the Golden Calf.[3] This doesn't mean they didn't love their brothers. It means they refused to let that love prevent them from telling their brothers the truth.

Nehemiah calls them "the Levites who caused the people to understand" (8:9)—teachers who didn't comfort their people with easy answers, but forced them to see clearly. In this book, I hope, in my own small way, to live up to the standard of my tribe.

But this book is also for non-Jewish readers, and not as an afterthought. Over one hundred years ago, Rabbi Abraham Isaac Kook wrote that the enormous upheaval of the modern world "has come about primarily and essentially for the sake of Israel," and that "in the birthing of new ideas, new laws, a new spirit—for all the nations—the hand of Israel must be at the center."[4] He was right then and even more obviously so today. Israel and the Jewish people increasingly stand at the epicenter of world events, just as the prophets said we would. "Thus says the Lord God: This is Jerusalem; I have set her in the center of the nations, with countries all around her" (Ezekiel 5:5).

The internal drama of the Jewish people—whether we understand who we are, whether we find the courage to become what we are called to be—determines the very course of world events in ways that most people, Jewish and non-Jewish alike, have not yet begun to understand. If you are not Jewish, you have a stake in this story. You may not know it yet. But you will.

"Thus says the Lord of hosts: In those days ten men from all languages and nations will take hold of the robe of a Jew, saying, 'Let us go with you, for we have heard that God is with you'" (Zechariah 8:23).

May the Jewish people become worthy of that moment—and may it come speedily, in our time.

Introduction

Late one evening during World War II, a young British Jew named Bernard Lewis sat on night watch somewhere in the Middle East. Lewis would later become one of the world's foremost historians of Islam and the Middle East, but at the time he was just another officer killing time through the long hours of the night. As he stood there with a fellow soldier, their idle conversation suddenly took a sharp turn.

"Forgive me," the soldier asked, "but am I right in thinking that you are Jewish?"

"You are right," Lewis answered. "I am Jewish, and there is nothing to forgive."

"Forgive me again," the soldier continued, "but I have the impression that you are not a devout and observant Jew."

Lewis admitted that was true.

"Then I don't understand," the soldier said. "Why do you bother?"[5]

Why bother being Jewish if you're not religious? Why hold onto an identity that's brought so much trouble if there's no faith behind it?

Lewis never forgot the question. He went on to become one of the world's foremost historians of the Middle East, but the soldier's question followed him for the rest of his life—because he didn't have a good answer. Why bother being Jewish if you're not religious? What holds the identity together when faith is gone, or was never there to begin with?

In the early years of the State of Israel, Prime Minister David Ben Gurion regularly urged American Jews to immigrate to Israel, where Jewish immigrants were desperately needed to help build up the country and maintain a Jewish majority. At the time, Israel had a population of only 600,000 Jews, while the American Jewish community numbered close to five million. New York City alone was home to nearly three times as many Jews as the entire Jewish state.

Ben Gurion's call for *Aliyah* infuriated American Jewish leaders. Jacob Blaustein, President of the American Jewish Committee (AJC), feared that talk of *Aliyah* and Jewish national destiny would hand antisemites exactly the ammunition they needed to call the loyalty of American Jews into question. In a speech to the AJC, he pushed back hard, rejecting not just Ben Gurion's call for immigration but the entire premise behind it:

"American Jews—young and old alike—Zionists and non-Zionists alike—are profoundly attached to this, their country. America welcomed our immigrant parents in their time of need. Under America's free institutions, they and their children have achieved that freedom and sense of security unknown for long centuries of travail. We have truly become Americans, just as have all other oppressed groups that have ever come to these shores. We repudiate vigorously the suggestion that American Jews are in exile. The future of American Jewry, of our children and our children's children, is entirely linked with the future of America. We have no alternative; and we want no alternative."[6]

Ultimately, Blaustein and Ben Gurion came to an agreement. American Jews would support the new state through lobbying, donations, and fundraising, while refraining from interfering in Israel's political decisions. In turn, Israel acknowledged the loyalty of American Jews to the United States and promised not to involve itself in the internal life of the diaspora. Those who chose to make *Aliyah* were valued and embraced, but Jews who remained in America were not to be dismissed as "exiles." Both communities agreed that neither would presume to speak on behalf of the other.[7]

It was a truce born of necessity. The fledgling State of Israel desperately needed the support of American Jewry. But the fundamental issue debated by these two obstinate Jews has remained a source of contention and confusion to this very day.

What, exactly, does it mean to be a Jew? For Jacob Blaustein, Judaism was a religion like any other. Jewish Americans attend synagogue on Saturday the way Christian Americans attend church on Sunday. Yes, most Jews share an ethnic background, but that background is incidental, not defining. He was a Jewish American, no different from the Irish Americans and Italian Americans who had come before him, assimilated, and become fully American within a generation.

Ben-Gurion had no patience for this. He was no believer—he worked on Yom Kippur and avoided synagogues like the plague. Yet he called the Bible "the single most important book in my life" and held it up before the Peel Commission as the Jewish people's title deed to the land.[8] For him, Jewish identity was never about faith. It was about belonging to an ancient people with a shared fate. The State of Israel was not just a refuge for persecuted Jews but the restoration of Jewish nationhood.

No other people wrestles with its own identity as we Jews do. The Ben Gurion-Blaustein debate never really ended. For a time it went quiet, buried under decades of Holocaust memory, Cold War solidarity, and the shared pride of Israel's early victories. But it never disappeared. The question of who Jews are—nation or religion, people or denomination—always simmered, just beneath the surface. But there are moments when it explodes onto the front page.

Now is such a time.

Since Hamas murdered 1,200 Israelis on October 7, 2023, Israel's enemies have not distinguished between Israelis and Jews. On the streets of London, New York City and Los Angeles, anti-Israel protesters regularly target Jews for harassment and violence. As the celebrated Arab "activist" Ahed Tamimi recently said, "My definition of Judaism, since my childhood, was that it and Zionism are one and the same. There's no difference between the two... I was raised to believe that Judaism is occupation. Today, tomorrow and in a million years, I will continue to say that... we are fighting Jews, not Zionism."[9]

Tamimi is not alone. Tucker Carlson, two months after October 7, said Ben Shapiro of the Daily Wire "[doesn't] care about the country at all" and is "focused on a conflict in a foreign country as their own country becomes dangerously unstable."[10] Megyn Kelly alleged that convicted sex offender Jeffrey Epstein worked for the Mossad—a claim she certainly would not have made had Epstein not been Jewish.[11]

The result left American Jews politically homeless in both directions. The left's contempt for Israel after October 7 drove many secular and assimilated Jews back toward a Jewish identity they had long neglected. The right's conspiratorial antisemitism gave traditionally conservative and religious Jews nowhere to turn.

American Jews can no longer avoid the question they spent decades carefully avoiding. "October 8th Jews"—those who woke up the morning after the massacre suddenly feeling Jewish—learned the hard way that "from the river to the sea" doesn't distinguish between Zionists and non-Zionists, religious and secular, Israeli and American. It means "death to *all* Jews"—even those living comfortably in America.

For many, this was their first real encounter with hatred. Not theoretical antisemitism from history books, but actual mobs on their college campuses and protesters screaming for their death in the streets of New York and Los Angeles. Some responded by exploring religious observance—Shabbat candles, Torah study, and synagogues they had spent years successfully avoiding. But many others responded differently. They started wearing Star of David necklaces and publicly identifying with Israel, feeling a connection to Jews they've never met and a land they've never visited. For these Jews, it wasn't about religion or ritual. It was something older and harder to explain—the same thing that makes a college student in Manhattan feel personally targeted when Hamas slaughters families in the Negev, the same thing their grandparents understood instinctively but never quite put into words.

"Remember the days of old; reflect upon the years of generations. Ask your father, and he will tell you; your elders, and they will inform you" (Deuteronomy 32:7). To understand what is happening to American Jews today, we have to look back—because this has happened before.

Different countries, different centuries, but the same story: a Jewish community that believed it had finally found a permanent home, that its story would end differently than all the others. It has not.

Throughout Jewish history, crisis has usually been a double-edged sword. The danger is real—American Jews are learning that now. But crisis is also God's invitation to redemption, if His people are willing to answer.

The invitation doesn't last forever. God uses crisis to create windows of opportunity—moments when His people can see clearly who they are and what they must do. But these windows close. When Mordechai urged Esther to risk her life by revealing her identity to the king, he warned her: "If you remain silent at this time, relief and deliverance will arise for the Jews from another place... and who knows whether you have attained royalty for such a time as this?" (Esther 4:14). Esther had a choice, but she also had a deadline. American Jews face the same test today—and the countdown has begun.

The stakes are higher than most realize. As we'll see, how Jews respond to this test will determine not only the fate of the Jewish people, but the fate of all nations.

But American Jews cannot answer God's challenge without first knowing who they are. The question they have spent generations avoiding is now unavoidable: Are Jews a faith or a people, a religion or a nation? Every other question - how to respond to the mobs, what Israel means to them, what to teach their children - depends on the answer.

The confusion runs deep. Young progressive Jews march with keffiyehs without recognizing the contradiction. Orthodox Jews who meticulously observe every detail of Jewish law twist themselves into knots finding religious justifications to avoid living in the land God promised their ancestors. And when accused of dual loyalty, they stumble in their response, unsure how to defend themselves.

Why are American Jews so confused about their own identity? The answer is more complex—and more troubling—than most realize. Something has been lost, edited out, carefully obscured over generations.

The question we face is not new. Abraham faced it when God first called him out of Haran. Moses faced it when he stood before Pharaoh. The prophets faced it in exile. We cannot understand the predicament of American Jews in a vacuum. The confusion of our generation is the culmination of four thousand years of Jewish history—a history shaped by exile, emancipation, and a deliberate effort to redefine what it means to be a Jew. Now, when American Jews need the answer most, they find themselves least equipped to give it.

The world insists on asking the question, but the force of the question does not come from the world alone. Nation or religion? People or faith? It presses upon us from within, shaping how we live as Jews in the Diaspora and in Israel. It is the question at the heart of Jewish destiny, the one that determines who we are and where we are going. Everything depends on the answer.

To answer it, we must go back to the beginning—to the Torah, and to Abraham, the first Jew.

A NATION, NOT A RELIGION

"Go forth from your land... to the land that I will show you. And I will make you into a great nation." (Genesis 12:1-2)

Israel365

1

When God Fired the Preacher

Long before Abraham received God's call, he was already engaged in a mission that would set the stage for all of human history. The Sages teach that Abraham recognized the folly of idol worship and took it upon himself to teach humanity the truth: there is only one God.

Working in his father Terach's idol shop, he smashed the merchandise and left only the largest statue standing. When Terach came in demanding answers, Abraham claimed that the big idol had destroyed the others. Terach scoffed—"Do you think they can act?"—to which Abraham replied, "Let your ears hear what your mouth is saying!"[12]

Abraham and Sarah gathered many followers, "the souls they had acquired in Haran" (Genesis 12:5). Abraham converted the men and Sarah the women, bringing them under the wings of God's presence. [13] Their vision was audacious: to create a universal faith, a community devoted to the One God. Had they succeeded, the world might have been filled with millions of believers.

And then, suddenly, God spoke: "Go forth from your land and from your birthplace and from your father's house, to the land that I will show you. And I will make you into a great nation..." (Genesis 12:1–2).

When Abraham heard the divine call, the command made no sense. He had spent years building a following of believers—why abandon them now? Why not continue as the wandering preacher, spreading the true faith wherever he went? Why not follow the path of his brother Nahor, who settled in, gave up his Hebrew identity and became Aramean?[14] Why did God want him to leave all of this behind and go establish a nation?

Yet this is precisely what God was asking of Abraham. "It is good that you have brought many to believe in Me. But now I call you to something greater, something altogether different. Leave behind all that you have built—even these first stirrings of faith—for I do not ask you to establish another religion, but rather to father a great nation. Not merely a faith, but a people. Not followers, but descendants."[15]

God's first command to Abraham is not to bring a sacrifice or fulfill any sort of ritual. It is simply to pack up and move from one land to another. And the promises that follow are equally concrete: not spiritual enlightenment or religious truth, but seed, descendants, and a covenant that would pass through them:

"This one will not inherit you, but the one who will spring from your innards—he will inherit you." (Genesis 15:4)

"And I will establish My covenant between Me and between you and between your seed after you throughout their generations as an everlasting covenant, to be to you for a God and to your seed after you. And I will give you and your seed after you the land of your sojournings, the entire land of Canaan for an everlasting possession, and I will be to them for a God" (Genesis 17:7–8).

The weight of this promise was not easy to bear. For decades, Abraham and Sarah remained childless, and as the years passed, Sarah's faith in the biological promise began to crack. She found herself drawn back to the mission she and Abraham had devoted their lives to before God's call—the universal religious movement, the gathering of believers, the spreading of monotheism through the world. Perhaps that had been the right path all along. And if so, what was needed was not a biological heir but a great student, someone who could absorb Abraham's teachings and carry them forward.[16] She gave her maidservant Hagar to Abraham, hoping that Ishmael might be that student—the one who would take the torch and run with it. But the plan failed. Ishmael could not inherit Abraham's legacy, and his descendants would go on to contest the Land of Israel to this day.

Finally, God reaffirmed the promise. After her name was changed from Sarai to Sarah, she bore Isaac. But Sarah only grasped the full magnitude of her mistake when she watched the two boys together. "And Sarah saw the son of Hagar the Egyptian, whom she had borne to Abraham, mocking" (Genesis 21:9). On the surface, it sounds like childish teasing. But the sages reveal that Ishmael's "mocking" took the form of idol worship, immorality, and violence[17]—acts that made a mockery of God's promise to Abraham. Ishmael turned the holiness of his father's mission into something profane, desecrating what was meant to be sacred. Sarah saw clearly: if this continued, Isaac would not only be endangered, but the entire purpose of Abraham's calling, to raise a nation devoted to God, would be lost.[18]

And so Sarah spoke decisively to Abraham: "Drive out this handmaid and her son, for the son of this handmaid shall not inherit with my son, with Isaac" (Genesis 21:10). Though this was a painful command, Abraham obeyed, and God affirmed her decision: "And God said to Abraham, 'Do not be displeased concerning the lad and concerning your handmaid; whatever Sarah tells you, hearken to her voice, for in Isaac will be called your seed'" (Genesis 21:12).

Through Isaac, the promise became real. Abraham's legacy would not be a religion, but a nation. Yet even after Isaac's birth, Abraham's understanding of nationhood was still incomplete.

"And it came to pass after these things, that God tested Abraham" (Genesis 22:1). The Torah introduces the Binding of Isaac with a vague reference to "these things" that occurred before. But what "things" is the Torah referring to, and why do they matter for this test?

Rabbi Samuel ben Meir explains that this test is directly linked to the story recorded in the verses immediately preceding the binding of Isaac: Abraham's covenant with Abimelech, the Philistine kin g.[19] In that agreement, Abraham promised that neither he nor his descendants would claim the land the Philistines occupied for four generations.

Though it seemed a prudent diplomatic move, God was displeased. Years earlier, in the Covenant of the Parts, God promised all the land of Canaan to Abraham and his descendants, including the very territory Abraham signed away to Abimelech: "To your descendants I will give this land" (Genesis 15:18). What right did Abraham have to give this land to the Philistines?

Abraham's mistake led directly to the binding of Isaac. "After these events, Abraham made a covenant with Abimelech for himself and for Abraham's son and grandson... God's anger was kindled over this, for the land of the Philistines was given to Abraham... Therefore, 'God tested Abraham.' He tormented and afflicted him. In other words: 'You became proud because of the son I gave you, making a covenant between you and their children. Now go and offer him as a burnt offering, and see what benefit your covenant-making has brought yo u.'"[20]

Why this punishment? Why, after Abraham willingly ceded territory that God had explicitly promised to his descendants, did God respond by demanding Isaac's life? The connection between giving away land and losing a son seems, at first glance, arbitrary and cruel.

Though the binding of Isaac was painful, it was not arbitrary, but rather a logical consequence of Abraham's mistake. In commanding Abraham to offer up his son as a sacrifice, God was saying: "Abraham, you treat the land as dispensable? Then you misunderstand what you are building. You think you can maintain your covenant through students and followers rather than sons and daughters? Then you still think like a religious teacher, not a national patriarch. If that is your vision—if you see yourself as founding a faith rather than a people—then Isaac is superfluous. Religions do not require biological succession."

By signing away the land, Abraham revealed that he still thought like a religious founder rather than a national patriarch. Religions do not require territory; its ideas can spread through students, texts, and rituals. A rabbi or pastor passes his wisdom to students who, in turn, become teachers themselves. The chain of transmission flows through intellectual and spiritual inheritance, not biological descent. For a religion, land is at best a convenience, at worst a distraction from higher spiritual pursuits.

But a nation? A nation cannot exist without both descendants and land. It occupies physical space, governs populations, and establishes borders. Its continuity depends on sons and daughters to inherit and sustain what has been built, and on territory to provide a home for the people and a foundation for the nation's future. Without children, there is no future; without land, there is no present or lasting structure to support that future.[21]

2

MEEK MEN DON'T BUILD NATIONS

Even before Jacob was born, God told his mother Rebecca what was growing inside her. "Two nations are in your womb, and two kingdoms will separate from your innards, and one kingdom will become mightier than the other kingdom, and the elder will serve the younger" (Genesis 25:23). Two *nations.* Two *kingdoms.* Not two religions or two different ways of worshiping God. The struggle between Jacob and Esau was national from the moment of conception.

The Torah describes Jacob in his youth as a "wholesome man, dwelling in tents" (Genesis 25:27). The Sages explain that Jacob lived apart from the world, immersed in study,[22] devoting himself to Torah while Esau pursued hunting and material prosperity.[23] Jacob embodied humility, meekness, and the quiet devotion of one content to live a purely religious life. He was the classic saintly figure who humbly accepts his lowly place and does not aspire to power or glory.

But that was never going to be enough. You cannot father a nation from inside a tent. Nations require land, power, and the willingness to fight for both. So Isaac and Rebecca sent Jacob into exile, to Laban's house, where there would be no Torah study and no shelter from the world's ugliness—only deception, competition, and the daily grind of survival.[24]

Before he left, Isaac gave him the blessing of his grandfather Abraham: "And may He give you the blessing of Abraham, to you and to your seed with you, that you may inherit the land of your sojournings, which God gave to Abraham" (Genesis 28:4).

Why is the land so important? Because outside of it, the descendants of Jacob are not a nation—they are merely communities. Scattered groups, each maintaining their own traditions, but with no center holding them together. A community in Brooklyn and a community in Paris and a community in Buenos Aires do not add up to a people. As we recite in our prayers every Shabbat: "Who is like Your people Israel, one nation in the Land." We are one nation—but only in the land.

The night Jacob fled from Esau and prepared to cross out of the land of Israel, he stopped at the place that would become Bethel, and there he dreamed: "And behold! a ladder set up on the ground and its top reached to heaven; and behold, angels of God were ascending and descending upon it" (Genesis 28:12). Why does the verse say the angels were "ascending first and afterwards descending"? Should it not say descending first, coming down from heaven? The Sages explain: "The angels who escorted him in the Holy Land do not go outside the Land, and they ascended to heaven, and the angels of outside the Holy Land descended to escort him."[25]

The angels of the land of Israel cannot leave its borders. At the very moment Jacob crossed out of the land, his escorts abandoned him.

Different angels, the angels of exile, came down to accompany him instead.

Many years later, when Jacob finally returned to Israel, he had another encounter with angels: "And Jacob went on his way, and angels of God met him" (Genesis 32:2). Rashi explains: "Angels of Israel came to greet him to escort him to the land."[26] Once again, at the border, the escorts changed. The angels of exile left him, and the angels of the Land came to meet him.

Why must Jacob be accompanied by different angels depending on where he stands? Because in exile, you are not the same man. Your identity is scaled down, restricted.[27] Jacob could grow in Laban's house. He could learn cunning, build wealth, father children, and become a man of the world. But he could not become Israel there. Jacob could not become the father of God's people while living in someone else's land. The angels knew it before he did. At the border, the escorts changed, because the land of Israel demanded a different and greater version of Jacob.

Jacob made his way to Haran, where he met Rachel at the well. He introduced himself in a curious way: "And Jacob told Rachel that he was her father's brother and that he was Rebecca's son" (Genesis 29:12). But Jacob was Laban's nephew, not his brother. Why does he call himself Laban's brother?

Rashi explains: "If he comes to deceive me, I, too, am his brother in deception, and if he is an honest man, I, too, am the son of his honest sister Rebecca."[28] Jacob was announcing the terms of engagement. He was no longer the naive boy who lived in the tents of Torah. He was entering Laban's world, and he would play by Laban's rules.

For the next twenty years, Jacob suffered under Laban's deceit. His father-in-law switched Leah for Rachel on his wedding night and changed his wages ten times. He was cheated, exploited, and forced to use cunning and strategy just to survive. This was not the life of a scholar. This was realpolitik. This was what would help Jacob become Israel, transforming him from a religious saint into the father of a nation.

As long as Jacob appeared to be putting down roots—building his future around Laban's world, becoming Aramean the way any sensible immigrant eventually becomes like the people he lives among—things were fine. Laban was his uncle, family, with all the warmth and obligation that word carries. He gave Jacob his two daughters, a livelihood, and a place in his household. But when Laban realized that Jacob viewed himself as a stranger under his roof, that he intended to take his family, his wealth, and his God and return to build his own national life in his own land—the warmth evaporated overnight. "And Laban's face was not toward him as before" (Genesis 31:2). Their relationship had always been conditional on Jacob becoming Aramean.

At the very beginning of the Passover *Haggadah*, before the story of Egypt even begins, the Sages insert a strange line: "Go and learn what Laban the Aramean sought to do to our father Jacob. For Pharaoh decreed only against the males, but Laban sought to uproot everything." What does Laban have to do with Passover?

Passover celebrates the Exodus, the foundation story of the nation of Israel. But the Sages understood that this national story nearly never happened. Had Laban succeeded, had Jacob and his family dissolved into Aramean life and lost themselves in someone else's national identity, there would have been no people to redeem, no Exodus to celebrate, and no nation to stand at Sinai. Pharaoh tried to destroy the nation after it existed. Laban would have prevented it from ever coming into being.

Laban nearly succeeded. Not through force, but through the slow seduction of comfort. When Rebecca sent Jacob to Haran, she expected him back in "a few days, until your brother's wrath has subsided" (Genesis 27:44). He stayed for twenty years. Jacob was not a prisoner; he *chose* to remain in Haran. Every year he stayed in Laban's house was an implicit concession to Laban's vision: that Jacob belonged in Haran, that his future lay there, that he had no pressing national destiny waiting for him elsewhere. It was tangible proof of his own identity confusion. Was he a Hebrew living temporarily in someone else's land, or an immigrant who left his homeland behind and made his peace with never going back?

Ultimately, God commanded Jacob to uproot himself from exile and return to his own land: "Now, arise, go forth from this land and return to the land of your birth" (Genesis 31:13). Jacob obeyed—but not without fear. When he finally broke free from Laban and heard that Esau was approaching with 400 men, "Jacob became very frightened and was distressed" (Genesis 32:8). But why was Jacob afraid? Only a few verses earlier, God promised him protection: "Return to the land of your forefathers and to your birthplace, and I will be with you" (Genesis 31:3).

The Sages explain that Jacob feared he was guilty of sin and that God's promise to protect him would therefore be revoked. But what sin was Jacob guilty of? The Talmud answers by way of comparison: just as the Jewish exiles in Babylon sinned by delaying their return to the Holy Land after Cyrus's proclamation, Jacob had done the same, staying in Haran for twenty years when he should have returned far sooner. And just as God withheld His miracles from the exiles because of that delay, Jacob now feared that his own delay had forfeited God's protection. Esau and four hundred men were approaching, and Jacob was no longer sure he deserved to be saved.[29]

Jacob sent messengers ahead to his brother Esau with a carefully worded message: "With Laban I have sojourned and remained until now" (Genesis 32:5). But why state the obvious? Esau knew perfectly well where Jacob had been for twenty years.

Jacob wasn't updating his brother on his whereabouts—he was telling him something about his identity. The word Jacob uses for "sojourned" is *garti*, from the Hebrew *ger*—a stranger, a foreigner who lives in a place that is not his own. He could have said *yoshavti*, "I dwelled," meaning he had settled, put down roots, made Haran his home. Instead, he says *garti*: I was never more than a stranger there. I never became one of them. "I did not become a prince or an important person, but merely a stranger."[30] Jacob did not rise to prominence in Haran because he never saw himself as a man of Haran. He carried himself as a perpetual outsider, as someone passing through, however long the passage took. Whatever confusion had kept him in Haran for twenty years, Jacob was done with it. This is what he was telling Esau: I spent twenty years in someone else's land and I never stopped being a Hebrew. This land still belongs to me. This is where I will build my nation.

The final transformation could only happen at the Jabbok River, on the very threshold of the land. That night, Jacob wrestled with a mysterious adversary until dawn. He could no longer run from his brother or disappear into someone else's house. At the border of the land, with nowhere left to go, he fought. And in that struggle, he became Israel.

"Your name will no longer be called Jacob, but Israel will be your name, for you have struggled with *Elokim* and with men, and prevailed" (Genesis 32:29).

The Torah stresses that "Jacob" would no longer be his name. Yet, in the very next verse, it says, "And Jacob asked..." (Genesis 32:30). The Sages resolve the contradiction: The name "Jacob" was not erased, but placed second. "Israel" became his primary identity, "Jacob" a secondary one.[31]

The Hebrew roots of each name reveal the difference between them. "Jacob" (*Yaakov*) derives from *ekev*—heel, reflecting lowliness, humility, and subservience. These are qualities that fit a private life of faith. But "Israel" (*Yisrael*) derives from *sarar*—struggle. It represents the man who stands tall, who strives and prevails, who carries the strength and pride of a nation.

The tension played out almost immediately. When the arrogant prince Shechem raped Dinah, Simeon and Levi didn't deliberate—they slaughtered the men of the city. Jacob was horrified. He condemned his sons, terrified of the bloodshed and what the neighboring tribes might do. But Simeon and Levi were unmoved: "Shall he treat our sister as a prostitute?" (Genesis 34:31). Their father was thinking like Jacob, a man of religion—cautious, humble, a man of the tent. His sons were thinking like Israel—a small but fearless nation. They understood that the restraint and silence that make an individual noble will get a nation killed.

The tension between Jacob and Israel has never disappeared. The Jewish people live with both names, both callings. But the Torah is clear about which must come first. Simeon and Levi were right. Fundamentally, we are Israel: a nation that cannot survive without pride and power, without the courage to fight when necessary. Secondarily, we are Jacob: a people of faith, humility, and Torah. Both are necessary, but the order is clear.[32]

Though the Torah is clear on this point, the descendants of Jacob often confused the order. Rabbi Shlomo Aviner once recalled an ultra-Orthodox rabbi telling him: "Let the Arabs establish a Palestinian state in Judea and Samaria. This will teach us humility." He responded that such thinking distorts the meaning of humility. For an individual, humility is a virtue—when rebuked by a parent, a rabbi, or a friend, silence is noble. But for a nation, humility is fatal. National survival requires pride, strength, and honor. If Israel lives only as Jacob, meek and submissive, it will not survive.[33]

On the eve of his descent to Egypt, God appeared to Jacob and called out his original name twice: "Jacob, Jacob." The man who wrestled with angels and became Israel was now, once again, reverting to "Jacob." This is the inevitable cost of exile.

The Torah confirms this shift in identity by placing two verses side by side. "And Jacob lived in the land of Egypt seventeen years" (Genesis 47:28). And then, in the very next verse: "And the days of Israel drew near to die" (Genesis 47:29). When Jacob and his children live in Egypt, Israel begins to die. The longer they stay, the more the exile identity takes over, and their national identity quietly disappears into the background.[34]

After all that Jacob went through in order to become Israel, why did God force him into exile and make him Jacob once again? This was no accident. It was God's plan, laid out in the Covenant of the Parts. Had Jacob and his family remained in Israel and grown into a nation there, they would have become a nation like any other. But Israel was never meant to be like other nations.

God put our forefathers through excruciating slavery in Egypt, what the Torah calls "the iron furnace" (Deuteronomy 4:20). He stripped them of everything: their land, their freedom, and their dignity. For 210 years, they suffered together, cried out to God together, and waited for redemption together. The tribes that sold their own brother into slavery emerged from that furnace as something new—one people, bound to each other and to God with a bond that no comfortable life in their own land could ever have forged.

When they left Egypt, Jacob's children became something new—no longer separate tribes, but one nation. Jacob had to become Jacob again so that his descendants could become Israel.

3

Would You Have Left?

Four out of five Israelites never left Egypt.

The Sages say that only twenty percent of the Israelites made it out, while the other eighty percent perished during the plague of darkness. They derive this from a single word: "And the children of Israel went up armed out of Egypt" (Exodus 13:18). The word "armed," *chamushim*, can also mean "one-fifth," and from this they concluded that only one in five Israelites walked out of Egypt alive.[35]

The Zohar adds an even more disturbing layer, arguing that even the one-fifth of the Israelites who left Egypt were idolaters. When God saved the people of Israel at the Red Sea and wiped out the Egyptian army, the angels questioned God: "Master of the Universe, what makes these [Israelites] different from those [Egyptians]? These are idol worshippers and those are idol worshippers."[36]

Viewed together, these two teachings demand explanation. If all of the Israelites in Egypt were idolaters, what distinguished the twenty percent who were redeemed from those who perished in Egypt? What made some worthy of salvation while others were left behind?

This is not an academic question. The same test that separated those who left Egypt from those who died there is playing out again today. Which Jews of our generation will merit to leave America and return to Israel, to participate in the final redemption? And who, tragically, will be left behind?[37]

The Sages tell us what separated those who left from those who didn't: "Israel possessed three good attributes in Egypt, by whose merit they were redeemed: they did not change their names, they did not change their language, and they separated themselves from licentiousness."[38]

Notice what is not on the list. Not prayer, not Shabbat observance, not sacrifice or ritual or any form of religious observance. Rabbi Yehuda Leon Ashkenazi explains that the three criteria for redemption are *national* in nature, not religious.[39] These three attributes are the foundations of national identity. Hebrew names marked them as members of the Israelite nation. Their distinct language, Hebrew, bound them together as a people. And marrying other Israelites ensured the continuation of their national story. Religious observance, while crucial, wasn't enough to guarantee inclusion in the Exodus. In order to be included in the redemption and leave Egypt, the Israelites had to identify themselves as part of the *nation* of Israel.[40]

In other words, the difference between those who were redeemed and those who perished was neither their religious beliefs nor their observance—they were all idolaters—but their national identity. The one-fifth who left Egypt did so because they identified as Israelites, not as Egyptians. Religiously, they were distant from truth, but they understood that they belonged to a people, to a covenant, and to the unique destiny of Israel, and that was enough. It was this commitment to the nation of Israel that made them worthy of redemption, while the others, who identified primarily as Egyptians, were left behind.

Ginnifer Goodwin, a Jewish actress with little religious background, was asked to speak out about the Israeli hostages taken by Hamas on October 7. She and her husband weighed what it might cost: her career, their house, becoming persona non grata in Hollywood. She spoke out anyway: "We would be okay if we lost the house and had to pull the kids out from school. The truth is, there's only one way this goes where I can sleep at night, and that's the way where I not only embrace Judaism, but fight for the continuation of our people."[41] Goodwin doesn't keep Shabbat or kosher. By conventional measures, she is not a religious Jew. But by the standard of the Exodus, she would qualify for redemption—because when it mattered, she stood with her people.

Jacob understood this distinction long before Goodwin did. On his deathbed in Egypt, when Joseph brought Ephraim and Manasseh to receive their grandfather's blessing, Jacob looked at the two boys and asked: 'Who are these?' (Genesis 48:8). He knew their names—they were his own grandsons. But they stood before him in Egyptian clothes, speaking Egyptian. What he wanted to know about these young men went deeper: Are you sons of Israel, or are you Egyptians who happen to worship the God of Israel? Only once they reassured him of their loyalty to the people of Israel did Jacob agree to bless them.

Moses grew up in Pharaoh's palace, raised as an Egyptian prince, but born a Hebrew. For years, he lived with the contradiction. Then one day he went out and saw an Egyptian beating a Hebrew slave—one of his own people. "Moses grew up and went out to his brothers and *looked at their burdens*" (Exodus 2:11).

The Sages explain: "He directed his eyes and his heart to be distressed over them."[42] It is easy to ignore the suffering of your fellow, to look the other way and concern yourself with the well-being of your small circle of family and friends. But Moses didn't glance and turn away. Something broke open in him. He couldn't look away.

What he saw was not random cruelty. The Egyptian officer wasn't punishing the Hebrew slave for being lazy or negligent—he was persecuting him because he hated the people of Israel.[43] Moses now understood: there is no neutral ground. To stand apart from Israel was to side with Egypt. The only path to redemption was to throw in his lot with his people, to make their fate his fate.

"He turned this way and that way, and he saw that there was no man; so he struck the Egyptian and hid him in the sand" (Exodus 2:12). "He turned this way and that way"—Moses looked at the Egyptian side of himself and then the Hebrew side. And "he saw that there was no man"—a man torn between two nations has nothing. And so Moses chose. "He struck the Egyptian"—he struck the Egyptian identity within himself—and buried that identity in "the sand" forever.[44]

Moses made his choice alone, with no one watching. But Egypt would soon demand the same choice from an entire people—and not everyone would choose correctly. The Passover *Haggadah* captures exactly who wouldn't. The wicked son asks: "What is this service to *you*?" The *Haggadah* explains: "To you, and not to him. Since he has excluded himself from the community, he would not have been redeemed."

Notice what the *Haggadah* does not say. It does not say the wicked son is denied redemption because he rejected God, or because he violated the commandments. Rather, it is because he separated himself from the nation of Israel.

The evil son represents a third kind of heresy. We usually think of heresy in two forms: denying God, or denying the divinity of Torah. But the *Haggadah* reveals another: the Jew who believes in God and keeps Torah, yet treats his worship as purely private, severed from the people of Israel.[45] As Rabbi Abraham Isaac Kook wrote, it doesn't matter how learned or pious this separatist is—the act of separation itself makes him wicked: "If the intention of the one who separates is to completely leave the community and follow their own path as they see fit, then even if they were the greatest of the great, they would be the most wicked of all."[46]

A Jew's worth is never measured in isolation. For Jews, holiness doesn't come from locking yourself away in pursuit of private spirituality. There's no place here for the monk in a monastery, the hermit in the wilderness, or the ascetic chasing solitary enlightenment. Jewish life insists on community. Every great leader in our history—whether freeing captives, teaching students, supporting families, or carrying the burdens of the people—has lived for others.

Maimonides codifies this: "One who separates himself from the ways of the community, even if he has not committed sins, but simply separates from the congregation of Israel... as if he were from another nation and not from Israel, has no share in the World to Come."[47]

This brings us back to the four out of five Israelites who perished during the plague of darkness—but not in the way we might imagine. They did not die a physical death; they died to the people of Israel. They chose Egypt over Israel, and in doing so ceased to exist as Israelites. Their lives went on, but the Israelite within them was extinguished.[48] The plague of darkness is the Torah's symbol for their fate: they died in confusion, unclear about who they were and where they belonged, and that confusion swallowed them whole. Today we would call it assimilation. Eighty percent of Israel's children vanished from Jewish history forever—not because they were wicked, but because they were lost.

But even for the twenty percent who identified as Israelites, leaving Egypt was not simple. Egypt was brutal, but it was familiar. It was the only home they had ever known. When Moses' initial confrontation with Pharaoh only made their slavery worse, the Israelites turned on him: "May the Lord look upon you and judge you! You have made us obnoxious to Pharaoh and his officials and have put a sword in their hand to kill us" (Exodus 5:21). They preferred the familiar misery of slavery to the risk of pursuing freedom.

God understood this. Between the ninth plague and the tenth, the Torah pauses for a command that seems strange in its timing: take a lamb, keep it for four days, then slaughter it publicly and apply its blood to your doorposts. This was no small thing. The lamb was the god of Egypt, the most sacred animal to the Egyptians. Now the Israelite slaves were commanded to take their masters' most sacred animal and slaughter it in the streets, in full view of the Egyptians. As Moses himself said, "We will be sacrificing the abomination of the Egyptians before their eyes" (Exodus 8:22).

The Israelites understood exactly what message this would send to their masters. The Egyptians would see their most sacred god slaughtered in the streets by their slaves. Yet they did it anyway. They brought the lambs into their homes with loud voices. They slaughtered the

Passover in groups, in large family operations, publicly. It was an act of extraordinary courage.

Why did God command this insulting act of provocation? Because words were not enough. If Israel wanted to leave Egypt, they had to cut the cord—completely and irrevocably. They had to show the Egyptians, in the clearest way possible: We are not Egyptian. We never were. We are leaving, and we will never bow to your gods again. The slaughter of the Passover lamb was Israel's declaration of independence.

Again and again, the Bible commands us to remember the Exodus. "Remember this day on which you went free from Egypt, the house of bondage, how the Lord freed you from it" (Exodus 13:3). "Remember that you were a slave in Egypt and the Lord your God redeemed you" (Deuteronomy 15:15). "So that you may remember the day when you came out of the land of Egypt all the days of your life" (Deuteronomy 16:3). God insists that we carry the memory of Egypt with us—*every single day.* To fulfill this command, our prayers recall the Exodus morning and night, "all the days of your life."[49]

But what are we actually commanded to remember? Not the plagues, not the splitting of the sea, not the fire on Sinai. Rabbi Judah Loew of Prague writes: "The Exodus from Egypt itself, aside from the miracles that were performed during the Exodus, is the foundation of faith upon which everything is built. For although the Holy One, blessed be He, performed countless miracles and wonders for the people of Israel, the Torah did not establish remembrance or commemoration for them..."[50]

The miracles were God's doing. What Israel did was walk out. That is what we are commanded never to forget—not God's awesome miracle at the sea, but simply that the people of Israel left. Every day we remind ourselves: we do not belong in exile, dependent on the goodwill of Pharaoh or any other power. God's purpose for the world demands that Israel live as a free nation in its own land. The Exodus is not just history; it is a command that has never been rescinded.

4

Why God Passed Over Abraham

Abraham was closer to God than anyone alive, and the same could be said of Isaac and Jacob in their respective generations. They spoke with God, ascended the altar at Mount Moriah and wrestled with angels. If God was searching for worthy recipients of His Torah, He had three obvious candidates standing right in front of Him.

Instead, He passed over all of them. God waited four hundred years and only then, when their descendants emerged from Egypt—emotionally broken, spiritually degraded, many of them still worshipping idols—did God give the Torah to them.

Why? Why give the Torah to a nation of former slaves rather than give it immediately to the greatest spiritual giants in human history?

The answer is simple, but one that must be articulated and understood. The Torah could not be given to Abraham, Isaac, or Jacob—not because they were unworthy, but because it wasn't meant for them. Abraham discovered God on his own, through reason and spiritual intuition. Isaac and Jacob followed in his path, each forging their own unique relationship with God. The Torah, with its 613 commandments governing every aspect of individual and collective life, would have been, for them, almost beside the point.

Abraham, Isaac, and Jacob were some of the greatest individuals who ever lived. But the Torah is not a document for great individuals. It is a constitution for a people. Only when six hundred thousand souls stood together at Sinai, when the nation of Israel was fully formed, could God give the Torah. From that moment forward, every Jew could reach spiritual heights impossible for any individual alone—not through personal greatness, but through membership in the nation.[51]

Still, we must be clear. The giving of the Torah, as awesome as it was, did not create the people of Israel. We were already a nation, the twelve tribes of Israel, before a single word of the Ten Commandments was given to us at Mount Sinai. We received the Torah because we were already God's people—not the other way around. Many people assume that Israel became God's chosen nation at Sinai, when we accepted the Torah. But this is not true. While we were still slaves in Egypt, before the Exodus and long before a single commandment was given, God already called us "*Beni Bechori Yisrael,*" "Israel, my firstborn son" (Exodus 4:22). We were His son before we were His students, His nation before He gave us His law. Sinai did not create us; it gave us our constitution. If we lose sight of this, we are not simply making a theological error. We are erasing the Jewish people entirely, replacing a nation with a "congregation of believers in the religion of Moses."[52]

Every morning, before studying even one word of Torah, we recite a blessing: "Blessed are You... who selected us from all the peoples and gave us His Torah." We don't say "who gave me His Torah." The Torah was given to *us*—to the nation of Israel—and each Jew receives his portion in it only through membership in the nation. We study and observe not as isolated individuals who happen to share a holy book, but as part of something larger than ourselves.[53]

Rabbi Yaakov Moshe Charlop goes even further. The people of Israel, of course, cannot survive without the Torah, but the reverse is equally true: "More than it is impossible for us to be a people while lacking one of God's commandments, it is even more true that no commandment can stand at all without our being a people."[54] The Torah and the nation are not two separate things. They rise and fall together.

Christians often miss this. Os Guinness argues that while Christians know the story of Sinai well, they frequently overlook its deeper meaning. They focus on God calling individuals rather than understanding His distinctive relationship with Israel as a nation. But the moment at Sinai is unlike any other in history: God's revelation was not to a single person, as at the burning bush, nor to a small group of leaders, but to an *entire nation* at once—men, women, and children.[55] As Moses later reflected, "Has anything as great as this ever happened, or has anything like it ever been heard of? Has any other people heard the voice of God speaking out of fire, as you have, and lived?" (Deuteronomy 4:32-33).

Rabbi Yehuda Leon Ashkenazi experienced this misunderstanding firsthand while growing up in France. When his Christian high school friends discovered he knew Hebrew, they were baffled. One boy, also Jewish, explained: "What do you want from him? He's the rabbi's son. He's religious!" Rabbi Ashkenazi shot back: "Is being religious some kind of disease?" His Hebrew, his observance of the Torah, his entire Jewish life had nothing to do with religiosity. They flowed from his identity. "The Torah was given to us not because we were religious, but because we are the children of Israel. This is the criterion—and there is no other."[56]

The blind spot shows up even in Theodor Herzl. No one understood more viscerally that being Jewish was not simply a matter of religion. The father of modern Jewish nationalism, Herzl devoted his life to the conviction that the Jews are a nation, not just a faith community. And yet, at the First Zionist Congress in 1897, he declared that religion in a future Jewish state would be "a private matter." He meant it, innocently, as a straightforward separation of church and state.

But as Rabbi Moshe Avigdor Amiel observed, Herzl was "assimilated in his spirit and soul" and didn't grasp that Torah is fundamentally different from religion. "Religion is for the individual alone, but Torah is, in its essence, directed toward the entire collective." And missing that distinction, Rabbi Amiel warned, means that "one who says that our Torah is a private matter is thereby destroying not only the foundations of the Torah, but also the foundations of our history." Herzl was a great man who understood that Jews are a people. But he never understood that their Torah is the soul of that people—and that you cannot separate the two.[57]

After the sin of the Golden Calf, God made Moses a compelling offer: "Now therefore let Me alone, that My wrath may burn hot against them and I may consume them. And I will make of you a great nation" (Exodus 32:10). Wipe out these idol-worshippers and start over. I built the first nation through Abraham, Isaac, and Jacob, and I can build another one through you.

Moses refused, which was exactly what God wanted. The offer was a test, and Moses passed it by fighting for his people, even when they seemed indefensible.[58]

But it's worth pausing to consider what would have been lost had Moses accepted. A nation descended from Moses would have been built on merit; you earn your place by meeting Moses' standards, and if you don't, you have no place. It would have functioned less like a nation than like a church, a community of believers where the wicked may be cast out. Membership would have been contingent, always up for review.

God chose differently. He gave the Torah to the nation that already existed—the descendants of Abraham, Isaac, and Jacob, a people bound together not by shared belief or personal virtue but by shared history and a destiny inherited at birth. Moses became their teacher, not their founder, which meant that every member of Israel kept their place in the covenant regardless of how they lived: the righteous, the mediocre, even the wicked. Belonging to the nation is not something you earn. It is something you are born into. "Israel, even though he sins, is still Israel."[59]

The Ten Commandments do not open with "I am the Lord your God who created the heavens and the earth." They open with: "I am the Lord your God who brought you out of the land of Egypt" (Exodus 20:2). It is no accident that God identifies Himself through the redemption of His people. As David declares, "Who is like Your people, like Israel, one nation in the world, whom God went to redeem for Himself as a people, and to make Him a name?" (II Samuel 7:23).

The same pattern appears in the central declaration of Jewish faith: "Hear O Israel, the Lord is our God, the Lord is One" (Deuteronomy 6:4). If this were simply a religion, it would say "Hear! The Lord is God, the Lord is One." But it doesn't. It begins with Israel. Faith and peoplehood cannot be separated.

The Hebrew word for congregation, *tzibbur*, captures this perfectly. It's an acronym formed from three types of people: *tzadikim* (the righteous), *beinonim* (the average), and *resha'im* (the wicked).[60] A voluntary fellowship of believers can exclude the wicked. The Jewish people include all three by definition, and always have.

Even Dathan and Abiram—the rebels who defied Moses and later tried to overthrow him—stood at Mount Sinai when the Torah was given. Any community built around shared conviction would have thrown them out long before. A nation has no such luxury. You don't get to resign from your family.[61]

God didn't give the Torah to the righteous alone, because the Torah was never meant to create a spiritual elite. It is meant to sanctify an entire people—saints and sinners, heroes and cowards—all of them part of the covenant, whether they deserve it or not. "For the Lord takes delight in His people" (Psalm 149:4). Not in His scholars or in His saints, but in His *people*.

But this only raises a deeper question: why create a particular nation at all? At first glance, a universal religion seems far more practical. Why bind one people to land, history, and law, rather than create a faith that anyone, anywhere, could embrace? Christianity and Buddhism both took that path—spiritual belief systems that could spread across continents without the complexities of territory and politics. Why did God choose one small and imperfect people instead?

Rabbi Shlomo Aviner tells the story of a Jew who sought spiritual truth in India, studying for ten years under Sri Aurobindo, the yogi who translated Hindu teachings for a Western audience. Eventually he returned to Israel, immersed himself in Torah, and became a deeply learned and observant Jew. He said to Rabbi Aviner: "Everything I learn in the Torah, I already learned in India in Hindu teachings." Stunned, Rabbi Aviner asked him: "If so, what is special about the Torah of Israel?" He replied: "In India there is sanctity of the individual, and in Judaism there is sanctity of the collective."[62] This unique focus on the sanctification of the collective is the key innovation of the Torah.[63]

What makes the Torah unlike anything that came before it is its sheer ambition. Every other spiritual tradition in history addresses the individual—how to pray, how to achieve salvation, how to purify the soul. The Torah provides a path for all of that, but it is clearly not the priority. The Torah's primary concern is the nation of Israel: how to govern it, how to structure its courts, how to conduct its wars, and how to organize its economy. It assumes you are running a country, and insists that every corner of that country falls under God's authority. The butcher and the farmer, the soldier and the judge—all of them serving God not through private piety but through the life of the nation. No civilization had ever attempted anything like it.

Ask most people what religion is for, and they'll tell you: to earn your place in the next world. What do I need to do to get to heaven? Jews believe in heaven, in personal reward and punishment—but strikingly, the Torah never explicitly discusses heaven or any sort of afterlife. They appear only in hints.[64] What the Torah does discuss, at length and in detail, is the fate of the nation of Israel in this world. "If you are careful to heed My commandments... I will provide rain for your land in its proper time"—and if not, "you will be swiftly removed from the goodly land" (Deuteronomy 11:13-17). This is not a promise to the righteous individual farmer that his fields will be blessed. God is speaking to the entire nation: when Israel is faithful, the land prospers; when Israel strays, the land suffers and the people are exiled. The Torah's focus is not my personal fate in the next world, but our collective fate in this one.

As Rabbi Abraham Isaac Kook wrote, the goal is to demonstrate to the world that "not only exceptional individuals—the wise, pious, monks, and holy people—can live by the divine ideal, but entire nations as well, down to the lowest levels of society."[65]

Rabbi Kook draws a sharp line between the "religious idea"—which leaves the world exactly as it is while people pray in corners—and the "Divine idea," in which God's presence fills every last corner of the earth.[66] "Could it truly be God's will for the world to remain desolate and corrupt, filled with evil, while we confine ourselves to a small corner of 'religious life' in synagogues and seminaries?"[67]

No nation other than Israel has ever tried to answer that question—not in theology or philosophy, but in the real world, through the existence of an actual state with borders, armies, courts, and taxes. Whether it is actually possible, whether an entire nation can be run according to God's will, is exactly what Israel's existence is meant to prove.

This is why the Torah was always meant to be lived in the land of Israel. The Sages compare God sending Israel into exile to a king who sends his wife to her father's house in anger: "Although I am exiling you from the Land to outside the Land, be distinguished in the *mitzvot*, so that when you return they will not be new to you."[68] Torah in exile is like a queen wearing her crown in her parents' living room—it is still a crown, still precious, still real. But ultimately, it is only practice for the real thing, not the real thing itself. The crown was designed to be worn at the royal court, beside the king, governing a kingdom. So too, the Torah was designed to govern a sovereign nation in its own land—not to be practiced in exile, however faithfully, in someone else's country.

For this reason, Rabbi Abraham Isaac Kook argued that "It should not be considered arrogance if we say that a small group in the land of Israel is more beloved than a great Sanhedrin in the Diaspora."[69] Imagine the greatest rabbinic court ever assembled—the finest legal minds and scholars of the generation—gathered outside the land of Israel. They are still missing the point. The Torah was given to a nation meant to govern itself in its own land. A Sanhedrin sitting in Vilna or Lakewood, however brilliant, is still wearing the queen's jewelry in her parents' house.

A nation in its land faces challenges that no diaspora community ever has to confront—how to run courts, wage war, govern an economy, and administer justice across an entire society. These are precisely the things the Torah was written to address.

The clearest example of what this looks like in practice is how the Torah treats war. War is unavoidable. Nations must defend their borders and their people or they will cease to exist. But war also creates moral chaos. Every army in history deals with the same problems: foul language that becomes the default mode of speech, gambling, heavy drinking, prostitution. Men raised with ethical standards find themselves doing things they'd never do at home. The stress of combat, the constant exposure to violence and death, separation from normal life—it all erodes boundaries.

Most nations treat this as the cost of doing business. You need an army, armies operate under brutal conditions, and those conditions produce moral damage. You can't prevent it, so you manage it and hope the soldiers readjust when they get home.

God expects more from the people of Israel. The Torah devotes three entire sections to the conduct of Israel's army in war, giving it more attention than almost any other subject.[70] The message is clear: even the stress of war does not excuse God's people from holiness.

Before battle, an anointed priest speaks to the troops, building their courage and reminding them of what they're defending. But he also reminds them to fear God, the true source of their strength.[71]

The Torah refuses to pretend that soldiers are angels. "If you go out to war against your enemies, and the Lord, your God, will deliver him into your hands, and you take his captives, and you see among the captives a beautiful woman and you desire her, you may take her for yourself as a wife" (Deuteronomy 21:10-11). The Torah doesn't pretend soldiers won't be attracted to captive women. It addresses the impulse directly, and provides a process for channeling that desire appropriately.

She must be brought to his home, where she shaves her head, cuts her nails, removes her captive's clothing, and mourns her father and mother for a full month. Only then may he marry her. And if he decides afterward that he doesn't want her, he must set her free. He is forbidden from selling her or treating her as a slave. She must be treated as a wife, not as a concubine or a sexual conquest to be used and discarded.

The same principle governs the camp itself. Soldiers must guard their speech and their ears from indecency. The camp must be kept physically clean. Why? "For the Lord your God walks in the midst of your camp to save you and to deliver your enemies before you; therefore your camp shall be holy, so that He shall not see anything indecent among you and turn away from you" (Deuteronomy 23:14). God's presence doesn't retreat to the synagogue when Israel goes to war. He is present in the military camp, and if the camp becomes defiled, He will turn away, and Israel will not succeed in battle.

This is what it means for a nation, rather than a religion, to live under God's law. There is nowhere to hide, no corner of life cordoned off from holiness—not even the battlefield.

But holiness without strength is fantasy. Israel cannot model anything for the world if it cannot survive in the world. Like every nation, Israel must be powerful enough to defend itself. But unlike ordinary nations, that power must be bound by *chessed*—by love, kindness, and moral restraint.

Rabbi Yehuda Leon Ashkenazi finds the key to this balance in the *Akeidah,* the Binding of Isaac. Abraham and Isaac are not just father and son; they represent two opposing forces that run through all of history. Abraham is *chessed*, the overflowing kindness and generosity that opens the world to blessing. Isaac is *din*, strict judgment, the demand for justice without compromise. Unchecked, each force destroys what it touches—pure kindness leads to indulgence and collapse, while pure judgment hardens into cruelty.

The command to Abraham was not to kill Isaac, but to *bind* him. "The main lesson... is that the attribute of kindness must restrain the unchecked spread of strict justice. Abraham is commanded to bind Isaac—to bind him and nothing more... This is not a story of human sacrifice, but a teaching about restraining the power of judgment with love."

This struggle to balance justice with kindness didn't end on Mount Moriah. Esau, Isaac's firstborn, inherited his father's fire but without Abraham's restraint. He is the prototype of raw power—*admoni* (ruddy, red), impulsive, and unrestrained. His strength is real, but he lacks the moral compass necessary to guide it.[72] Jacob was the opposite: morally great but physically weak, a man whose spiritual depth was real but who struggled his entire life to fully live up to the name Israel. He earned the name in one night of wrestling, but then spent much of the rest of his life slipping back into being Jacob. The harmony that eluded the patriarchs—strength bound by justice, power tempered by love—finally found its expression in King David.

Superficially, David is like Esau; he is the only other man in the entire Bible described as *admoni*. Yet there is a crucial difference between them: David is *admoni*, but with "beautiful eyes" (I Samuel 16:12). The same strength and fire is there, but it is tempered by vision, wisdom, and compassion. The same redness that in Esau meant uncontrolled violence, in David becomes holy strength, directed toward justice and service of God.

This is the model for Jewish nationhood. Israel must be *admoni*, capable of fire and force, but always with "beautiful eyes," guided by compassion, justice, and reverence for life. Power itself is made holy.

This ideal of sanctified power runs against everything the modern world believes about statecraft. Charles De Gaulle was not being cynical when he said "No nation worthy of the name has friends—only interests." He was simply describing how states function. Ethics may govern individuals, but nations operate by different rules entirely.

This assumption has deep roots. From Thucydides to Hobbes, the classical understanding of statecraft was built on one premise: power is all that matters. The strong dominate the weak, the state exists to impose order through force, and human life without that force is, in Hobbes' famous formulation, "nasty, brutish, and short."[73]

Aristotle gave this intuition its philosophical foundation. In his *Nicomachean Ethics* and *Politics*, he drew a fundamental distinction between two domains: ethics, which governs how an individual should live to achieve virtue and happiness, and politics, which governs how a state maintains order and survives. Because their goals differ, their standards must differ as well. A ruler may need to deceive an enemy to save his city, execute criminals, and order actions in war that would be unconscionable in private life. Aristotle wasn't celebrating cruelty, but he believed the standards that govern a good person are not the same as the standards that govern a good ruler. Political necessity can justify actions that personal morality condemns.[74]

This became the bedrock of Western political thought, reaching its apex in Machiavelli's *The Prince*. Here was a handbook for rulers that explicitly rejected morality in politics. The prince must learn "how not to be good." He must be willing to break his word when keeping it would destroy him. He must know how to use cruelty well—not sadistically, but strategically. Half-hearted violence is worse than none at all. Strike hard once, then rule in peace.

Machiavelli was deeply cynical about his fellow man's motivations. Better to be feared than loved, because people will abandon you the moment it costs them something. Love is unreliable, but fear keeps them in line. The successful ruler must be both fox and lion—clever enough to spot traps, fierce enough to terrify wolves. Above all, he must master the performance of virtue while being ruthless in practice. "It is unnecessary for a prince to have all the good qualities, but it is very necessary to appear to have them." Outwardly, you must seem merciful, faithful, honest, and religious—especially religious. Just don't let any of it stop you from doing what needs to be done.[75]

Writing in the early twentieth century, Rabbi Yitzchak Nissenbaum looked at the great powers of Europe and saw exactly what Machiavelli had described. "Whoever looks at any kingdom, great or small, at how it was built and how it rose to power, will read concerning them the words of our prophets: 'Woe to him who builds his house without justice and his upper chambers without righteousness' (Jeremiah 22:13)." The enlightened democracies of Great Britain and France were no better than the ancient empires; they were just better at packaging the same brutality. "This spirit of impurity, this spirit of tyranny that crushes every lowly and weak person, so fills their hearts that even the most enlightened peoples and the most advanced nations cannot free themselves from it."[76]

The logical endpoint of this tradition is a world where legality defines morality, where the only question that matters is not "is this right?"

but "is this legal?" But who writes the laws if not people driven by their own interests and desires? Under Roman law, a soldier could forcibly occupy land for years with his comrades, then claim permanent ownership through "possession," completely displacing the rightful owner. That was legal.[77] But was it moral?

Where does this lead? If legality defines morality, if the only question is "is this legal?" rather than "is this right?", then nothing is off limits. Change the law, and any atrocity can be committed with a clear conscience. The Holocaust was legal under German law.

The Jewish vision rejects all of this. Israel cannot be passive or purely spiritual, but it also must not embrace the amoral statecraft that treats law as the ultimate authority. Like David, Israel must be *admoni*—capable of fire and force—but always with "beautiful eyes," guided by compassion and justice.[78]

The challenge is enormous. Nations will always argue: "Individuals can afford the luxury of private morality, but running a state is a different matter. When you face war, economic crisis, crime, and enemies who play by none of your rules, idealism becomes a liability. Come back and talk to us when you've succeeded not in theory, but as farmers, soldiers, judges, and leaders of an actual country — then we'll take your claim to morality seriously."

The world will always assume that "man is wolf to man" when it comes to real-world affairs. The only way to overturn this assumption is through living proof: a tangible national example that it is possible to build and sustain a modern, developed country whose citizens are happy, just, and moral. As Rabbi Joseph B. Soloveitchik said, "Indeed, we must have a state... a legal-political nation with all its accoutrements, for the state and the nation will serve as the laboratory in which the great ideals and values of [Israel]... will be realized."[79]

Israel exists not to preach to the world but to prove that a righteous nation can actually function, survive, and flourish. Not through words, but through its very existence. This is how a particular nation serves a universal purpose.

God promised Abraham at the very beginning: "All the families of the earth will be blessed through you" (Genesis 12:3). Rabbi Ovadiah Seforno explains that Israel wasn't chosen *from* the nations but *for* them—to serve as a "treasure from among all the nations" by teaching all of humanity to call upon His name. Not by conquering the world, but by building within it a society that the world could not ignore.[80]

God did not call Israel to be a conquering empire. Nowhere in the Bible does He promise the patriarchs an empire.[81] The Torah is explicit about Israel's borders, and equally explicit about what lies beyond them: "Take good heed of yourselves therefore. Meddle not with the children of Esau, for I will not give you of their land" (Deuteronomy 2:4–5). The same instruction applies to Moav and Ammon: "Do not harass them, nor contend with them in battle, for I will not give you of their land for a possession" (Deuteronomy 2:6, 9, 19). In the ancient world, when powerful nations naturally became conquering empires, these commands were radical. Israel is holy not because it dominates the world, but because it restrains itself, respects the boundaries God set, and acts with moral purpose.

The model was never conquest, but admiration. When the Queen of Sheba visited Solomon's court, nobody forced her to come. She came because she had heard of Israel's wisdom and wanted to see it for herself. After witnessing the order of his kingdom and the justice of his courts, she declared: "Blessed be the Lord your God, who preferred to place you on the throne of Israel" (I Kings 10:9). A conquering empire breeds resentment. A holy nation can inspire other countries to transform themselves.

This is the purpose of Israel's sovereignty: secure the land God gave, build a holy society, and let the example speak for itself.[82]

That example has already shaped the world more than most people realize. The constitutional structures that protect individual freedom in the modern West—limited government, rule of law, rights that no ruler can simply annul—don't trace back to Athens or Rome.[83] Athens had democracy and slavery simultaneously. Rome had law, but the emperor's word was final. The Torah introduced something neither had: a nation where even Moses and the kings of Israel stood under God's law, where the powerful were answerable to legal limits, where the widow, the orphan, and the stranger had rights that could not be trampled.[84]

The American founders spoke of these rights as "self-evident" truths. But how did these truths become "self-evident" in the first place? Not from thin air. These are *Israel's* gifts to the world.

The Torah's influence on Israel shows most clearly in how the nation treats minorities. In July 2025, Syrian jihadists began slaughtering Druze villagers in southern Syria. Israel had no legal obligation to intervene—these weren't Israeli citizens. But Israel's own Druze population has served loyally in the IDF for generations, and the bonds between Israeli Druze and their Syrian relatives run deep. When the slaughter began, Israel acted. It bombed the jihadist positions and stopped the massacre—not for strategic gain, but out of loyalty to a minority that has long stood steadfastly with the Jewish state.[85] The world condemned the strikes. Even the United States criticized Israel's intervention. The UN gave no credit for stopping a genocide in progress. Israel was the only country willing to act.

Why was Israel the only nation on earth to care about the Syrian Druze? How has Israel built the kind of mutual loyalty with its minorities that led them to risk international condemnation to protect people who aren't even its own citizens? And how has Israel managed what neighboring states like Syria and Iraq cannot achieve except through brutal terror—a society where minorities flourish rather than face persecution?

The answer isn't found in the UN Charter or international law, but in the Torah itself.

The Bible commands Israel to "love the stranger" thirty-six times. It commands the people to “love their neighbor” exactly once. This disproportion isn't accidental. God roots the obligation in Israel's own suffering: "You yourselves know how it feels to be strangers, because you were strangers in Egypt" (Exodus 23:9). Israel’s own national memory is its foundation for forming a nation dedicated to justice.

The framework gets more specific. In Leviticus, God establishes the law of *ger toshav*—the resident alien who accepts the seven Noahide commandments binding on all humanity—and grants him full standing in Israelite society: "If any of your fellow Israelites become poor and are unable to support themselves among you, help them as you would a resident alien, so they can continue to live among you" (Leviticus 25:35). Maimonides codified what this means in practice:

Jews must establish courts for resident aliens and "act towards resident aliens with the same respect and loving kindness as one would to a fellow Jew."[86] You don't have to be Jewish to have rights in a Jewish state. You simply have to be a moral, God-fearing human being—and that is enough.

Arrogant Western nations like Great Britain and France take great pleasure in lecturing Israel about minority rights—even as their own multicultural experiments are destroying the social fabric of their own countries. Meanwhile, everyday life in Israel is an example of what works: a strong Jewish national identity combined with biblical principles of justice for the stranger. Other nations could learn from this model, but first they would have to admit that the Jews might have something to teach them.

None of this reaches its fulfillment in some otherworldly future. Maimonides is characteristically blunt about what the Messianic era actually looks like: "Let it not enter your mind that in the Messianic times anything from the world's natural order will be nullified, or that there will be any innovation in the work of creation, but rather the world continues according to its custom."[87] People will still farm, trade, raise families, and govern cities. The difference is that all of it will unfold through a nation living under God's law—which means that every Jew who attaches themselves to that collective has a role, whatever their personal level of observance.

Rabbi Kook goes even further. "The soul of the sinners of Israel in the footsteps of the Messiah, those who connect with love to matters of the collective of Israel, to the land of Israel and to the life of the nation, is more perfected than that of the wholesome believers of Israel who do not have this advantage of self-feeling for the benefit of the collective and the building of the nation and the land."[88]

The secular kibbutznik draining swamps in the Galilee, the atheist soldier defending the borders, the non-observant engineer building roads through Judea—if they love the people of Israel and dedicate themselves to building the nation, their souls are loftier than the Torah scholar who studies in isolation, concerned only with his own spiritual perfection. Redemption comes through the nation, not through private piety alone. The imperfect Jew who builds up the nation is advancing God's plan for the world. The righteous Jew who ignores the nation—no matter how scrupulously he observes every commandment—is not.

This is why Rabbi Kook insisted that the generation of redemption must draw on all of Israel's strength, even from those who seem furthest from holiness. "He who does not know how to turn bitter into sweet and darkness into light will not enter the hall of the Messiah."[89] The coarse must be transformed, not discarded. Even imperfect forces can be channeled toward God's purpose—and in the generation of redemption, they must be.

Israel Eldad once compared the Jewish people to a locomotive. The engine pulls forward, and the other cars—the nations—follow. But humanity won't be redeemed by theology or sermons. People are too materialistic, too hungry for power. What the world needs is proof: a real nation, living under God's law, showing that it actually works. Only such a nation can drag the rest of humanity toward something better.

"I have separated you from the nations to be Mine" (Leviticus 20:26). When the Torah forbids intermarriage and commands Israel to remain separate from other nations, it is not arrogance, but rather necessity. You can't pull someone out of a pit while you yourself are standing on quicksand. Only by standing firmly apart—distinct, unassimilated, rooted in its mission—can the Jewish people acquire the spiritual strength necessary to fulfill our mission as a light unto the nations.[90]

Israel's insistence that it was chosen by God is frequently misread as supremacy. The determination of traditional Jews to maintain a separate identity, even while living among other peoples, breeds suspicion and resentment. These accusations aren't new, and they won't go away. They are the price of refusing to dissolve into the majority.

But this resentment stems from a fundamental misunderstanding of Israel's purpose. Rabbi Yehuda Leon Ashkenazi explains it through a metaphor. After the Flood, humanity divided into seventy distinct nations. "Humanity... is like a bouquet composed of seventy different flowers. Every flower in the bouquet has its place and importance, and if a particular type of flower is missing, the bouquet is incomplete." Each nation contributes something unique to the world. "If that contribution is missing, the bouquet is not the bouquet that the Creator intends it to be."

Every empire in history tried to create its own version of the bouquet by making all the flowers identical to itself. The Spanish, English, and French empires claimed universality while forcing every nation into its mold. "The imperialist approach is immoral because it seeks to erase the uniqueness of each flower. According to it, there is only one type of flower in the bouquet. That is not moral."

Israel's mission is the opposite: "to assemble the bouquet while giving a unique place to each flower." Israel doesn't try to remake other nations in its image, but rather to be the thread that holds them together. "Israel is not part of the bouquet. Israel is not part of the seventy nations. For the bouquet to be a bouquet, there must be a thread that ties the flowers together. That is our role. We are the connecting thread." You can't tie flowers together if you're trying to be one of the flowers. "To do this, we must avoid at all costs taking sides in favor of any particular flower. We must remain the thread—in other words, truly universal."[91]

Israel refuses both paths other nations have taken: it will not conquer the world and force others to become like Israel, nor will it assimilate into the world and become like everyone else. This is what Israel was chosen for: to help all nations learn to live together and appreciate one another's unique contributions. The true United Nations—not the corrupt institution in New York—must be centered in Jerusalem. Only when this gathering of nations is centered in the holy city and run by God's people according to the Torah will Israel become God's vehicle for bringing peace among the nations.

This is what Isaiah prophesied: "In the end of days, the mountain of the Lord's house shall be established as the top of the mountains... and all the nations shall flow unto it... For out of Zion shall go forth the law, and the word of the Lord from Jerusalem. And He shall judge between the nations, and shall decide for many peoples; and they shall beat their swords into plowshares, and their spears into pruning hooks; nation shall not lift up sword against nation, neither shall they learn war any more" (Isaiah 2:2–4). Nations quarreling with one another will no longer go to war. They will come to Jerusalem, where Israel will help them work out their disagreements in peace, according to the Torah.

Zechariah saw what lies ahead: "Ten men from every language of the nations shall grasp the garment of a Jewish man, saying, 'Let us go with you, for we have heard that God is with you'" (Zechariah 8:23). When Israel fulfills its calling—when it builds a nation where power is bound by justice and holiness shapes public life—the world will stop resenting and start learning. As Rabbi Kook wrote, "All cultures in the world will be renewed through the revival of our spirit. Abraham's blessing to all nations of the earth will begin its work with strength and revelation."[92] Israel will teach the world by being the nation it was meant to be.

God's decision to pass over Abraham was not a strange detour. It was the whole plan. The world has never lacked for holy individuals, and so the Torah was not designed for them. It was designed to make an entire people holy, so that people could show the rest of the world that holiness is not the private possession of saints. God wants more than that. He wants holy nations, holy societies, holy civilizations—and Israel is how He intends to get there.

“Fortunate is the world to have such a nation in it.”[93]

5

No Going Back

What makes a Jew? Is it belief? Practice? Birth?

For most nations, the answer is straightforward: you're French if you're born in France or become a naturalized citizen. You're American if you're born there or if you pledge allegiance and pass the citizenship test. But the Jews are different. From the very beginning, the people of Israel were a *family*—the children of Abraham, Isaac, and Jacob. The nation of Israel began as one particular household that God Himself chose to carry forward His mission in the world.

Unlike Abraham, whose son Ishmael was excluded, or Isaac, whose son Esau went his own way, all of Jacob's children were included in God's promise. God told Jacob: "I am the Lord, the God of your father Abraham's house and the God of Isaac's house; the land on which you are lying I will assign to you and to your offspring" (Genesis 28:13). Later God promises Jacob directly: "A nation and a congregation of nations shall come from you, and kings shall come out of your loins. The land that I gave to Abraham and Isaac I give to you; and to your descendants after you I will give the land." (Genesis 35:11–12). And when Jacob summons his sons, he frames them as a single people: "Assemble and hear, O sons of Jacob; listen to Israel your father." (Genesis

49:1–2). Israel begins as a family—Jacob's household—which becomes a nation.

Jewish law reflects this reality. If your mother is Jewish, you are Je wish—automatically.[94] No conversion needed, no faith required, no baptism, no confirmation, no questions asked. You are born into the people of Israel the same way you're born into any other people: by descent.[95] Similarly, being a Jew is permanent; though a Jew might abandon his faith in the Torah, he remains a Jew. Family ties can never be severed.[96]

The *bar mitzvah* and *bat mitzvah* are often misunderstood as Jewish versions of baptism or confirmation—religious rites that formally bring you into a religion. But they could not be more different. They are not verbs; a Jewish teen is not "*bar mitzvahed*" or "*bat mitzvahed.*" *Bar mitzvah* means "son of the commandment" and *bat mitzvah* means "daughter of the commandment." The terms describe a legal status, not a ritual that makes you Jewish. When a Jewish boy reaches the age of 13 and a Jewish girl reaches the age of 12, they automatically become *bar mitzvah* or *bat mitzvah*—officially obligated by Jewish law to fulfill the commandments—whether they celebrate it or not, whether they even know about it or not. The obligation to fulfill the commandments simply attaches to them, because they are members of the nation and always have been. They were Jewish the moment they were born. The party doesn't make them Jewish. Nothing makes them Jewish. They already are.

By this logic, joining the Jewish people from the outside should be impossible. No matter how much I might love my neighbor's family, no matter how much I admire their warmth, share their values, and even feel at home at their dinner table, I can never truly become one of them. You're either born into a family or you're not. By all normal standards, Israel should be no different. And yet, the Torah makes room for exactly that impossibility. There *is* a way to become part of the family of Israel—through a process called "*giyur.*"

Giyur is almost always translated as "conversion," but that translation is misleading. The word *giyur* derives from the Hebrew root *gimmel-vav-reish*, meaning "to sojourn"—to leave where you came from and take up residence among a people not your own. It is not a word about belief or spiritual transformation. It is a word about relocation, in the deepest sense of the term.

When a Christian converts, he professes a new creed. When a Muslim converts, he submits to divine law. But the person who undergoes *giyur* does something that has no real parallel in any other tradition: he changes his national identity, abandoning his people and casting his lot permanently with another.

The Torah uses the word *ger*—sojourner—to describe anyone who dwells among a people not their own. Abraham called himself a *ger* among the Hittites (Genesis 23:4). A *ger toshav* is a non-Jew who lives among the Jewish people in the land of Israel while remaining a non-Jew. A *ger tzedek*—a "righteous sojourner," the rabbinic term for a full convert to the Jewish people—goes further still. He doesn't come to visit or to live alongside the Jews. He comes to stay, permanently and completely, forever binding his fate to Israel's fate as though he had been born into it.

Although the Jewish nation began as a family, it was never racially or ethnically exclusive. From the moment Israel became a nation, others joined. When the Israelites left Egypt, a "mixed multitude" went with them and stood at Sinai to receive the Torah.[97] Jethro the Midianite joined Israel's camp,[98] and throughout history, people of every background have done the same. Jews have never been defined by race or color. What unites all Jews is not blood or appearance, but national loyalty—a shared story and destiny.

During his February 2026 interview with Mike Huckabee, the US Ambassador to Israel, Tucker Carlson demanded that Israelis undergo genetic testing to prove their claim to the land. "Why don't we do genetic testing on everybody in the land and find out who Abram's descendants are?" he asked. "We've cracked the human genome. We can do that. Why don't we do that?"[99] The question reveals a complete misunderstanding of what the Jewish people are. Israel is not a bloodline with a deed attached. We are a nation—one that others have always been able to join, and have joined, across every generation of our history. No genetic test can measure national belonging.

No single story in the Bible captures this better than the Book of Ruth.

Ruth was a Moabite princess. When her Jewish husband died young, every practical and social consideration pointed in one direction: go home, return to her family, and return to the life she came from. Instead she did the opposite. When Naomi urged her to return home, Ruth refused: "Do not urge me to leave you, to turn back and not follow you. For wherever you go, I will go; wherever you lodge, I will lodge; your people shall be my people, and your God my God" (Ruth 1:16).

The order of her words is critical. Ruth first pledges loyalty to the people of Israel—"your people shall be my people"—and only then to the God of Israel—"your God shall be my God." Her conversion begins not with theology, but with belonging, with an act of national allegiance that precedes and grounds everything else.

Orpah's choice confirms this from the other direction. When Orpah turned back, Naomi said to Ruth: “Behold, your sister-in-law has returned to her people and to her gods” (Ruth 1:15). The Sages noticed the sequence: first her people, then her gods. From this they concluded: “Since she returned to her people, she returned to her gods.”[100] Orpah did not abandon Israel's God and then choose to return to Moab. She returned to the nation of Moab, and inevitably returned to the Moabite gods as well. In the Book of Ruth, national allegiance is not the consequence of religious belief. It is its precondition.

Ruth did not say to Naomi, "Teach me your laws and I will consider joining your people." She said nothing about laws at all. What she saw was Naomi herself—a woman who carried herself with a sense of purpose and mission unlike anyone Ruth had ever known in Moab. As Rabbi Moshe Miller puts it, Ruth was saying: "The laws are not really what I'm interested in. They aren't the real point. What I care about is that when you left town, the lights went out in Moab. I want to be part of that light."[101] Whatever Naomi was, Ruth wanted to become it. "Your people shall be my people" is not a legal declaration. It is the cry of someone who has fallen in love with an entire nation and will do whatever it takes to belong to it.

The Torah deliberately sets Ruth's heroic decision against an earlier choice made by Naomi's family. The Sages explain their sin: "Elimelech and his sons Mahlon and Chilion were prominent members of their generation and were leaders of their generation. And for what reason were they punished? They were punished because they left the land of Israel..."[102] When famine struck and the nation suffered, the wealthy Elimelech abandoned his people and fled to Moab. Ruth made the opposite choice. She left Moab—her home, her comfort, her status as a princess—to join Israel when it had nothing to offer her but hardship. Elimelech's family line was nearly destroyed by his abandonment; Ruth restored it through her loyalty. Her unwavering loyalty to the nation of Israel earned her a place at the center of Israel's story: she became the great-grandmother of David, the founder of Israel's royal line.

The sages make clear that conversion is first and foremost about joining the destiny of the Jewish people, not mastering or even accepting principles of faith. When a potential convert comes before a *beit din*, a conversion court, the judges do not begin by quizzing him on Jewish law or doctrine. Instead, they ask: "What did you see that motivated you to come to convert? Don't you know that the Jewish people at the present time are anguished, suppressed, despised, and harassed, and hardships are frequently visited upon them?"

The focus is entirely on the gravity of joining the people of Israel—accepting its responsibilities, sharing in its suffering, and taking on its fate. The candidate is tested first in his willingness to bind himself to the destiny of the nation. Only after he replies, "I know, and although I am unworthy of joining the Jewish people and sharing in their sorrow, I nevertheless desire to do so," do the judges move to the next stage and explain the religious obligations of being a Jew. "And then the judges of the court inform him of some of the lenient commandments and some of the stringent commandments..."[103]

The traditional sequence as laid out by the Talmud is strange. The court accepts the candidate *before* teaching him the fundamentals of faith. Religiously speaking, he is "in" before he knows what he is getting into. All he needs to know is one thing: that he is choosing to cast his lot with a unique and persecuted people, and that he wants to join them anyway. That is enough for acceptance; religious belief and practice can be taught later.[104]

For Christians, this process seems strange. Picture a young man at a revival meeting. The preacher calls sinners to repentance, the worship band plays, and suddenly he feels it—the presence of God, undeniable and overwhelming. He walks down the aisle, declares Jesus as his savior, and the pastor embraces him while the congregation celebrates. He is born again. It's personal, emotional, transformative—a moment between the individual and God. The spiritual experience *is* the conversion.

But a *beit din* is nothing like that. Three rabbis sit in judgment. They ask hard questions and test the potential convert's resolve. They warn him about the suffering that has so often been the fate of the Jewish people. They even try to discourage the candidate. The process is formal, legal, and deliberate. Yes, when the court finally accepts the convert, when he immerses in the *mikvah* and emerges as part of the Jewish people—it is deeply emotional, often overwhelming. But the emotion *follows* the conversion. It's the joy that comes after a long and complex naturalization process, the relief and celebration of finally belonging to the nation you've fought so hard to join.[105]

Becoming a Jew begins with accepting the people of Israel and its history; observance of the commandments comes next. As Michael Wyschogrod wrote: "Judaism involves a set of ideas, beliefs, values, and obligations... but these are, in a sense, superstructure rather than foundation. The foundation of Judaism is the family identity of the Jewish people as the descendants of Abraham, Isaac, and Jacob."[106]

Rabbi Joseph B. Soloveitchik describes this as the acceptance of the "Covenant of Fate," the bond that unites all Jews across time and space. This is the covenant that every convert enters first: "We are all in the realm of a shared fate that binds together the different strata of the nation and does not discriminate between nobility and commonfolk, between rich and poor, between a prince dressed in royal purple velvet and a poor man who goes begging from door to door, between a pious Jew and an assimilationist. Even if we live in different lands, speak different languages, or look different, we have but one fate. When the Jew in the cave is attacked, the security of the Jew standing in the courtyard of the king is jeopardized."

Joining Israel means taking on everything that comes with it—the people's burdens, its history, its exile, its suffering, and its triumphs. Shared fate is lived through empathy and moral responsibility: "If boiling water is poured on the head of a Moroccan Jew, the prim and proper Jew in Paris or London must scream, and by feeling the pain, shows himself loyal to the nation." A convert must internalize this bond. Only after accepting this national destiny does a convert take on the "Covenant of Mission"—the religious and theological calling expressed through Torah observance.[107]

Can someone accept the Torah of Israel without accepting the destiny of Israel? Can a person say, "Your God is my God" without first saying, "Your people are my people"? Rabbi Aharon Lichtenstein answers with an emphatic "no": "In the 'I and Thou' encounter that takes place in conversion, the convert meets two 'Thous': the Master of the Universe and the people of Israel." One cannot accept the Torah's commandments while standing apart from the people who came out of Egypt, wandered in the desert, conquered the Land, flourished in it, were exiled, and returned in our own time. A convert who embraces the Torah but refuses to join the people of Israel is not a true conver t.[108]

Rabbi Yehuda Leon Ashkenazi goes even further. He argues that genuine conversion should take place primarily in the land of Israel—because there, and only there, can one truly join the nation of Israel. To convert in exile is to join a religious community detached from its land. But in Israel, conversion becomes what it was always meant to be: "an act of citizenship and attachment to the Israeli nation, when the religion encompassing this process is Judaism."[109] The Torah itself assumes this national context: "And if a convert sojourns with you *in your land*, you shall not oppress him" (Leviticus 19:33). The verse presumes that a convert will join the people of Israel within their land, living as part of the nation God created, something that is not possible in exile, where Jews do not fully live as a nation.

A convert who binds themselves to Israel in this way becomes fully and completely part of the people—a Jew through and through, equal in status and responsibility to the physical descendants of Jacob. By joining the nation in its land, they enter the covenant of fate and take their place in Israel's history and destiny. And like those born Jewish, the choice is permanent. A convert who later abandons the Torah, rejects the commandments, even walks away from the Jewish community entirely—remains a Jew. They joined the nation. There's no going back.[110]

6

The Land that Devours

When disaster strikes, we look for someone to blame. The rebels, the troublemakers, the corrupt at the bottom of society—these are the usual suspects. But not always. Sometimes the most destructive errors come from the top, from respected leaders and elites. This is what happened in the tragic episode of the spies.

The Torah goes out of its way to establish the credentials of the spies: "Each one shall be a chieftain... all of them were men of distinction, heads of the children of Israel" (Numbers 13:2–3). The sages emphasize that "everywhere that the word 'men' (*anashim*) is used, it is referring to righteous men... Moses did not wish to send the spies at his own initiative until he consulted with the Holy One blessed be He regarding each and every one, so-and-so from tribe such-and-such, and He said to him that they were worthy."[111]

The spies were not common scouts. They were princes of Israel, Torah scholars, leaders who dedicated their lives to guiding their respective tribes.

And yet it was precisely these men who brought back the evil report that turned the people against the land of Israel and ultimately condemned an entire generation to die in the wilderness. Which forces us to ask: what went so terribly wrong? How could men of such stature, righteous in every way, have made such a destructive choice?

Though some argue the spies were corrupt and self-serving, this misses the deeper lesson of their failure. Their sin was not one of temptation or greed. It was ideological: they recoiled from the very idea of Jewish nationhood.

The spies were not only afraid of the giants that awaited them in the Holy Land. Their deeper fear was of becoming a normal nation. In the wilderness, Israel's existence was sustained entirely by miracles—manna from heaven, water from the well of Miriam, and clouds of divine protection. It was a life of clarity and simplicity, shielded from the complications of politics, agriculture, and war. Though the desert was physically perilous, Israel could live there focused entirely on serving God. But crossing into the land would change everything. There, they would have to plow fields and defend their borders, like every other nation.

Rabbi Menachem Mendel Schneerson explains that there are two types of righteous people: "There are those who dedicate their lives to individual purity and personal spiritual growth, detaching themselves from the world and its material interests. And there are those who are leaders of their generation, who do not focus primarily on their personal spiritual level but instead devote themselves to the needs of their people, even if this requires engaging with matters that are beneath their spiritual rank."[112]

The spies belonged firmly to the first category. They sought a life of uninterrupted spiritual work, and the desert gave them that. What they resisted was the Torah's demand to take on the messy job of nationhood and to reveal God's presence not in isolation from the world but within it.

This is what they meant when they said: "It is a land that devours its inhabitants" (Numbers 13:32). The land consumes time, energy, and focus, leaving less space for Torah and spiritual connection. From their perspective, this was not a rejection of God but a defense of His Torah: better to remain a religion in the desert than to risk losing everything as a nation in the land.

Their logic had one further implication. If God's plan was for Israel to enter the natural order—tilling fields, building governments, fighting wars—then Israel must submit to the laws of nature. And under those laws, the few and the weak cannot defeat the mighty and the many. By this reasoning, even God Himself could not help them defeat the Canaanites,[113] for He had chosen to place them under natural law.[114] In their thinking, the moment Israel became a nation on its land, God Himself could no longer intervene miraculously without undoing His own purpose. Understood this way, their sin was not self-serving nor cowardice but a tragic refusal to believe that Israel could build a holy nation within the natural world.

At first, the spies sounded like patriots. "Look at this fruit! The land flows with milk and honey, just as God promised!" But then came the turn: "We cannot go up against the people, for they are stronger than we are" (Numbers 13:31).

Their fear, Rabbi Yitzchak Nissenbaum explains, had nothing to do with losing battles. The Canaanites weren't just militarily powerful—they were civilized. They had cities, courts, sophisticated legal systems, and centuries of cultural refinement. The spies looked at themselves, former slaves who had spent forty years wandering in the desert, and feared what would happen when those two worlds collided. How could Israel's fragile identity survive contact with such a civilization? In their eyes, the people faced an impossible choice: Torah or the land. Better to remain in the desert, preserving the purity of Torah in isolation, even if it meant renouncing the inheritance of the land.

This was the true danger of the spies. The spies didn't say, "Let us rebel." They said, "Let us protect the Torah." By framing Torah and the land of Israel as opposites, they created a false dilemma that has haunted Jewish history ever since: the claim that Torah can only thrive in exile, detached from the burdens of national life. But God never intended that separation. The Torah wasn't given to wandering tribes in the wilderness. It was given to a people on their way to build a nation in a specific land.

The spies' mistake was to cling to Torah while rejecting the land. But just as dangerous was the opposite mistake, made by the *ma'apilim*—the Israelites who tried to storm Canaan on their own. When God decreed that the generation of the spies would die in the wilderness, a group rose up defiantly, proclaiming, "Here we are, we will go up!" (Numbers 14:40). They were bold, even zealous — but they went without Moses' approval, without the Ark, and without God's command.

Their attack collapsed almost immediately. The Amalekites and Canaanites struck them down and crushed them, pursuing them all the way to Hormah. The message was clear: you cannot conquer the land while abandoning God. But the spies had made the opposite error—trying to preserve Torah while abandoning the land. Both failed, because God never meant to separate the two.[115]

God rejected both the spies and the *ma'apilim*. An entire generation—the people who had walked through the sea and stood at Sinai—were condemned to die in the wilderness. Only their children would cross the Jordan and claim the land.

Israel would indeed go on to conquer and settle its homeland, because nations must. But the broken perspective planted by the spies, that Torah and the Land could be separated, did not die in the desert. It lingered in the heart of Israel and would return with a vengeance in later generations. Again and again, Jews would be tempted to choose one without the other: Torah without the land, or the land without Torah. And each time, the cost would be catastrophic.

7

The Unmarked Grave

Moses led the people out of Egypt. He stood before Pharaoh, the most powerful man in the world, and stared him down as plague after plague shattered Egypt. He led his people through the sea and brought down the Torah from Sinai. For forty years, he led an infuriatingly stiff-necked people through the wilderness, defending them selflessly before God when they sinned. He taught them God's law, judged their disputes, and bore their complaints. He was the shepherd of his generation, the greatest prophet who ever lived, the man who spoke to God face to face.

And yet, when the time came to cross into the Promised Land, God refused to let him enter.

"And the Lord said to Moses, 'Go up... and see the land of Canaan, which I am giving to the children of Israel as a possession. And you shall see the land from afar, but you shall not enter there'" (Deuteronomy 32:49-52). Moses died on Mount Nebo, gazing across the Jordan at the land he would never walk upon. "And Moses, the servant of the Lord, died there, in the land of Moab, by the mouth of the Lord. And He buried him in the valley, in the land of Moab, opposite Beth

Pe'or. And no person knows the place of his burial, unto this day" (Deuteronomy 34:5-6).

The greatest prophet in Israel's history is buried outside the Holy Land in an unmarked grave. Why? Why was Moses, who dedicated his entire life to leading Israel to the Promised Land, denied burial there? How could God treat His most faithful servant this way?

The question only deepens when we compare Moses to Joseph. Joseph spent most of his life in Egypt, rising to become Pharaoh's viceroy, yet he merited burial in the land of Israel. When the Israelites left Egypt, it was Moses himself who ensured Joseph would not be left behind: "And Moses took the bones of Joseph with him: for Joseph had made the children of Israel swear, saying, 'God will surely visit you; and you shall carry up my bones away hence with you'" (Exodus 13:19). Years later, when the conquest of the land was complete, Joseph's dying wish was fulfilled: "The bones of Joseph, which the children of Israel brought up out of Egypt, buried they in Shechem, in a parcel of ground which Jacob bought of the sons of Hamor the father of Shechem" (Joshua 24:32).

Why was Joseph's body brought home, while Moses—Israel's greatest leader—was left behind?

Troubled by this question, the Sages point to a fascinating distinction between these two great leaders of Israel. Even while enslaved in Egypt, Joseph openly identified as a Hebrew from Israel. When Potiphar's wife accused him before her household, she called him "a Hebrew man" (Genesis 39:14). Later, imprisoned and forgotten, Joseph told Pharaoh's butler, "I was stolen from the land of the Hebrews" (Genesis 40:15). Joseph made it unmistakably clear: though he currently found himself in Egypt, he was not an Egyptian. He belonged to the people and land of Israel. For this reason, God rewarded him. His bones—his *atzamot*, a Hebrew word that means both "bones" and "essence"—were brought back to rest in Israel.

Moses never made that declaration. When he first fled Pharaoh's wrath and escaped to Midian, he rescued the daughters of Jethro from hostile shepherds. They went home and reported to their father, "An Egyptian man saved us" (Exodus 2:19). Moses presented himself as an Egyptian, and never corrected it. He allowed a foreign identity to attach to him without protest. And so, taught the Sages, God decreed that his *atzamot* would not be buried in Israel.[116]

Both Joseph and Moses lived out their lives in exile. But Joseph's heart was anchored in the land of Israel, while Moses allowed himself to be defined as an Egyptian. The difference was not geography but orientation—where each man saw himself as truly belonging.

This seems harsh. Moses had just arrived in Midian, exhausted and alone. He was forced to flee for his life after killing an Egyptian taskmaster who was beating a Hebrew slave. Of course Jethro's daughters saw him as Egyptian—he had grown up in Pharaoh's palace, spoke Egyptian, and dressed like an Egyptian. What was he supposed to say? Can he really have been expected to interrupt his hosts and immediately correct them, declaring his Hebrew identity to strangers in a foreign land?

The Sages say yes. A Jew, no matter where he lives, no matter how far he wanders, must never allow himself to be defined by exile. Even when it is easier to blend in, even when openly identifying as a Hebrew might invite danger or suspicion, the choice of identity matters. Joseph was enslaved, imprisoned, and powerless—and still he proclaimed, "I was stolen from the land of the Hebrews." Moses was a fugitive in a strange land—and still, the Sages say, he should have corrected the daughters of Jethro.

Exile is not just a place. It is a state of mind. A Jew can live his entire life in Jerusalem and still be in exile if his heart is not anchored to his people. And a Jew can live his entire life in a foreign land and still belong to Israel if he never allows that land to define him.

Moses brought Israel to the edge of the land. He gave them the Torah, taught them God's law, and prepared them to enter as a nation. But he could not cross over himself. The man who would lead the Jewish people into nationhood had to be Joshua—a man who never forgot where he truly belonged.

8

The Seduction of Normalcy

Joshua shattered the Canaanite armies. First, Jericho fell, then Ai. In the north and south, one miraculous victory followed another, and the people of Israel entered the land God had promised their fathers. Winning the battles, in retrospect, was the easy part.

The real test came next: could Israel live among the very cultures they had just defeated without becoming like them? God knew the danger before they ever crossed the Jordan, and He was explicit about it. "Do not follow their statutes" (Leviticus 18:3). "Do not intermarry with them" (Deuteronomy 7:3). "I have separated you from the nations to be Mine" (Leviticus 20:26).

Two thousand years later, Rabbi Moshe Isserles would explain the principle: "A Jew must remain distinct from the nations in his clothing and in his actions. But all this is forbidden only when the practices of non-Jews are adopted for reasons of immodesty—or when a practice is followed as a custom with no rational basis, which raises concern for the ways of the Emorites"—one of the very nations Israel now lived among—"and suggests a trace of idolatrous influence."[117] Nachmanides warned that without this separation, a nation could become "a scoundrel within the bounds of Torah,"[118] technically obedient yet indistinguishable from its neighbors.

The commands were clear, but Israel failed them almost immediately. Tribe after tribe stopped short of completing the conquest. "Manasseh did not drive out... Ephraim did not drive out... Zebulun did not drive out..." (Judges 1:27-33) They allowed the Canaanites to live among them.

A messenger of the Lord confronted them: "You shall make no covenant with the inhabitants of this land; you shall tear down their altars... But you did not obey Me. What is this you have done? Therefore I also said: I will not drive them out before you; they shall become traps for you, and their gods shall be a snare to you" (Judges 2:2-3).

It happened exactly as God warned. "The children of Israel lived among the Canaanites, Hittites, Amorites, Perizzites, Hivites, and Jebusites. They took their daughters as wives and gave their own daughters to their sons, and they served their gods" (Judges 3:5-6). Living among the pagan tribes, the people of Israel became like them. The cycle repeated throughout the era of the judges: "The children of Israel did what was evil in the eyes of the Lord and served the Baals. They abandoned the Lord, the God of their fathers... and followed other gods, from among the gods of the peoples around them" (Judges 2:11-13). Israel absorbed everything around them—the gods of Aram, Sidon, Moab, the Ammonites, and the Philistines (Judges 10:6-7).

Their national identity dissolved. God delivered them into the hands of their enemies, and the oppression awakened them—barely. Without it, they would have vanished entirely.

The Sages paint a picture of just how far Israel had fallen. In Ephraim, only a few miles from Shiloh where the Tabernacle stood and the presence of God rested among His people, a man named Micah built a shrine for idol worship. The two sites were so close that the smoke from Micah's altar and the smoke from the Tabernacle intermingled in the sky above Ephraim.[119]

Most of Israel went to Micah.

This spiritual collapse left Israel defenseless. When the Philistines attacked at Aphek, Israel's army fell apart. In just two short battles, thirty-four thousand Israelite soldiers were killed, including the sons of Eli the high priest. The Philistines captured the Ark of the Covenant. When the elderly Eli heard the horrific news, he collapsed and died. In short order, Shiloh and the Tabernacle were destroyed.[120] For the first but not the last time, it appeared that Israel's national experiment was over.

But out of the ruins of Shiloh came Samuel, a prophet unlike any Israel had seen since Moses. He traveled throughout the land for twenty years, educating and inspiring the people of Israel to return to God. It took time, but the people responded to his call. They rejected idolatry, and ultimately came to Samuel to ask him to appoint them a king. They were tired of the tribalism and internal tensions that made Israel vulnerable to the attacks of neighboring peoples. “Now, set up for us a king to judge us like all the nations” (I Samuel 8:5).

The people were right to yearn for unity, but by asking for a king "like all the other nations," they revealed how far they still were from grasping God's vision for Israel. The Sages draw a sharp distinction between two very different requests hidden within the same demand.

Rabbi Eliezer taught: "The elders of the generation made a fit request, as it is written, 'Give us a king to judge us.' But the common people acted unworthily, as it is written, 'That we also may be like all the nations and that our king may judge us and go before us.'"[121] The elders wanted a king who would govern them according to God's law. The masses wanted something else entirely—a ruler who would make Israel safe, stable, and indistinguishable from every other nation around them.[122] Samuel warned them of what they were asking for, but God instructed him to grant the request, and Israel set out on the difficult path of monarchy.

Saul was chosen: a man of courage, stature, and personal piety who has been judged harshly by posterity, perhaps too harshly. He united the tribes for the first time in generations, built Israel's first truly national army—the original Israel Defense Forces—and led them into battle against enemies on every side, usually successfully. He died as he lived, fighting the Philistines on Mount Gilboa rather than surrender. By any normal measure, he was a great king.

But Israel's king was never meant to be normal. "He shall write for himself two copies of this Torah... and he shall read it all the days of his life... so that he may not turn away from the commandment" (Deuteronomy 17:18-20). An Israelite king is not meant to rule by his own judgment or by popular will. His entire legitimacy rests on his willingness to execute God's will, and the moment he substitutes his own calculations for God's commands, he ceases to function as Israel's king in any meaningful sense.

Saul could not make that leap. When God commanded him to destroy Amalek completely, he hesitated, sparing the Amalekite king and the best livestock. When Samuel confronted him, he betrayed his fundamental flaw: "I feared the people and hearkened to their voice" (I Samuel 15:24). As Rabbi Yigal Ariel explains, "If a king acts as a messenger of God... then he will sit on the throne of God as king. But if he takes authority for himself, it is as if he has inherited the throne of his Creator. Royalty is, all at once, an opportunity and a great danger."[123] A messenger rules in God's name, holding authority in trust. An heir, by contrast, takes ownership; he doesn't serve the previous master, he replaces him. When Saul chose what the people wanted over what God commanded, he stopped being a messenger and became a usurper. That cost him the throne.

Saul's name comes from the Hebrew "*shaul,*" "borrowed." He borrowed the throne for a time, laying the groundwork for what would come next. He was the necessary first step toward the king Israel truly needed: David.

From his first moment in the public eye, David saw things differently than Saul. When Goliath taunted Israel's army, the soldiers saw a terrifying enemy. Saul saw a threat to national security. But David saw something else: "Who is this uncircumcised Philistine, that he should taunt the ranks of the living God?" (I Samuel 17:26). Not "the army of Israel", but "the ranks of the living God." For David, Israel's army was not a national military force that happened to worship God. It was the mighty arm of God, and its honor was God's honor.

Rabbi Shlomo Aviner explains the difference: "For Saul, the nation is a means to an end—a union, an association of people. There is disorder and the enemy threatens us; we cannot live in peace and tranquility. Therefore, we must establish order and strike the enemy so that we can dwell securely and observe Torah and commandments. This is the level of 'a king like all the nations.'"[124] Saul understood kingship as a practical necessity: defeat the enemies, create stability, protect the people so they could get on with their lives. It was a worthy goal. It was simply not enough.

In most countries, that would be more than sufficient. When James Carville ran Bill Clinton's 1992 presidential campaign, he summed up the entire logic of democratic politics in one phrase: "It's the economy, stupid." Keep people safe and prosperous, and history will judge you a success. But David understood that Israel existed for something higher. Not just to survive or even thrive, but to become a nation through which God's presence would be visible and real in the world.

This is why David's first act as king of a united Israel was to conquer Jerusalem and bring the Ark of the Covenant to its center. He didn't prioritize fortifications or tax policy. He put God at the heart of the capital, because he understood that Israel is the vessel through which God's will enters the world.

David's reign, followed by Solomon's, brought about a brief golden age. Under Solomon, Israel's influence stretched from Egypt to the Euphrates. The Queen of Sheba traveled from the ends of the earth to see this kingdom for herself. What she found astonished her: "You have wisdom and goodness in excess of that which I have heard. Blessed be the Lord your God, who preferred to place you on the throne of Israel" (I Kings 10:7-9). Kings from across the known world sought Solomon's counsel (II Chronicles 9:23). They came because Israel had become what David envisioned: a kingdom where power served holiness, where wealth and wisdom both pointed toward God.

The glory didn't last. The wise and brilliant Solomon stumbled, led astray by his idol-worshipping wives. After his death, the kingdom split in two — ten tribes broke away under Jeroboam and established a rival kingdom in the north, while only Judah and Benjamin remained under Solomon's son Rehoboam in the south. The united nation David built fell apart, and most of the kings who followed—north and south—ruled as if Israel were just another petty kingdom scrambling for power. The prophets raged at them: sacrifices in the Temple meant nothing if widows and orphans were abandoned, if justice was cast aside. This was not what God intended. This was not the nation David built.

Amid this long decline, one king stood out: Hezekiah. When he looked north at the remnants of the ten tribes—those who survived the Assyrian conquest and remained in the land—he saw brothers who needed to come home. They had been separated from Judah and Jerusalem for centuries, steeped in idolatry and corrupted religion. Others might have written them off as heretics, but Hezekiah was willing to break the Torah's law to bring them back.

Hezekiah made an audacious decision. He would invite the remnants of the northern tribes to celebrate Passover, the festival of Jewish nationhood, together with the people of Judah in Jerusalem. But there was a problem: the priests were not yet sanctified, the people had not gathered, and many who might come would not be ritually pure in time for the festival. So Hezekiah did something shocking: he postponed Passover by an entire month.

This was no small matter. The Sages later counted this among three actions "which the sages did not approve."[125] Jeroboam had also shifted dates of the festivals, earning eternal condemnation as one who "uprooted the Torah."[126] Hezekiah knew the risks, but pressed forward anyway. He sent messengers throughout northern Israel to the remnants of the ten tribes to invite them to Jerusalem for the delayed Passover.

Hezekiah's plan worked. Huge crowds of people came from the tribes of Asher, Manasseh and Zebulon. Many of them were ritually impure; by the letter of the law, they had no business eating the Passover offering. Yet Hezekiah prayed: "May the good Lord grant atonement to all who set their hearts to seek God, the Lord, God of their fathers, even if not according to the purity required for the sanctuary" (II Chronicles 30:18-19).

Around Hezekiah stood rabbis and other righteous men who understood the urgency of the situation but could not bring themselves to act. Their fear of violating religious law held them back. Hezekiah understood that he was crossing a line, temporarily setting aside the letter of the law to take advantage of a critical moment in Israel's national history. When he prayed, "May the good Lord grant atonement," he was not only praying for those who arrived impure. He was praying for himself. He was asking God to forgive him for a decision he believed was necessary, even though, by the letter of the law, postponing Passover was forbidden. But he also understood that uniting the nation mattered more than religious ritual. Unlike Saul, who bent God's word for his own benefit, Hezekiah was bending the rules in service of God's purpose.

And for one brief, awesome moment, it worked. "And there was great joy in Jerusalem, for since the days of Solomon the son of David, king of Israel, there had not been the like in Jerusalem" (II Chronicles 30:26).

But the moment passed. The kings who followed lacked Hezekiah's vision. The Temple stood for another hundred years, but yet again, the nation forgot why God brought them to the land of Israel in the first place.

By the time of Jeremiah, Judah had become a small, vulnerable state caught between two powers: Egypt to the south and Babylonia to the north. Each empire fought for control of the region, and Judah lay directly in their path. Judah's kings frantically tried to survive by shifting alliances, trusting diplomacy, treaties, and military calculations to keep the kingdom intact.

The prophets rejected this line of thinking. Judah's weakness was not merely political. God was using the great empires of the age to chastise and awaken His people. As Isaiah said in Hezekiah's time, "Woe to the Assyrian, the rod of my anger, in whose hand is the club of my wrath! I send him against a godless nation, I dispatch him against a people who anger me" (Isaiah 10:5-6). Foreign domination was not an accident; it was God's way of calling out to His wayward people.

As Babylon's armies advanced on Judea, thousands of terrified Jews fled south to Egypt, away from Nebuchadnezzar. Rabbi Jonathan Eibuschitz argues that this flight was the central failure of the generation. They didn't reject God, but they abandoned their nation at the moment it needed them most. Egypt offered safety, stability, and the illusion of comfort. They could build mini-temples and worship God there, but only as scattered individuals and communities, not as a people in their land.[127]

Ultimately, fleeing to Egypt would not save them. "Thus said God of Hosts, the God of Israel: If you turn your faces toward Egypt, and you go and sojourn there, the sword that you fear shall overtake you there, in the land of Egypt, and the famine you worry over shall follow at your heels in Egypt too; and there you shall die" (Jeremiah 42:15-16). As assimilationist Jews would learn over and over again throughout history, abandoning Jewish nationhood doesn't protect Jews from their enemies. The antisemites will come for you anyway.

As Jeremiah prophesied, Nebuchadnezzar's armies crushed Jerusalem, burned the Temple, and dragged the people into exile. But unlike other nations that were quickly absorbed into the conquering empire, the people of Judah did not lose their national identity in exile. Jeremiah also prophesied that the Jewish people would return to their land after seventy years,[128] and return they would.

9

A Civil War for the Jewish Soul

Nebuchadnezzar's court had a plan for conquered peoples: take their brightest young men, feed them well, educate them in the empire's language and culture, give them new names, and within a generation, you won't have a conquered people anymore—you'll have Babylonians.

Daniel didn't cooperate. He was a teenager, far from home, with no power and no allies, in a palace where everything was designed to remake him into a Babylonian nobleman. When offered the king's food and wine, he "resolved in his heart that he would not defile himself" (Daniel 1:8) and insisted on maintaining a kosher diet that would set him apart from the rest of the palace (Daniel 1:12-16). It was a small act of defiance, but it was also a declaration: you can dress me in Babylonian clothes and teach me the Babylonian language, but you cannot make me into something I am not.

Jerusalem lay in ruins, the Temple was ash, and the people of Judah were servants in a foreign empire. The central question of Jewish survival had already announced itself: how does a nation hold together when everything around it is designed to pull it apart?

Daniel rose to prominence anyway. His brilliance and integrity earned him influence under Babylonian rule, and when Babylon fell and the Medes took over, he kept his position. For the men around him, however, an incorruptible rival with the king's ear was an intolerable problem.

They couldn't find anything to accuse him of, so they set a trap. They went to Darius the Mede with a proposal: issue a decree that for thirty days, no one could pray to any god or man except the king. Anyone who violated it would be thrown into the lions' den.

The proposal appealed to Darius. He wanted to test his subjects' loyalty, to identify anyone who might resist Persian authority. Daniel's enemies knew this. They also knew Daniel prayed three times a day and would keep praying. Darius signed the decree.

"When Daniel learned that the decree had been put in writing, he went to his house, in whose upper chamber he had windows facing Jerusalem, and three times a day he knelt down, prayed, and made confession to his God, as he had always done" (Daniel 6:11).

Why did Daniel keep praying? Jewish law doesn't require martyrdom for prayer. He could have prayed in secret. He could have waited thirty days. Instead, he opened his windows toward Jerusalem and prayed in full view of the public. Not because he had a death wish, but because this was never just about prayer. Daniel was making a declaration: I belong to the Jewish people. My capital is Jerusalem, not Babylon or Persia. No king can change that. Even facing death, he would not hide his allegiance to his nation.

Daniel's enemies caught him praying and dragged him before the king. Darius had no choice—his own law demanded Daniel's execution.

They threw him into the lions' den, but God was with Daniel, and saved him from the lions.

When Cyrus succeeded Darius, he did something no conqueror had ever done: he issued a decree allowing the Jews to return home and rebuild the Temple, and returned the sacred vessels that Nebuchadnezzar had seized from Jerusalem and kept in the Babylonian treasury for decades.

What moved a foreign king to act with such urgency on behalf of a small, conquered people at the very start of his reign? The Cyrus Cylinder,[129] discovered in the ruins of Babylon, confirms that this was his general policy: he allowed conquered peoples across his empire to return to their lands and restore their temples. But his decree regarding Israel was different in kind. He did not only permit the Jews to return. He charged them with rebuilding the Temple, returned the sacred vessels by name, and invoked the God of Israel as the source of his own authority. Something convinced him that this people and this God were not like the others.

The most compelling answer is Daniel. By this point an elderly man who had served in the palace for decades, he may well have shown Cyrus the Hebrew prophecies that named him specifically. Isaiah had written more than a century earlier: "Thus says the Lord to His anointed, to Cyrus, whose right hand I take hold of to subdue nations before him... I will go before you and will level the mountains; I will break down gates of bronze and cut through bars of iron... so that you may know that I am the Lord, the God of Israel, who summons you by name" (Isaiah 45:1-3). Isaiah had even prophesied that Cyrus would declare of Jerusalem, "Let it be rebuilt," and of the Temple, "Let its foundations be laid" (Isaiah 44:28).

Imagine reading your own name in a prophecy written a hundred and fifty years before your birth. Cyrus understood something that many Jews themselves had forgotten: the Jewish people were different from other conquered nations. They belonged to their land, and God was calling them to return home.

But when the gates finally opened, only a handful of Jews answered Cyrus' call to return to Israel. Most chose the comfort of life in exile over the hard, uncertain work of rebuilding a land they knew only from their grandparents, a place they themselves had never seen and that lay in ruins since Nebuchadnezzar's armies destroyed it seventy years earlier.

A small group—only 42,360 people—led by Zerubbabel ben Shealtiel, a descendant of King David, and the high priest Joshua, left behind the comforts of Babylonian prosperity to make the journey home. It was this committed remnant, not the many who remained in exile, that would shape the future course of Jewish history.

Under Zerubbabel and later Ezra, the returning exiles worked to restore both their political institutions and their national character. The Temple was rebuilt, reestablishing the center of Jewish worship. Ezra made Torah study central to Jewish life and insisted on maintaining the nation's distinct identity—even forcing the dissolution of mixed marriages that threatened to blur the boundaries between Jews and neighboring peoples.[130] Later, Nehemiah restored Jerusalem's walls, returning dignity and honor to the city after centuries of ruin and neglect, rekindling a sense of national pride among the people.

For several centuries, the Jews lived in Judea, but always under foreign rule. The Persians allowed them limited self-governance as a small province within their empire. Later, Alexander the Great swept through the region, bringing with him Greek language and culture. After his death, Judea passed back and forth between the Ptolemaic rulers of Egypt and the Seleucid kings of Syria. At times, life was stable and even prosperous, but the Jews never enjoyed full independence. They were always semi-autonomous at best—able to maintain the Temple, laws, and communal life, yet ultimately subservient to imperial powers. Generation after generation, the people endured this uneasy balance, never forgetting the glorious era of David and Solomon and awaiting the day when their national freedom would be restored.

The greatest danger during this period did not come from the Seleucid armies, but from within. Greek culture was dazzling, sophisticated, and powerful. Entire segments of Jewish society became enamored with Hellenism, adopted Greek names, frequented the gymnasiums that their Greek overlords built, and slowly began to see themselves less as members of a distinct people and more as participants in the universal culture of Greece.

This spread of Greek culture in the Holy Land created deep divisions among the Jews themselves. Traditional Jews remained committed to their Torah way of life and refused to bend. But Hellenized Jews adopted Greek ways and saw themselves as Greeks—much as earlier generations of assimilated Jews in exile identified as Babylonians and Persians.

One of the great early Zionist thinkers, Rabbi Yitzchak Nissenbaum, explained the existential danger that the Hellenizers introduced: "Over time, the national element in Judaism and the religious element within it were once again separated... The Hebrew language was forgotten... They apparently considered all these things to be of minor importance and placed the entire weight of Jewish identity on religion and its commandments alone... opening the door to assimilation."[131]

The very word "Judaism" reflects this distortion. The term does not appear even once in the Bible, nor in the Mishnah or Talmud. It entered Jewish vocabulary only during the Hellenistic era, when Jews living under Greek influence began describing their way of life using the Greek term *Ioudaismos.* The early Church later adopted this term, and it eventually returned to Hebrew through Enlightenment-era Jews, who translated it as *Judentum* in German and *Yahadut* in H ebrew.[132] The concept of "Judaism" as a religion detached from the Jewish people—a system of beliefs and practices— is entirely a Greek invention.

Just as the Bible contains no word for "Judaism," it also contains no word for "religion" as we understand it today.[133] The modern Hebrew term for religion, *dat*, was chosen by modern scholars. "*Dat*" appears only once in the Hebrew Bible, in one of its latest books, the Book of Esther. There, Haman condemns the Jews to King Ahasuerus: "There is a certain people scattered and separate among the peoples throughout all the provinces of your kingdom, and their laws (*dat*) differ from those of every people, and they do not keep the king's laws (*dat*); it is therefore of no use for the king to let them be" (Esther 3:8). While *dat* could theoretically be translated as "religion," its plain meaning is closer to "ways," "laws," or "practices." As Gersonides explains, Haman was condemning the Jews precisely because "they do not have customs and practices similar to the customs of any other people, and their practices are distinct."[134] The word refers to the Jews' unique national customs and laws, not to a religion in the modern sense. This is precisely what the Hellenizers sought to change — stripping Jewish identity of its national character and reducing it to religion alone.

The danger came from inside. Jason and Menelaus were both Jewish high priests in Jerusalem in the decades before the revolt. Jason, originally Yehoshua, bought the high priesthood from Antiochus IV Epiphanes by bribing him. He used his position to transform Jerusalem into a Greek polis, building gymnasiums that lured priests away from Temple service to compete naked in Greek athletic contes ts.[135] Menelaus went further. He outbid Jason for the office, financed his bribes by looting the Temple treasury, and was implicated in the murder of the legitimate high priest Onias III. These hellenized Jews weaponized the high priesthood to force their Greek views on the Jewish people.

They spoke Greek, gave their children Greek names, and called themselves pious followers of Moses while promoting a version of Jewish identity stripped of everything that made Israel a nation — just a portable set of religious practices you could perform anywhere, in any language, under any ruler. But some traditional Jews, people like Mattathias and his sons, saw through the charade and were sickened by the hypocrisy of hellenized Jews role-playing as devout priests in the Temple.

Their fury finally erupted in the Hasmonean revolt. The Maccabees rose up against Seleucid oppression, defeated their overlords, drove the Greeks from the Temple, and restored Jewish sovereignty in the land of Israel. It was the first time in centuries that the Jewish people had governed themselves in their own land, and they established a holiday to mark it: Chanukah.

As Maimonides explains, the essence of Chanukah is not primarily the miracle of the oil lasting for eight days, but the national victory that preceded it. He writes: "The sons of the Hasmoneans... overcame them, slew them, and saved the Jews from their hand. They appointed a king from the priests, and sovereignty returned to Israel for more than 200 years, until the destruction of the Second Temple."[136] The Roman Jewish historian Josephus, writing his Antiquities of the Jews only a century after the events, never mentions the miracle of the oil—that the small cruise which should have lasted one day burned for eight—at all. For him, as for Maimonides, the point of Chanukah was the victory itself.

But after the Romans destroyed the Second Temple and drove the Jews into exile, the memory of what Chanukah actually celebrated began to fade. A people living under foreign rule, scattered across the earth with no army and no sovereignty, could barely imagine national independence, let alone speak of it openly. The miracle of the oil moved to the center of the holiday, while the military victory and the restoration of sovereignty quietly faded from our collective consciousness.

Today, that distortion has reached absurd extremes. Ironically, Chanukah is often the one holiday celebrated by secular Jews in the diaspora—even though it is the holiday that most concretely and specifically rejects their way of life. Few see the irony in assimilated Jews celebrating the anti-assimilation holiday.

In December 2023, Douglas Emhoff—then Second Gentleman of the United States and a thoroughly ignorant American Jew—posted a video "explaining" the holiday of Chanukah in a way that said more about his own hellenized views than the actual story itself: "In the Hanukkah story, the Jewish people were forced into hiding. No one thought they would survive or that the few drops of oil they had would last... During those eight days in hiding, they recited their prayers and continued their traditions."[137]

Emhoff's version of the Chanukah story is pure fiction. The Maccabees didn't light candles in hiding. They rebelled against the Greeks and used guerilla tactics to kill Seleucid soldiers in the hills. "For it is better for us to die in battle, than to behold the calamities of our people and our sanctuary."[138] The miracle of the oil occurred *after* they killed the Hellenizers and drove out the Greeks, when they purified the Temple they had just recaptured by force. Emhoff erased the entire military victory and invented a story about refugees huddled in the dark and praying for survival. He turned a story about Jews killing other Jews who betrayed their nation into a therapeutic tale about resilience and hope.

Why? Not because Emhoff set out to rewrite the story, but because, like many assimilated American Jews, he inherited a version of "Judaism" that sees it primarily as a religion—a set of rituals and traditions practiced in synagogues and living rooms. A nation fighting for sovereignty in its homeland doesn't fit that framework, so he simply erased it. To him, being Jewish means lighting candles and reciting prayers, not killing Greeks and Jewish collaborators in the hills of Judea. His distorted version of Chanukah flows directly from his distorted understanding of what Jews are—which is to say, it is completely wrong. What Emhoff cannot bring himself to acknowledge is that Chanukah is, at its core, the celebration of a civil war in which pious Jews slaughtered their assimilated brothers—people with views quite similar to those Emhoff himself holds today. And so he twists Chanukah into a benign story of Jewish victimhood, tolerance and inner light.[139]

The *Al HaNissim* prayer, the main passage added to Jewish liturgy on Chanukah, makes the point better than any argument can. It focuses entirely on the military victory—"You delivered the mighty into the hands of the weak, the many into the hands of the few"—and concludes with the restoration of Temple worship. The miracle of the oil is not mentioned at all. The oil was God's confirmation that the victory was His, that Israel defeated its enemies not merely through courage or military brilliance, but through divine providence. It was a sign, not the story. Emhoff got it exactly backwards.

The Sages highlight the uniqueness of this victory by contrasting it with the salvation of Purim.[140] On Purim, when Esther and Mordecai saved the Jews from annihilation, the people survived but remained subjects of the Persian Empire—still in exile, without sovereignty in their land. For this reason, *Hallel*, the psalms of praise and thanksgiving, is not recited on Purim. But on Chanukah, *Hallel* is recited, because the miracle took place in the land of Israel, where the Jewish people not only survived oppression but reclaimed independence and rededicated the Temple.[141]

The significance of Jewish sovereignty over the land of Israel is reflected in Jewish law. Rabbi Elazar taught: "One who sees the cities of Judea in a state of destruction must tear their garments."[142] What qualifies as a "state of destruction"? The answer is fascinating: it is not empty streets or ruined buildings, but the loss of self-rule. As Rabbi Israel Kagan explains: "Even if Jews are living in these cities, since the Ishmaelites rule over them, it is considered destruction."[143] A city can be full of life, with thousands of people going about their day, but if the Jewish people do not govern it themselves, it is legally considered "destroyed." Survival alone is not enough; sovereignty is what defines whether a city truly belongs to the Jewish people.

10

The Self-Induced Death of Jewish Sovereignty

The Hasmoneans won independence. They drove out the Greeks, reclaimed the Temple, and reestablished Jewish sovereignty. For a brief period, the nation was free again. And then they destroyed it—in exactly the same way it had almost been destroyed before they saved it.

They rose to power fighting Hellenizers, yet within a few generations, the Hasmoneans became what they had fought against. The grandchildren of Mattathias and Judah the Maccabee embraced the very Hellenism their grandparents worked so hard to destroy. They adopted Greek names, such as Alexander Jannaeus instead of Yannai. They minted coins with pagan motifs. They filled their courts with Hellenized appointees and launched wars mimicking the Seleucid kings they had overthrown. Worst of all, they claimed both the kingship and the high priesthood, even though Jewish tradition strictly separates those roles, concentrating power in ways that bred resentment and division.[144]

All it took was three generations to fall apart. The Hasmoneans went from brave guerrilla fighters bleeding in the hills of Judea to

Greek-named kings who feasted while their rivals died on crosses. Alexander Jannaeus crucified 800 rebels and watched them die over dinner. They saved the nation from Hellenization, then Hellenized themselves.

When Queen Salome Alexandra died in 67 BCE, her sons Hyrcanus II and Aristobulus II tore the kingdom apart in civil war. Both invited outside help. Rome answered.[145] In 63 BCE, Pompey the Great entered Jerusalem—ostensibly to mediate between the Hasmonean brothers, but in reality to seize control. His legions stormed the city, slaughtered over 12,000 Jews, and placed Hyrcanus on the throne as a Roman puppet. Within a generation, Herod, backed by Rome, ended Hasmonean rule entirely. The Maccabees had fought the Greeks to free Judea. Their grandchildren handed it to Rome for free.[146]

Rome had a standard playbook for conquered peoples: let them keep their local rulers, allow them to worship their own gods, collect the taxes, and move on. For most nations, that was enough. Local identity survived, temples stayed open, and within a generation or two the conquered people learned to live within the imperial system.

The Jews rejected this arrangement. Not because they were uniquely stubborn, but because the Roman bargain missed the point entirely. A Jew praying in Judea under Roman rule was not truly free—he was a citizen of a subject province, not a member of a sovereign nation in his own land. But Rome never understood this. They kept trying to pacify a religious community when they were actually fighting a nation that refused to disappear.[147]

And so the revolts kept coming. For over two centuries, the same pattern repeated: uprising, crushing defeat, temporary quiet, then another rebellion. Always with the same demand: complete independence in their own land.

The Great Revolt of 66 CE exploded out of this tension. Roman governors plundered the Temple treasury and humiliated the people. The Jews responded by forming their own government, raising an army, and minting coins stamped with the words "freedom of Zion." They were not demanding religious tolerance. They were fighting for independence. The revolt ended in ruin: Jerusalem destroyed, the Temple burned, hundreds of thousands dead.

Josephus Flavius, the great historian of the era, embodies the tragedy of his time. He remained a religious Jew until the day he died, faithful in belief and practice. And yet, he is remembered as a traitor, the Benedict Arnold of the Jewish people. Why? Because while he clung to Judaism as a religion, he abandoned the Jewish nation. Once a leader of the Great Revolt, he surrendered to Rome and concluded that the Jewish people's national story had reached its end. In Rome, he lived as a client of the Flavian dynasty, writing his works under imperial patronage. He became what later generations called a "Roman of the Mosaic faith," a man who kept the rituals but forsook the people. For the Jews, that was the ultimate betrayal.[148]

The people had not yet forgotten what they were. Sixty years after the destruction of the second Temple, Bar Kochba, a military commander so formidable that Rabbi Akiva believed him to be the Messiah, led another revolt. He declared a Jewish state, minted coins proclaiming "freedom of Israel" and "for the freedom of Jerusalem," and built a national army. For three brief years, Israel lived free again—until Rome returned with overwhelming force, crushed the rebellion, slaughtered much of the population, and renamed Judea *Syria Palaestina* to erase the memory of Judea itself.[149]

Even as the Jews kept fighting Rome, something was rotting from within. The rebellions demonstrated that the nation hadn't given up. But the leadership was fracturing into competing factions, each with a different answer to the same desperate question: how will Israel survive?

The Sadducees were the Temple aristocracy, priests and wealthy elites who controlled the Temple service and cooperated with Rome to preserve their position. The Zealots drew the opposite conclusion: compromise was treason, and the only path forward was armed revolt, whatever the cost. The Pharisees were the rabbinic scholars and teachers who focused on Torah study and legal interpretation as the bedrock of Jewish identity.[150] And the Essenes went furthest of all. They withdrew from the world entirely, retreating to isolated communities near the Dead Sea to achieve spiritual perfection while the nation fought and bled around them.

The Essenes were genuinely pious men who devoted themselves entirely to Torah study, ritual purity, and spiritual discipline. Convinced they were the righteous remnant preparing for divine redemption while the rest of the nation wallowed in corruption and compromise, they lived in voluntary poverty near the Dead Sea, maintained the highest standards of observance, and saw themselves as the "Sons of Light" locked in a cosmic battle against the "Sons of Darkness."[151]

But there was a fatal flaw at the core of their belief system: they prioritized holiness over peoplehood. While their fellow Jews were fighting and dying to preserve the nation's independence, the Essenes were perfecting their purity rituals in desert caves. They believed that withdrawing from the contaminated world and achieving spiritual perfection was the path to redemption.

When Rome destroyed Jerusalem in 70 CE, the Essenes simply vanished—not because Rome bothered to destroy them, but because they had already removed themselves from the story. The Essenes thought that detaching from concrete reality made them better Jews. Instead, it was the reason they inevitably disappeared from Jewish history.[152]

The Essenes weren't alone in losing sight of nationhood. But while the Essenes withdrew and the Sadducees collapsed with the Temple they had controlled, the Pharisaic rabbis survived—and it was they who would carry Jewish life through the long centuries of exile ahead. Their path forward was necessary and brilliantly conceived, but it came at a great cost.

As Jerusalem burned, Rabbi Yochanan ben Zakkai had himself smuggled out of the city in a coffin and went to the Roman general Vespasian. He requested only one thing: permission to establish a Torah academy at Yavneh. Vespasian granted it. While the Temple lay in ruins, Rabban Yochanan rebuilt Jewish life around the study hall. Prayer took the place of sacrifice, Torah study became the axis around which Jewish life turned, and the Sanhedrin reconvened at Yavneh instead of Jerusalem. Jews had found a way to survive without the Temple, without sovereignty, and even without the land. This saved the Jewish people. Without Rabban Yochanan's foresight, Torah and Jewish identity would have died with the Temple.

Still, something irreplaceable was lost along with the Temple, something greater than the sacrificial service. As long as the Temple stood, a Jew always knew who he was. He had an unambiguous point of reference. The Temple in Jerusalem was far more than a religious site. It was the heart of the Jewish people's national life. Even if a Jew personally never made the arduous trek to the Temple, even if he was not meticulous in observing all the commandments, the very existence of the Temple gave him his identity as a Jew. Without it, the question of Jewish identity—who are we, and who do we intend to be?—suddenly had no self-evident answer.[153]

Rabban Yochanan's solution saved the Jewish people—but in doing so, it quietly reframed what being Jewish meant. It created a form of Jewish life that could thrive anywhere. Prayer didn't require Jerusalem. Study halls could be built in any city. Jewish law could develop in Babylon as easily as in Judea. The rabbinic system was portable, adaptable, resilient. Jews could be Jews in exile indefinitely.

But that very portability made it easier, over time, to forget God's original plan for the people of Israel. If Torah life could flourish in exile, then maybe national sovereignty didn't matter as much. Maybe being Jewish was primarily about belief and practice, not land and independence. Maybe the nation could gradually become a religion. Rome was destroying Jewish nationhood from the outside. But the rabbis, trying to save the people, were inadvertently creating a framework that would allow later generations to lose sight of it from the inside.

The destruction of the Temple and the defeat of Bar Kochba forced the Sages to confront the most painful question in Jewish history: how could God allow His Temple to burn and His people to be driven into exile? Their answers went beyond military failure or poor strategy. They probed the spiritual failures that made exile inevitable.

The Sages asked: "The Second Temple, during which people were engaged in Torah study, in observing the commandments, and in acts of kindness—why was it destroyed? Because there was baseless hatred among them. And baseless hatred is weighed as equivalent to the three cardinal sins: idolatry, sexual immorality, and bloodshed."[154]

This teaching is often misunderstood as a plea for all Jews to simply "get along." But the Sages never meant that conflict should disappear. Jews who recognize the uniqueness of Israel must be willing to fight for the nation's direction and survival. We cannot act as though every perspective is equally valid.

The key is conducting this struggle without tearing the nation apart. We must "win" without turning fellow Jews into enemies. David fought Saul for the kingdom, yet refused to kill him: "How can I harm my lord, the LORD's anointed?" (1 Samuel 24:10–11). A nation must resolve conflict without tearing out its own heart.

A religion can afford to cast out those who disagree or hold different beliefs. A nation cannot. By definition, it must hold together a diverse mix of right and left, wise and foolish, righteous and sinful. In the Roman period, Jews lost that sense of national cohesion. Sadducees opposed Pharisees, Essenes withdrew, Zealots assassinated moderates, and the Sicarii killed fellow Jews within Jerusalem itself. By the time the Romans finally breached the city walls, they found a people already consumed by civil war. This collapse of collective unity—the willingness of Jews to turn on one another—is the deeper meaning of the Sages' warning against "baseless hatred."

The Sages demonstrate how baseless hatred led directly to devastation: "Because of Kamtza and Bar Kamtza, Jerusalem was destroyed."

Here's the story: A wealthy man was preparing a grand banquet and sent his servant to invite his friend, Kamtza. But by mistake, the servant brought the wrong guest—Bar Kamtza, the wealthy man's enemy. When the host saw him, he was infuriated. "Get out!" he shouted. Humiliated, Bar Kamtza pleaded to stay. First, he offered to pay for his own meal. When that failed, he offered to pay for half the banquet. Still, the host refused. Finally, he offered to pay for the entire feast—but it made no difference. The host turned him away, shaming him in front of everyone.

Even worse, the leading rabbis of Jerusalem were present and did nothing. Bar Kamtza took their silence as agreement with his humiliation. In anger, he traveled to Rome for an audience with the emperor and claimed that the Jews were rebelling against Rome. To test the Jews' loyalty, the emperor sent a choice calf to be offered in the Temple—a practice not unusual at the time, since foreign rulers and dignitaries occasionally presented sacrifices there. If the Jews offered the calf as a sacrifice, it would demonstrate their loyalty to the Empire; if they refused, it would provide proof that they were rebelling against Rome.

On the way to Jerusalem, Bar Kamtza secretly inflicted a minor blemish on the emperor's animal—something that would disqualify it under Jewish law but would seem insignificant to the Romans. When the calf arrived at the Temple, the rabbis faced a dire crisis. Accepting the offering would violate Jewish law, but rejecting it risked angering the emperor and provoking deadly retaliation. Some of the rabbis argued that the sacrifice should be accepted in violation of Jewish law, to preserve peace with Rome. But Rabbi Zechariah ben Avkulas objected: "If we accept this sacrifice, people will think blemished animals are allowed on the altar." Others suggested killing Bar Kamtza before he could report back to the emperor. Again, Rabbi Zechariah refused: “Making a blemish on consecrated animals is not a capital crime.” Trapped by Rabbi Zechariah’s rigid interpretation of the law, the rabbis ultimately refused to offer the emperor’s sacrifice. Bar Kamtza returned to the emperor with his “proof” that the Jews had rejected his offering, and the emperor responded with war.

The Sages sum up the tragedy: “Because of the scrupulousness of Rabbi Zechariah ben Avkulas, our House was destroyed, our Temple burnt, and we ourselves exiled from our land.”[155]

Rabbi Zechariah saw only the law. He couldn't see, or refused to see, the national catastrophe barreling toward them. One man's grudge escalated into a national crisis, and the rabbis responded with legal technicalities while the nation crumbled around them.

This was the rabbis' second failure. The first came earlier, when they stood by silently as Bar Kamtza was publicly humiliated at that banquet. They watched a Jew be shamed and expelled, and said nothing. Then, when that humiliation turned into treason and treason into an imperial crisis, they still couldn't see what was actually at stake. They debated whether a blemished calf violated Temple law when they should have been asking how to hold the Jewish people together when one embittered man was trying to tear them apart. The question wasn't one of Jewish law—it was existential. Not "what does the law permit?" but rather "how do we survive this?" The rabbis treated a rupture in the national body as a problem of ritual purity, and by the time they realized their mistake, Roman legions were already marching toward Jerusalem.

The Sages offer another explanation for why the Temple was destroyed: "This matter was asked of the Sages, but they could not explain it; it was asked of the prophets, but they could not explain it—until the Holy One, blessed be He, Himself explained: 'Because they abandoned My Torah which I placed before them.'... This means that they did not recite the blessing over the Torah before studying it."[156]

At first, it seems trivial: would God really allow the Romans to destroy the Temple simply because the Jews neglected a blessing? Rabbi Zvi Yehuda Kook explains that this blessing is far more than a ritual formula; it expresses the essence of what it means to be a Jew. Before studying Torah, a Jew recites: "Blessed are You... Who has chosen us from all the nations and given us His Torah." The order is deliberate: first, God chose Israel as a people, and only afterwards was the Torah given.

In Rabbi Kook's words: "They studied Torah and were devoted to it, but their learning did not flow from Israel's national essence—from the sense of chosenness expressed in the blessing, 'Who has chosen us from all the nations,' recited before Torah study. When the Torah is detached from Israel's identity as a people, it cannot endure."[157]

This misplaced priority led directly to the catastrophe of the Temple's destruction. The Temple was not merely a religious holy site; it was the central institution that unified the entire nation of Israel across all tribes and regions. Once the leadership abandoned their role as guardians of Jewish nationhood, there was no longer any purpose for a Temple, and so God allowed it to be destroyed.

11

The Nation that Refused to Die

When Shmuel Yosef Agnon, Israel's greatest novelist, rose to accept the Nobel Prize for Literature in 1966, he stood before King Gustaf VI Adolf of Sweden, the royal family, and the assembled elite of Europe—academics, politicians, and fellow laureates in evening dress. And there, in that glittering hall in Stockholm, this bearded Jew from Jerusalem made sure the audience understood exactly who he was:

"As a result of the historic catastrophe in which Titus of Rome destroyed Jerusalem and Israel was exiled from its land, I was born in one of the cities of the exile. But always I regarded myself as one who was born in Jerusalem. In a dream, in a vision of the night, I saw myself standing with my brother-Levites in the Holy Temple, singing with them the songs of David, King of Israel, melodies such as no ear has heard since the day our city was destroyed and its people went into exile..."[158]

Agnon was born in Galicia in 1888, nearly two thousand years after the Temple burned. He had never seen Jerusalem in its full glory. And yet he stood before the King of Sweden and described himself as a Levite who had just stepped off the Temple steps.

In the late 1980s, Rabbi Yehuda Leon Ashkenazi met with the Dalai Lama, who said to him: "You are finishing a two-thousand-year exile while we are just beginning ours. We need to know your secret. How did your people survive?"[159]

It is a question worth answering.

No other nation in history has survived the long-term exile of their people. The Babylonians, the Philistines, the countless tribes of Europe and the Middle East—once uprooted from their land, they vanished. Their gods were forgotten, their languages died, their identities dissolved into whatever empire swallowed them. Mark Twain noticed this about the Jews: "All things are mortal but the Jew; all other forces pass, but he remains. What is the secret of his immortality?"[160]

Rome's destruction of Jerusalem was the most catastrophic event in our people's history. Jewish history divides into two unequal parts: the shorter span when we inhabited our land as an independent nation, and the much longer era of exile, when we were dispersed throughout the world and ruled by others. Heinrich Graetz, the great 19th-century German Jewish historian, argues that the Torah and our way of life were never meant to be a religion but rather "a constitution for a body politic." Only after the exile, he argued, did the religious elements take precedence, so that "Judaism ceased to be the constitution for a state and became a religion in the usual sense of the word."[161]

In the vision of the dry bones, Ezekiel compared the exile of Israel to a graveyard, and the longed-for redemption to resurrection from death. "Behold, I will open your graves and raise you from your graves, My people, and I will bring you to the land of Israel. And you shall know that I am the Lord, when I open your graves and raise you from your graves, My people" (Ezekiel 37:12–13). Jeremiah used the same metaphor: "He has made me dwell in darkness like those long dead" (Lamentations 3:6).

When a person dies, two things happen simultaneously: the body disintegrates, its parts no longer held together as a living whole, and the soul departs. Exile inflicted both on Israel. The scattering of the nation across a hundred countries was the disintegration of the body — the same people, the same blood, but no longer one organism, just fragments. And the soul? That was the Temple, the Sanhedrin, prophecy, the full living structure of Torah law practiced by a sovereign nation in its land. All of it gone. A body without its soul and a nation without its land are the same thing: not weakened, not wounded, but dead.[162]

Rabbi Jonathan Eibuschitz explained why Jewish prayers so often went unanswered in exile. The Sages teach that God accepts prayer recited with a congregation of ten, as the Torah says: "He redeems me unharmed from the battle against me, for those with me are many" (Psalms 55:19).[163] But in exile, God no longer regarded Israel as a "congregation"—as a nation—but as scattered individuals. Their prayers lost power because they were no longer truly united as a people. This is reflected in the singular voice of Lamentations 3:8: "Though I cry out and plead, He shuts out my prayer." The "I" and "my" emphasize that even when Jews were physically gathered in prayer, exile reduced them to isolated voices, not the united national voice they were meant to be.[164]

Israel's mission—the very reason God formed our nation in the first place—cannot be fulfilled without sovereignty in the land. How could we fulfill the prophetic dream of Isaiah, "from Zion shall go forth Torah" (Isaiah 2:2), if we were not in Zion? How could Israel serve as a model of holy nationhood for the world while subjected to foreign rule in lands not our own?

The exile of our people was not only a disaster for Israel and the nations meant to learn from us. It was also a tragedy for God Himself. When Israel is diminished, so is His glory. The prophet Ezekiel describes what happened when Israel was scattered among the nations: "And I scattered them among the nations, and they were dispersed through the countries... They profaned My Holy Name, inasmuch as it was said of them, 'These are the people of the Lord, and they have come out of His land'" (Ezekiel 36:19-20). Israel's enemies looked at this exiled, degraded people and drew the obvious conclusion—that God had no power to save His own nation.[165] The humiliation of Israel is a public humiliation of God.

This was not a new insight. When the people prepared to strike Midian, Moses declared that this was not only Israel's revenge but "the Lord's revenge" (Numbers 31:3). To strike at Israel is to strike at Go d.[166] "Why should they say among the peoples, 'Where is their God?'" (Joel 2:17). Pharaoh mocked Israel's God in Egypt for the very same reason: "Who is the Lord that I should heed His voice?" (Exodus 5:2). When Israel is enslaved, God Himself is mocked and shamed.

Why would God allow this? If Israel's purpose is to be a holy nation in its land, why scatter His people across the earth for two thousand years?

The Sages answer with a strange story set at the very moment the Romans destroyed the Second Temple. A Jew was plowing his field when an Arab passing by heard a voice declare: "Jew! Untie your ox and your plow, for the Temple has been destroyed." The voice spoke again: "Jew! Bind your ox and tie your plow, for the Messiah King has been born."[167]

Who is this Messiah born the very moment the second Temple was destroyed? Is there a 2,000-year-old person wandering around, hiding in the shadows, waiting to be revealed?

This story is not a prophecy about an actual human Messiah, but rather a message from God to His people: "Yes, you have sinned, and yes, your enemies have destroyed the Temple. But do not for a moment think that I am rejecting you. Even as the Temple burns, I am already planting the seeds of your national restoration." As the nation collapsed and exile began, the vision of the Messiah, the third Temple and a restored people was already taking shape. The fires of Rome might consume Jerusalem, but they could not sever the eternal bond between God and Israel. "For the Lord will not forsake His people, nor will He desert His inheritance" (Psalm 94:14).

Rabbi Shlomo Aviner explains that exile was not only a punishment but also a cure. God scattered us among the nations and dismantled our national institutions because they had rotted from within. We needed to start over. For the first time in generations, stripped of courts, borders, economy, and political factions, we could focus entirely on the foundations: families observing Shabbat together, communities caring for their poor, individuals working on their character, deep study of Torah. Before we could return and build a truly holy nation in our land, we first had to heal—as individuals, as communities, as a people. Only after this long process of spiritual repair could the scattered tribes reunite and establish the kind of holy sovereignty that had eluded us throughout the First and Second Temple periods.[168]

The exile was never meant to be permanent, and God said so long before it began. Moses warned in Deuteronomy that Israel would be scattered among the nations for betraying God—but he immediately promised that when they returned to Him, He would gather them again: "For the Lord your God is a merciful God; He will not let you loose or destroy you; neither will He forget the covenant of your fathers, which He swore to them" (Deuteronomy 4:31). Later in Deuteronomy, the promise is even more explicit: "Then, the Lord, your God, will bring back your exiles, and He will have mercy upon you. He will once again gather you from all the nations where the Lord, your God, had dispersed you. Even if your exiles are at the end of the heavens, the Lord, your God, will gather you from there... and will bring you to the land which your forefathers possessed" (Deuteronomy 30:3-5).

Centuries later, Isaiah prophesied: "Any weapon whetted against you shall not succeed, and any tongue that contends with you in judgment, you shall condemn; this is the heritage of the servants of the Lord and their due reward from Me, says the Lord" (Isaiah 54:17). The verse speaks to both kinds of danger. "Any weapon whetted against you" points to the threats against Israel's physical existence—Rome, Crusaders, Nazis and jihadists. "Any tongue that contends with you" points to the spiritual assaults—to those nations and religions who claim that they have replaced Israel as God's chosen people. Both the sword and the word were turned against the Jews, but God's promise stood: "No weapon formed against you shall prosper."

God refused to give up on His people. And we, against all reason, refused to give up on ourselves. We refused to accept foreign soil as home, refused to let the nations write our ending, refused to believe that God's covenant had been broken. From the very beginning of the exile, mourning the destruction of Jerusalem and the loss of sovereignty became central to Jewish life. The Sages established fast days—the 9th of Av, the 17th of Tammuz, the 10th of Tevet, the Fast of Gedaliah—each marking a stage in the destruction of the Temple and the fall of Jewish nationhood. Their goal was not only to grieve but to instill a permanent dissatisfaction with exile, a refusal to feel at home outside the land of Israel. They wanted the wound to stay open, so that the Jewish people would never forget that their wholeness could only be restored through sovereignty in their own land.

Even as generation after generation of Jews lived their entire lives in other countries, the Sages insisted that exile was fundamentally temporary. They expressed this through vivid metaphors. "Exile is like the night, and redemption is compared to the dawn."[169] "The Jewish people in exile are like widows and orphans—but not actual widows and orphans. Rather, they are like a woman whose husband has traveled to a distant land, or children whose father has gone away, with the intention of returning."[170] Exile is painful, dark, and lonely, but never final. The night will end, the husband will return, the father will come home.

Though it was only natural that many Jews longed for material comfort and a sense of stability in their host countries, this very desire ran counter to the direction the Sages sought to instill. They insisted that exile could never be treated as permanent or fulfilling. To truly sustain Jewish life, we must regard our existence outside the land as temporary, even suffocating, never allowing foreign soil to feel like home. Only by cultivating this unease could we preserve this unbroken connection to our land and our national identity.

Though we were exiled from our land, we carried our national institutions with us, shrinking them down but never letting them disappear. Rabbinical courts, led by local judges and rabbis, became the heirs of the Sanhedrin. The synagogue was a "minor Temple," where priests still raised their hands to bless the people and cantors sang words and tunes that were once sung in the Temple. The era of prophecy ended, but their voices lived on in the preachers and moral teachers, the *magidim*, who rebuked and inspired their communities.

Kingship survived, too, in a way. Every town had its "seven finest of the city," community leaders who could levy taxes on the Jews living there and, when necessary, even put a Jew on trial if his actions threatened everyone else's survival. The nation was scattered and weakened, but the structures that made us a nation didn't disappear.

A Jew taken hostage, even one his community had never met, living in a distant land, was still their brother—and his life was their responsibility. Communities would empty their treasuries to ransom a single soul, to the point that slave traders learned to take advantage of this—much as terrorists in our own time take Israeli hostages because they know that Israel will make unreasonable concessions to purchase their release. Such sacrifice was rare in the ancient or medieval world. Others might speak of brotherhood, but we acted on it: scattered across continents, we still lived as one people, carrying ourselves in exile as a nation waiting to be restored.

Yet at various points during the long exile, Jews became overly comfortable in their host countries, settling into stability and prosperity while the land of Israel remained distant from their lives. Rabbi Judah HaLevi, author of the *Kuzari* and one of medieval Spain's greatest Jewish thinkers, criticized them for growing too comfortable in

Spain and for treating Israel and Jerusalem as distant, almost mythical places—lands they would never seriously contemplate returning to.

In his work, the fictional king of the Khazars confronts the Jews: "You have not made the land of Israel your goal, nor your place of living and dying… I see that all your kneeling and bowing toward the land of Israel is mere flattery or some insincere custom."

HaLevi's fictional rabbi, who defends the Jews throughout the book, is forced to agree with the king on this point. While Jews remained distinct as a people, most, whether in Babylon, Spain, or elsewhere in the diaspora, did not seriously contemplate returning to Israel. He writes: "This very sin prevented us from achieving that which God promised us for the Second Temple… Only some returned, while the majority—including the greatest scholars—remained in Babylon. They preferred subservience in exile, so that they would not have to part from their homes and businesses."

He compares this passivity to sleep: "I am asleep… [God's] voice knocks, yet the Jewish people are slow to answer." Even prayers meant to express longing for Jerusalem—"Bow down to the mount of His holiness" or "Blessed are You Who returns His divine presence to Zion"—become empty words, "merely like the chirping of birds."[171]

HaLevi himself never stopped longing for the land, which he expressed poetically in his famous poem, *"My Heart is in the East"*:

"My heart is in the east, and I in the uttermost west— How can I find savour in food? How shall it be sweet to me? How shall I render my vows and my bonds, while yet Zion lieth beneath the fetter of Edom, and I in Arab chains? A light thing would it seem to me to leave all the good things of Spain— Seeing how precious in mine eyes to behold the dust of the desolate sanctuary."

But HaLevi did not stop at longing. He lived up to his own teaching, leaving the comfort and security of Spain to journey to the land of Israel. HaLevi's quixotic mission to the land had little practical purpose—he almost certainly died shortly after arriving.[172] But his journey burned itself into Jewish consciousness across the centuries that followed. It reminded every generation that the land of Israel was not an ethereal fantasy of distant messianic hopes, but a real place that Jews had an obligation to return to and rebuild.

Rabbi Isaiah Horowitz of 17th-century Prague lamented the ease with which many Jews had settled into comfortable lives in the diaspora, building grand houses while forgetting their true home. "My heart was always burning when I saw the children of Israel building houses like the fortresses of princes, making permanent dwellings in impure lands... and it appears, God forbid, as if you have forgotten about the [future] redemption. Therefore, my sons, even if God gives you great wealth, build houses according to the necessity of your needs and no more, and do not build towers in pride and grandeur, but only to have a dwelling befitting your honor, and places to seclude yourselves in them for Torah study and repentance."[173]

Counterintuitive as it may sound, persecution in exile was better than comfort, for it awakened the people and reminded them that they were not truly at home. Rabbi Abraham Isaac Kook explained the benefits of hardship and persecution: "The troubles that come upon us outside the land—these actually deepen our awareness of the inner spiritual connection to the land of Israel and its holiness. The longing to see [the land] grows stronger, and the engraving of the sacred forms of the land—upon which God's eyes rest constantly from the beginning of the year to the end of the year—becomes deeper and deeper."[174]

Some Jews went further, making exile into an ideal. They stopped merely tolerating exile and began celebrating it. Being scattered among the nations, they argued, was not a punishment but an opportunity: a chance to fulfill Israel's mission to be a light unto the nations from within the world's most powerful societies. Why go back to a small, struggling nation in the Middle East when you could reshape history from Russia, Germany, or America? Karl Marx sought a workers' revolution in Europe. Leon Trotsky tried to remake the world by building a Bolshevik state in Russia. Liberal American Jews planned to repair the world—*tikkun olam*[175]—by marching for social justice in America.

None of it worked. As individuals, Jews inspired and helped countless people wherever we lived. But none of our grand plans to reshape the nations from within ever succeeded—not one. Not one host nation became more moral or righteous because of our efforts. Quite the opposite: every Jewish attempt to transform the world from exile ended with Jews being expelled, persecuted, or slaughtered.[176] Jews can survive in exile, but we cannot shape nations and societies without first forming our own model society in our own land.

Rabbi Yehuda Leon Ashkenazi captures this confusion with a simple parable. A man sets out on the road to Jerusalem, but along the way a wheel on his wagon breaks. He stops to repair it. The repair takes so long that by the time he finishes, he has completely forgotten where he was going.[177]

This is the story of two thousand years of exile. The wheel kept breaking—persecution, poverty, emancipation, revolution, assimilation—and each crisis demanded attention. Each generation of Jews was so consumed with fixing the wagon that they forgot Jerusalem was the destination.

Jerusalem is not just home. It is the only place from which we can fulfill our mission to the world.

Whether living under persecution or in comfort, even the most vibrant Jewish communal life in exile could never substitute for sovereignty in Israel. Rabbis, teachers, and leaders built schools, synagogues, courts, and community institutions that held Jewish communities together for centuries—but all of it rested on borrowed ground.

As Rabbi Steven Pruzansky put it: "For all the dedication of rabbis, teachers and professional leaders in the Jewish world—and for all the vast investments in Jewish infrastructure that make the United States such a hospitable and pleasurable exile—life in exile is a holding pattern. We are trying to hold on to something—powerful in its own right and indispensable for almost two centuries—that cannot be sustained in perpetuity. We are not building as much as we are trying not to fall. We are walking on a ledge rather than on solid footing."[178] Exile allowed Jewish life to continue, but it was never secure, never whole, and never permanent.

The Dalai Lama asked how the Jewish people survived two thousand years of exile. The answer is that we never forgot where we came from, or where we were supposed to go. But survival carried within it a danger that no persecution ever could. The enemy that nearly destroyed us was not Rome or the Crusaders. It was comfort.

THE LONG FORGETTING

"Let us be like the nations, like the families of the lands." (Ezekiel 20:32)

Israel365

12

Faith Without a People: Christianity's Turn from Israel

After Fox News fired him in 2023, Tucker Carlson spiraled into a world of conspiracies—and his favorite obsession was the Jews. Again and again, he set up a neat contrast: Christianity is the religion of peace, while Judaism is the religion of war.

"It's the Old Testament versus New Testament," he told one guest. "The New Testament is universalist. Jesus says it again and again: I'm here for everybody. It doesn't matter what your bloodline is. And I'm also opposed to violence... There's this effort to pretend they're the same story, but they're completely different stories." Jesus preaches love and nonviolence, he says, while Jews—just look at Israel—worship power.

When Mark Levin called on President Trump to bomb Iran's nuclear sites, he said, "You watch Mark Levin talk about killing people and it's really dark. Christians are not for killing people, period."

Tucker nodded along as Marjorie Taylor Greene—the congresswoman who claimed California wildfires were started by "space solar generators" funded by Jews—quoted the commandment "do not murder" and insisted, "If someone hits you in the face, turn the other cheek. That's from Jesus. So Christians care above all what Jesus says... How do we get to a point where good people like that are making the case that Jesus wants more bombing?"[179]

The implication was clear: Jews are violent tribalists, while Christians are pure and peaceful. It's a nasty accusation—but is there any truth to it?

The Gospel of Matthew opens with a genealogy tracing the ancestry of Jesus, from Abraham to David, through the kings of Judah, and finally to Joseph, the husband of Mary. At first glance, it looks like a simple family record. But Rabbi Yehuda Leon Ashkenazi argues that the New Testament begins with Joseph because Christianity chose to model itself on the original Joseph—the Bible's archetype of exile.

In the Hebrew Bible, Judah and Joseph represent two very different visions of redemption. Judah embodies kingship and the destiny of Israel as a nation in its land. He understood that Israel could only fulfill its mission as God's chosen people by becoming a holy nation in its own land, and then teaching the world from there. "Out of Zion shall go forth the law, and the word of the Lord from Jerusalem" (Isaiah 2:3). In Judah's vision, God's people bring redemption to the wider world by first building a holy society in Israel.

Joseph took another path. He sought to bring God's word to the world immediately, and so he embraced life in Egypt. He dressed like an Egyptian, spoke their language, rose to power, and began teaching Egyptians about God. According to the Sages, he even required the Egyptians to circumcise themselves during the famine—making this covenant with God a condition for receiving grain—and introduced them to Torah principles.[180] Joseph believed that Israel could most effectively spread God's truth by gaining influence at the very center of it—in Egypt, the superpower of the ancient world.

Yet Joseph's story does not end there. At the end of his life, he reversed course. He began to see that all of his efforts to bring the people of Egypt to God had failed, and that all the influence he had accumulated during his lifetime would not outlive him. Though the enslavement of his people would not begin for some years, Joseph saw what was coming. Before he died, he bound his descendants with a final oath: "God will surely remember you, and you shall carry up my bones from here" (Genesis 50:25). Joseph finally understood that the people of Israel can only fulfill their mission by building a holy nation in their own land. Judah was right.

The Christian church made the opposite choice. It rejected Joseph's final decision and instead implemented his initial strategy to the very end—creating a universal religion that anyone could join, detached from any particular nation or land. It chose Joseph the Egyptian over Joseph the Hebrew, Joseph the Roman over Joseph the Jew, the path of a world religion over the path of peoplehood. It replaced the covenantal story of the Jewish people with a universal church of believers. Instead of twelve tribes forming a nation, it created twelve apostles forming a church. Anyone, anywhere, could join simply by believing.

This is why Matthew begins with a genealogy that most people gloss over. But the genealogy matters because it ends with Joseph—not Judah.

For Jews, redemption comes through Judah. Judah carries the royal line and the promise of a kingdom in the land of Israel. Christianity went a different way. It went with Joseph: the exile who rose to power in Egypt, who brought God's word to Pharaoh's court while living far from home. The details in Matthew reinforce the point. An angel commands Joseph, Jesus' father, to take his family and flee to Egypt to escape Herod. None of this is accidental. By invoking Joseph—both the patriarch who brought God's word to Egypt through exile and influence, and the father who carried the infant Jesus into Egypt—Matthew is making a theological argument. Christianity follows Joseph's path. Not Judah's vision of redemption rooted in the land, but Joseph's vision of shaping the world from within the empires of exile.

That path took on institutional form at what became known as the Jerusalem Council, described in Acts 15. The question before the Council was fundamental: must Gentile followers of Jesus become Jews—accepting circumcision, the Law of Moses, and membership in Israel's story—or could they enter the covenant as Gentiles? "Certain men came down from Judea and taught the brethren, 'Unless you are circumcised according to the custom of Moses, you cannot be saved'" (Acts 15:1). After much dispute, Peter declared that faith alone was sufficient: "We believe that through the grace of the Lord Jesus we shall be saved, even as they" (Acts 15:11). James issued the ruling that would define Christianity's future: Gentiles would not be required to join Israel's covenant at all.

At that moment, Christianity separated itself from the story of the nation of Israel and became something entirely different: a religion. Circumcision, the mark of belonging to the nation of Israel, was replaced by baptism, the mark of personal belief. Christianity developed councils, creeds, and an institutional hierarchy because, at its core, it is a system of belief. If you don't accept the creed, you don't belong. The church exists, among other things, to define and enforce that boundary.

The Jewish people never built any of this, and not by accident. The Torah sees personal perfection as growing out of a life rightly lived, not one rightly thought, which is why our tradition never sought to express itself in terms of dogmas until the Middle Ages. There is not a single verse in the Torah that begins "Thou shalt verily believe that..."[181] We have no papacy, no councils, no synods of bishops to determine and enforce what Jews must believe. Maimonides' Thirteen Principles—the closest we ever came to a creed—were the work of one philosopher, never formally adopted, never made binding, never accepted by all Jews. Eight centuries later, they still aren't.[182]

This is what Paul set out to change. As Joseph Klausner observed, "In spite of the fact that the foundations of all the teachings of Paul are Jewish, his own teaching is both the contradiction of the Jewish religion and the rejection of the Jewish nation."[183] Paul used Jewish ideas—covenant, redemption, holiness—but tore them away from the Jewish people. What remained was a faith that could belong to anyone, anywhere.

Paul believed, as Isaiah did, that Israel was called to be a light to the nations — that God's promise to Abraham, "all the families of the earth will be blessed through you" (Genesis 12:3), demanded fulfillment beyond Israel's borders. On this, every Jew would agree with him. Where Paul parted ways with Jewish tradition was in his conviction that the end times had already arrived, and that the moment for Israel to actively carry its light to the world was now. He believed he himself was the instrument of that mission. As Pamela Eisenbaum explains: "Paul's understanding of himself as the Apostle to the Gentiles is his interpretation of God's commissioning to be a light to the nations. God had promised that all the nations would be blessed through Abraham. That promise had to be fulfilled in order for redemption to be realized, because God always fulfills God's promises."[184] For Paul, the hour had struck. The mission could no longer wait.

The Jewish people's disagreement with Paul is not about the goal. It is about the precondition he overlooked. Isaiah's promise—"out of Zion shall the Torah go forth, and the word of the Lord from Jerusalem" (Isaiah 2:3)—requires sovereignty. Israel's unique contribution to the nations is not theology or philosophy; other peoples can offer those. It is something only a nation can demonstrate: what it looks like when an entire society attempts to live under God's law. Paul launched his mission to illuminate the world at precisely the moment when the Jewish people had no sovereignty and no Jewish state to point to. He wanted Israel to teach the nations how to build what Israel itself was not permitted to build. The light does not go forth from a people under Roman occupation. It goes forth from Zion, and only when Israel is sovereign in Zion.[185]

The Jerusalem Council decision was Christianity's turning point moment. From this point on, Christianity could spread across empires precisely because it no longer depended on any one nation's survival. The covenant was no longer something you were born into; it was something you chose through faith.

The consequences of this shift were enormous. Redemption was no longer tied to building a moral society in a specific land under specific laws. It was universalized. The Church, not a nation, became the vehicle for collective redemption. "Render unto Caesar what is Caesar's and unto God what is God's" captured this new reality: Christians belonged to God's kingdom while living under earthly rulers. The state could remain brutal and corrupt—but the community of believers might still be redeemed. This created a permanent tension that Judaism never had to face: How do you transform the world when you're not responsible for running it?[186]

The Gospel writers replaced Israel's collective vision of redemption with something entirely new: the faith of the individual in a single universal figure of salvation. Instead of rooting redemption in the story of a people, Christianity proclaimed that it depends solely on each person's relationship with Jesus. This appealed not only to philosophers and thinkers, but to the poor, the slaves, and the masses ground down by Roman society—people who had no nation, no land, and no collective story to belong to, but who could still have faith.

It is true that some early Christians raised demands for social change and even suffered martyrdom for it. But very quickly, these demands faded. The dominant line became dualistic: morality belonged to the realm of private faith, while politics was left to the Caesars and emperors. This approach was a radical departure from the teachings of the Jewish sages, who insisted that both the individual and the nation are called to sanctify every aspect of the world, including the elements that seemingly belong to Caesar.[187]

When Christianity became the state religion of Rome, it inherited not only Rome's roads and symbols but its imperial dream. What began as a faith of the persecuted became, in time, the faith of the greatest empire the world had ever seen. As Yoram Hazony writes, "Christianity eventually succeeded in establishing itself as the state religion of Rome. In the process, it adopted the Roman dream of universal empire... For more than a thousand years, Christianity thus aligned itself, not with the ideal of setting the nations free as had been proposed by the Israelite prophets, but with much the same aspiration that had given rise to imperial Egypt, Assyria, and Babylonia."

This was no small shift. The prophets of Israel envisioned a world of independent nations, each serving God in its own way: "He shall judge between the nations, and shall decide disputes for many peoples... and nation shall not lift up sword against nation" (Isaiah 2:4). Christianity, through its fusion with Rome, replaced that mosaic of free nations with the dream of a single global order united under one faith and one law. To be part of this new order meant accepting baptism and church authority—everyone was welcome, but only if you became a Christian. The language of redemption, which in the Hebrew Bible meant the liberation of an enslaved people and their return to their land, became the language of empire and conversion.[188]

Jews believe that redemption is inseparable from the nation of Israel: "I will gather the children of Israel from every nation where they have gone, and bring them into their own land. And I will make them one nation in the land" (Ezekiel 37:21-22). Redemption happens when the people of Israel are living as one, in the Holy Land, following the Torah—not as isolated individuals scattered across empires. That's why Jesus' own Jewish disciples asked him: "Lord, is this the time when you are to be established once again over the sovereignty of Israel?" (Acts 1:6). As Jews, they expected the Messiah to do what Judaism had always said he would: restore Israel's national sovereignty.

The Jerusalem Council made a radical break with Israel's vision. As the Italian Jewish philosopher Rabbi Elijah Benamozegh explains, Christianity's claim is that the Jewish people are unnecessary to the plan of redemption. What matters is the individual believer or the Church, not the covenantal people. Redemption no longer flows through a particular people in history, but through each person's faith in Jesus.[189]

This contrast becomes especially clear when we compare how Jews and Christians respond to enemies. The prophet Jeremiah calls on God to avenge His people against the nations who devoured Israel: "Pour out Your fury upon the heathen, and upon the families that call not on Your name: for they have eaten up Jacob, and devoured him, and consumed him, and have made his habitation desolate" (Jeremiah 10:25). Jeremiah speaks as a representative of the nation of Israel, praying for vengeance and justice.

Jesus, on the other hand, addresses the individual believer: "You have heard that it was said, 'You shall love your neighbor and hate your enemy.' But I say to you, Love your enemies and pray for those who persecute you, so that you may be children of your Father in heaven" (Matthew 5:43–45). Here, the focus is no longer national destiny or collective justice. It is the private spiritual life of the believer, detached from the fate of his people.

In practice, of course, Christian soldiers go to war and kill enemies in battle like anyone else—they just separate it from their faith. Christian nations wage war, execute criminals, and defend their borders with the same force as any other civilization. The difference is that these actions are not integrated into Christian theology as sacred duties. War is a political necessity, nothing more.

This helps explain what Ruth Wisse calls "the otherwise astonishing discrepancy between the teachings of Jesus and the brutality of so many rulers acting in his name." Christianity deliberately universalized Israel's teachings by detaching them from the people of Israel. By doing so, it "released its adherents from political constraints. The most consequential of all its differences from Judaism was that it did not require a nation to adopt the religious standards of an individual."[190]

To be clear, Christians throughout history have often engaged deeply in politics and social reform out of Christian conviction—but Christianity itself does not mandate this the way Judaism does. A Christian can be perfectly faithful without ever engaging in politics. Israel's Torah governs both the person and the nation, binding the political and moral spheres together as a theological requirement. Christianity separated them. Christians as individuals were called to holiness, but Christian nations were not bound to live by the Sermon on the Mount.

Christianity's opposition was never to Moses, the giver of the Torah, or to the philosophical truths of the Jewish people. Rather, its target was Abraham, the *biological* father of the Jewish people. Christians who embrace replacement theology agree with Jews about Moses—they honor the divinity of the Torah—but they reject the Jewish understanding of Abraham. To Jews, Abraham is much more than a spiritual model; he is our grandfather, the literal forefather of the Jewish people. But Christianity isn't interested in who our grandfather might be; all that matters is the person standing before God, right here, right now.

Christianity's universal vision, by design, transcends particular national belonging. The argument is that true universal faith cannot be tied to a specific people or land. The Pontifical Biblical Commission states this explicitly: "The Church is conscious of being given a universal horizon. The reign of God is no longer confined to Israel alone, but is open to all, including the pagans, with a place of honor for the poor and oppressed."[191] Christianity presents itself as the universal faith that welcomes everyone, while Judaism is cast as narrow and exclusive.

But there's a problem with this picture. Christianity presents itself as welcoming all people, but only on condition that they abandon their own identities and convert. "Outside the Church, there is no salvation."[192] The Great Commission commands believers to "make disciples of all nations" and baptize them "in the name of the Father and of the Son and of the Holy Spirit" (Matthew 28:19). As church father Cyprian put it: "You cannot have God for your Father unless you have the Church for your mother."[193] Everyone is welcome—so long as they submit to baptism and church authority.

The Jewish people do not demand this kind of submission from other nations. We are a people, not a universal religion, and it would be absurd to require other peoples to become like us in order to serve God properly. The Talmud makes explicit what the Torah implies: all human beings, regardless of nation or background, are bound by seven basic moral laws—the Noahide commandments—a framework that allows every nation to remain distinct while living righteously before God. Other peoples don't need to adopt Jewish law, join the Jewish nation, or abandon their own identities. They can serve God as they are.[194]

Yet in the telling of history, the Jewish people, who let other nations be themselves, are labeled exclusive and ethnocentric, while Christianity, which demands that all people join one universal church through baptism, is celebrated as welcoming and inclusive.[195]

Christian universalism even overrides family and kinship. In the New Testament, Jesus uses striking, even shocking language to insist that loyalty to him and to the kingdom of God must come first. When his mother and brothers come seeking him, he points to his disciples and declares, “Here are my mother and my brothers!” (Matthew 12:46–49). Similarly, he warns that anyone who loves their father or mother more than him is not worthy of him (Matthew 10:35–37). He even tells a man who wishes to bury his father before following him, “Let the dead bury their own dead, but you go and proclaim the kingdom of God,” and dismisses another who wants to say goodbye to his family before discipleship (Luke 9:59–62). Christian commentators generally understand these sayings as hyperbolic calls to radical discipleship—placing faith above every other attachment—rather than as a literal command to abandon one's family. But even as a metaphor, the priority is clear. The bonds of faith supersede the bonds of blood.

This could not be more foreign to Jewish teaching. When the prophet Elijah called Elisha to become his disciple, Elisha was plowing his family's field with twelve yoke of oxen. He asked permission to say goodbye to his parents first. Elijah let him go (I Kings 19:20). There was no demand to abandon family, no test of ultimate loyalty. A man could serve God and still honor the people who raised him.

The Torah recognizes that real love is preferential. Imagine getting down on one knee to propose. You pull out the ring, look into your beloved's eyes, and say: "I love you as much as I loved my last girlfriend, and the same as that girl from camp three years ago, and as much as that woman over there who works at the Laundromat." Universal love is not real love. It doesn't inspire loyalty or sacrifice. If someone tells you he loves your children as much as he loves his own, don't let him babysit. Love means preference. I love certain people more than others—and that is what makes it love.

For Jews, this preferential love extends from family to nation. Jews are obligated to show greater love and care for the Jewish people than for anyone else. That's not evil or ethnocentric, but rather healthy and natural. Critics who condemn Jews for caring more about their own people either misunderstand what love and nationhood mean, or they're simply jealous that their own nations don't feel this kind of loyalty toward one another.

A father who loves all children equally is not a good father; he's neglecting his own. A nation that cares as much about strangers as about its own citizens has abandoned its responsibility. Jews are commanded to love the stranger and treat him justly, but we are also commanded to prioritize our own people. "If your brother becomes poor and his means fail with you, then you shall uphold him" (Leviticus 25:35). The Torah doesn't pretend that all obligations are equal. Some bonds are closer, and those bonds create duties that matter precisely because they are particular.

This bond extends across every border. When Hamas took hostages on October 7, Jews in New York, London, and Sydney felt the pain of those captives as if they were their own children. They demanded their release, organized rallies, and refused to let the world forget their names. That's not tribalism; it's what a healthy nation looks like. When one Jew suffers, all Jews suffer. When one is freed, all rejoice.

Christians don't experience this kind of bond with fellow Christians around the world—not because they're less caring than Jews, but because Christianity is a religion, not a nation. An American Christian feels the pain of fellow Americans, whether Christian or not. A French Christian feels loyalty to France. But a French Christian doesn't instinctively feel a Nigerian Christian's suffering the way an American Jew feels an Israeli Jew's pain.

For Jews, meeting another Jew anywhere in the world is like discovering you have a brother you never knew existed. If he were in danger, you wouldn't hesitate to protect him. How could you not? He's your brother. This is the bond Jews feel across every border, even with those they've never met.

In January 2026, Alex Pretti, a 37-year-old nurse from Minneapolis, was shot and killed by federal agents during a protest. Americans erupted in fury—massive protests filled the streets, videos went viral, members of Congress from both parties demanded investigations, and his death dominated news coverage for weeks.[196]

Meanwhile, jihadist groups in Nigeria have slaughtered thousands of Christians over the past few years, burning their churches, beheading villagers and massacring entire communities. American Christians barely noticed. Advocacy groups worked hard to raise awareness, but with little success. There were no mass protests, no viral outrage, no congressional hearings. One American dead in Minnesota generated more fury among Americans, including American Christians, than thousands of Nigerian Christians butchered in their own churches. Again, this is not because American Christians are callous. It's because national bonds are real.[197] Religious bonds, absent nationhood, are weak.

By now, it should be obvious that the notion of "the three monotheistic religions"—Judaism, Christianity, and Islam as variations of the same faith—is not just a modern invention. It is a fiction.

New Testament scholar Anders Runesson notes that "although Christians have, through the ages, tried to redefine Judaism as a 'religion,' a negative mirror image of themselves, mainstream Jews never accepted this rewriting of their identity."[198] That resistance was well-founded. It was only in the emancipation era—when Jews desperate for equality began redefining themselves as members of a "religion" alongside Christians and Muslims[199]—that the fiction finally took hold. The Torah, however, knows nothing of this framework. Moses was not a religious reformer like Jesus or Muhammad; he was the leader of a people, the founder of a nation under God.

None of this should be understood as an attack on Christianity itself. On the contrary—from a Torah perspective, Christianity has played an indispensable role in God's plan for humanity. Maimonides writes that "all the deeds of Jesus of Nazareth and the Ishmaelite who arose after him will only serve to prepare the way for the coming of the redemption and the improvement of the entire world, motivating the nations to serve God together."[200] Christianity and Islam, in other words, were part of God's design—not for Israel, but for the nations. They helped billions of people abandon idolatry and recognize the God of Israel, bringing the world closer to the messianic vision described in Zephaniah: "I will transform the peoples to a purer language that they all will call upon the name of God and serve Him with one purpose" (Zephaniah 3:9). God did not ask all peoples to become Israel; He asked Israel to be Israel, and the nations to find their own path toward Him.

The problem arises only when Christianity is forced upon the Jewish people. God designed two different paths: one for Israel, and one for the nations. Christianity offered the world a faith that could transcend borders and bloodlines, a spiritual identity independent of any particular nation or homeland. For the nations, this was exactly what God intended. For us, it was a demand to abandon everything we were.

History has proven this repeatedly. When a Jew converts to Christianity, he loses his national identity within a generation or two. His children marry Christians, and his grandchildren know little of the Jewish people. Within a short time, he is gone—assimilated, absorbed, and lost to the Jewish nation forever.[201] Christianity is simply incompatible with a people whose relationship with God is grounded in a unique, national covenant.

This is why Tucker's attack is so off base. He compares Christianity, a religion, to Israel—as if Jews were just another faith choosing violence over Jesus' teachings. But Jews are a nation, like Americans or Frenchmen, with a land to defend and a people to protect. Israel isn't a congregation that can "choose" to turn the other cheek; it is a country that must defend its children from those who would murder them. Killing in self-defense isn't "really dark," as Tucker claimed. What would be dark—and deeply immoral—is standing by while jihadists slaughter innocents. Christianity long ago outsourced national defense to Caesar, separating faith from politics. The Jewish people never did.

When Golda Meir met Pope Paul VI at the Vatican in 1973—the first meeting between a Pope and an Israeli prime minister—the conversation was tense. "The Pope said to me at the outset," Meir later recalled, "'that he found it hard to understand how the Jewish people, which should be merciful, behaves so fiercely in its own country.'"

Golda didn't flinch. "Your Holiness," she said, "do you know what my earliest memory is? A pogrom in Kiev. When we were merciful, when we had no homeland, and when we were weak, we were led to the gas chambers."[202]

The Pope was speaking as a man of religion; Golda was speaking as the leader of a nation. For the Church, mercy meant turning the other cheek. For Israel, mercy meant ensuring there would never again be Jewish victims.

The founding of the modern State of Israel made this difference impossible to ignore. As Rabbi Ashkenazi put it, the rebirth of Israel proved that Jews could never be classified as just a religion. "There is a history of faiths, but the Hebrews have no place therein; rather, they belong to the history of mankind... The contemporary Christian world is discovering that the Jews... are a nation, a society and not characters in a religious novel."[203]

Israel's very existence shatters Tucker's false dichotomy. Judaism isn't a religion in the same category as Christianity. We are a people—a family that became a nation. And we must never apologize for defending our children—or destroying our enemies.

13

Liberty, Equality... Oblivion

On the morning of September 28, 1791, Isaac Berr of Loraine sat down to write. The French National Assembly had just passed the decree that would change Jewish life forever: emancipation. For the first time in nearly two thousand years, Jews in France were citizens, equal before the law.

Overwhelmed with emotion, Berr wrote: "At length the day has come when the veil, by which we were kept in a state of humiliation, is rent; at length we recover those rights which were taken from us more than eighteen centuries ago. How much are we at this moment indebted to the clemency of the God of our forefathers! We are now, thanks to the Supreme Being and to the sovereignty of the nation, not only Men and Citizens, but we are Frenchmen!"[204]

It was a cry of joy, and who could blame him? For centuries, European Jews were walled into ghettos, despised, taxed, and persecuted. Suddenly the gates were thrown open. The humiliations of exile seemed to dissolve overnight. Jews could now walk the streets as free men and women, citizens of the new Republic of France.

But the price of that freedom was steep. Count Stanislas de Clermont-Tonnerre spelled it out in the National Assembly debates of December 22–24, 1789: "The Jews should be denied everything as a nation, and granted everything as individuals." The Assembly went further, declaring that "the existence of a nation within a nation is unacceptable to our country." The ghetto walls may have crumbled, but in their place arose a new demand: assimilation. Jews were expected to shed their identity as a people and become French citizens—Frenchmen who merely practiced the "Jewish religion."[205]

The Revolution's universalist motto—*liberty, equality, fraternity*—opened the ghetto gates. But the ticket of entry into French society was clear: the death of Jewish nationhood.

Twenty years later, Jewish leaders sat uneasily before Napoleon Bonaparte. The ghetto walls were gone, but the questions remained. The emperor himself wanted answers.

"Who are you," he demanded, "Jews or Frenchmen? When you pray for the coming of the Messiah and the return to Zion, what loyalty do you owe to France? If war breaks out between France and England, will you fight against your English Jewish brothers?"

For centuries, such questions never arose. No one expected Jews to show loyalty to the nations they lived in—they were outsiders confined to ghettos and denied citizenship. But emancipation changed everything. Now Jews were citizens, expected to give full allegiance to their new nations. And with that, the old attachment to Jerusalem and their fellow Jews in other countries suddenly looked like a dangerous conflict of loyalties.

France's rabbis and notables answered Napoleon without hesitation. After the Assembly of Jewish Notables and the Grand Sanhedrin, they declared: "The bond which united the sons of Jacob into a social body for political unity has been severed. Homeland is a human concept that changes according to place and time. Yesterday the land of Israel, today France." They insisted that Judaism was a religion only, not a people. "It is true; we are no longer a nation."[206] France was now their homeland, and Paris their Jerusalem.[207]

This was not a momentary slip of the tongue. Jewish leaders repeated it openly: the old covenant of peoplehood was gone. "The bond that once united Jacob's sons into a social body for political unity has been severed," one rabbi explained. "Homeland is a human concept that changes according to place and time. Yesterday the land of Israel, today France."[208]

In 1852, the chief rabbi of Paris made the point even more directly: "The Jewish people are dead. Its national form is dead. But what has not died and will never die is the spirit of Judaism."[209] What earlier generations viewed as the tragic consequences of exile, many Western European Jews now defended as the highest expression of Judaism—turning the loss of nationhood into a religious ideal.[210]

The pattern repeated across Western Europe. But the Germans, true to form, framed their demand in philosophical terms. And so German Jews went even further in their capitulation, completely changing the Torah's theological foundations to satisfy German academics.

A towering figure in German intellectual life, the German philosopher and theologian Friedrich Schleiermacher was deeply engaged in debates over religion, society, and citizenship. He viewed Jewish integration into German society as a test case for modernity itself. Schleiermacher insisted that for Jews to be accepted as full Germans, Judaism had to be fundamentally transformed: the parts of the Torah that made the Jews a functioning nation—the legal system, communal institutions, and national vision—had to be abandoned. Instead, the Jews must become a classic "religion."

"Religion's essence is neither thinking nor acting, but intuition and feeling... Religion maintains its own sphere and its own character only by completely removing itself from the sphere and character of speculation as well as from that of praxis."[211] In other words, faith must be separated from law, politics, and public life. Jewish rituals were fine, but the Torah's claim to govern society contradicted everything Schleiermacher believed about religion and the modern state.[212]

Abraham Geiger heard the message—and went even further. The founder of Reform Judaism declared that the Bible was a human document, written by men responding to their times, not the word of God for all time. Revelation was "progressive." Every generation could remake Judaism as it saw fit. Torah no longer carried divine authority, and Jewish law no longer bound the Jewish people. Geiger discarded whole realms of Jewish practice as outdated relics, reducing Jewish life to vague categories like "spirit" and "ethics" that could be remade into whatever modern Jews wanted them to be.

At the core of Geiger's program was his effort "to rid the Judaism of his day of any concept of Jewish collective politics or messianic hope."[213] He wanted to make Jewish life resemble the dominant Protestant Christianity of his era: a religion and nothing more. Jews were no longer a people with a shared destiny; they were "Germans of the Mosaic faith." This redefinition of Jewish identity—from nation to religious denomination—was just as radical as his rejection of Torah's divine authority. Both served the same purpose: to make Jews acceptable in an Enlightenment Europe that could tolerate religious minorities but not rival nations.

Gabriel Riesser, a prominent Reform Jew, did not hesitate to declare where his allegiance lay. Addressing the Frankfurt synagogue, he declared: "Where else is there a state that could claim our loyalty? What other homeland calls upon us for its defense? We are not immigrants to Germany—we were born on this soil. We are either Germans, or we are a people without any homeland at all. There is but one sacred act that can truly consecrate a person to their nation: the willingness to shed their blood in common cause for the freedom of their fatherland."[214]

Not everyone agreed. Rabbi Mordechai Benet, Chief Rabbi of Moravia, denounced the Reform movement's omission of prayers for the restoration of Jewish sovereignty in Israel: "These deliberate omissions will inflict incalculable harm on coming generations. For whatever our present obligations may be, we are persuaded of the ultimate restoration of Jerusalem and its Temple, and of the coming of the Messiah to redeem us. These prayers keep that belief alive in us and plant it in our children. Without them, the belief itself will wither, and when the Messiah does come—as come he must—he will find a generation to whom the thought of restoration appears strange and incomprehensible, a generation cut off from the larger body of Israel."[215]

The crisis of Jewish nationhood in the era of emancipation did not stop with Reform. Even many Orthodox leaders and communities, while fiercely loyal to Torah, lost sight of Israel's collective mission.

Rabbi Samson Raphael Hirsch, the towering 19th-century Orthodox leader of Frankfurt, fought the Reform movement tooth and nail. He petitioned the Prussian government for the right of Orthodox Jews to form their own separate community. He defended every detail of Jewish law and ritual. But even he could make a comment like this: "It is precisely the purely spiritual nature of Israel's nationhood that makes it possible for Jews everywhere to tie themselves fully to the various states in which they live."[216]

What did Rabbi Hirsch mean by "spiritual nationhood"? It was his way of saying that Jews could be loyal Germans while remaining religious Jews—the same bargain Reform offered, just with stricter observance of the Torah. In fighting to preserve tradition, he adopted the framework of both Schleiermacher and Geiger, bringing Jews closer to the Christian model of religion.[217]

Orthodox leaders became so consumed with defending the Torah against Reform's changes that they lost sight of everything else. Within their Orthodox communities, they succeeded in preserving traditional Jewish rituals like Shabbat, kosher food and prayer. But the Torah's larger vision of Jewish peoplehood faded into the background. What remained was private devotion, sectarian community life, and the hope that if Jews just kept the laws carefully enough, God would one day bring the Messiah. They meant to preserve Jewish life, but what they created instead was a religion.[218]

This shift in identity had real, practical consequences. Rabbi Yissachar Shlomo Teichtal described the "exile-Jew" who no longer lived as part of a nation but only as a loyal citizen of his host country. "In exile you do not lead a nationalistic life... you dedicate your entire heart and soul [only] to the citizens amongst whom you dwell. Thus, you have detached and separated yourself from the holy nation and its collectiveness, and you have become isolated in your place of dwelling in exile."[219]

Rabbi Teichtal saw this mindset even among pious Jews. The Hasid bound only to his rebbe's circle, the scholar who cared only for his own study hall—both had lost a sense of responsibility for the broader nation of Israel. German and Hungarian Jews looked down on Polish Jews as if they were foreigners, belonging to another nation entirely. When Emancipation broke open the ghetto walls, it shattered Jewish unity along with them. Jews stopped seeing themselves as one people and splintered into separate communities, each absorbed in its own concerns.

14

The Illusion of Acceptance

In neighborhoods of Berlin and Paris, Jewish families built lives that seemed indistinguishable from their neighbors. They spoke the language of the city, kept up with its latest fashions, and sent their children to public schools. They believed that they were true Germans and Frenchmen of the Mosaic faith. As Albert Einstein noted in 1921, "up till about a generation ago the Jews in Germany did not regard themselves as belonging to the Jewish people. They felt themselves only members of a religious commu nity."[220] They believed that by blending in and abandoning their unique national identity, they could finally be safe.

The freedom was real. But the welcome was not what it seemed.

Emancipation opened doors to professions, commerce, and public life, and the Jews ran through those doors as fast as they could. They studied, worked, and built businesses faster than anyone expected, seizing every opportunity the new freedoms offered. But their rapid success drew attention and envy, making them convenient scapegoats during economic downturns.

In Vienna, Mayor Karl Lueger masterfully used Jewish success to propel his own rise to power. He depicted Jews as monopolists, controlling finance, the press, and industry. In an 1899 speech he warned: "Here in our Austrian fatherland the situation is such that the Jews have seized a degree of influence which exceeds their number and importance... the greater part of the press is in their hands, by far the largest part of all capital and, in particular, high finance, is in Jewish hands, and in this respect the Jews operate a terrorism of a kind that could hardly be worse."[221]

Lueger's populism was strategic. He sometimes rewarded individual Jews, but only to fuel resentment against the community as a whole. He went so far as to say, "I decide who is a Jew."[222]

In France, the Dreyfus Affair exposed a similar pattern on a national stage. Alfred Dreyfus, a Jewish officer in the French army, was falsely accused of passing military secrets to Germany in 1894. Despite evidence of his innocence, a court-martial convicted him. The French public didn't care about evidence—it wanted a Jewish traitor.

The affair divided the nation. People of conscience like Émile Zola spoke out—his famous "J'accuse...!" letter accused the government and army of judicial corruption and antisemitism[223]—but the trial also revealed how deeply ingrained Jew-hatred was, even in the supposedly enlightened republic of France. Jews learned that the legal protections of emancipation were not an effective shield against mass hysteria and conspiracy theories.

Across Europe, Jews were beginning to realize that no amount of assimilation or success would make their neighbors see them as anything but outsiders. Jews who thought they'd earned acceptance discovered they were more exposed than ever—visible, successful, and without the old community networks that had once offered some protection. In Vienna, Paris, Berlin, and beyond, emancipation made Jews more vulnerable, not less.

Why did the supposedly advanced, "liberal" societies of Western Europe respond this way? While sociologists offer many explanations for modern antisemitism, the leading rabbis of the late 19th and early 20th centuries saw the rise in Jew hatred in theological terms: as the inevitable result of our people forgetting their own identity and destiny.

Rabbi Meir Simcha of Dvinsk warned that assimilation was a trap. When Jews forgot they were a nation in exile and treated foreign lands as permanent homes, the host countries would eventually remind them—painfully—that they were outsiders. Those who "think that Berlin is Jerusalem... will be uprooted and set down in a distant land whose language they do not know, and they will remember that they are strangers."[224]

German Jews didn't listen. They became more German than the Germans—distinguished professors, decorated war heroes, loyal patriots. In the end, they were dragged from their homes, packed into cattle cars, and murdered by their German neighbors in the Holocaust.

Writing from Jerusalem, at the heart of the Jewish people's renewal in their land, Rabbi Yaakov Moshe Charlop addressed the Jews of the exile. He taught that antisemitism was not random hatred, but God's way of jolting Jews awake when they forgot who they were. "When the Jewish people forget their own holiness and greatness ... even though they are 'the Lord's portion, Jacob is the lot of His inheritance', that is when antisemites come and attack them, striking and trampling them with arrogance."

The solution, Rabbi Charlop insisted, was not assimilation but its opposite—Jewish pride. "The way to be delivered from all this is only through Israel remembering the sublimity of their souls and being careful to lift up their glory, to set their greatness upon a banner and to take pride in this."[225]

Stop apologizing for being Jewish. The more Jews hide, the more violently they're reminded that hiding won't save them.

The truth is, the explosion of modern antisemitism should not have been so surprising, for it had all happened before, in the days of Joseph. Joseph rose higher than any Jew in exile could dream. He was viceroy of Egypt, second only to Pharaoh, the savior of the empire. He had wealth, power, and fame. Yet to the Egyptians he was never one of them. Even as he ruled over them, "they set for him separately and for them separately, and for the Egyptians who ate with him separately, because the Egyptians could not eat food with the Hebrews, because it is an abomination to the Egyptians" (Genesis 43:32). Despite the crown on his head, he remained an abomination—the Hebrew outsider.

In the end, all of Joseph's accomplishments evaporated. A new Pharaoh arose who knew nothing of Joseph, and the people he had saved enslaved his descendants.

German Jews proudly called themselves "Germans of the Mosaic faith," yet the Germans themselves never bought it. Even the greatest antisemites viewed Jews not as a religion, but as a distinct people. It didn't matter how much Jews assimilated or embraced local culture; their identity could not be erased.[226]

The Jews who convinced themselves that they had truly become Germans, French, or citizens of any land were blind to reality. To the world, they remained Jews. And that illusion only made it worse when the antisemites came for them.[227]

15

The Sickly Girl Awakens

In February 1840, a Catholic monk named Father Thomas disappeared in Damascus along with his Muslim servant. The French consul, Ulysse de Ratti-Menton, immediately blamed the Jews. He revived the medieval blood libel—the grotesque fantasy that Jews murder Christians to bake their blood into Passover matzah.

With the backing of Ottoman authorities, the French consul arrested prominent Jewish leaders and tortured them until they confessed. He imprisoned over sixty Jewish children to force their parents to talk. Several prisoners died in custody, and mobs pillaged synagogues throughout the city.

This was Damascus, one of the Ottoman Empire's most cosmopolitan cities, in the middle of the nineteenth century. If Jews could be tortured and killed on medieval accusations even there, what did that say about Jewish security anywhere? The Damascus Affair exposed the precarious position of Jews throughout the Muslim world. They lived as *dhimmis*—protected but subordinate to Muslims. They could maintain their communities and preserve their way of life, but were legally inferior to Muslims, paying a special tax (*jizya*) and subject to social restrictions, including dress codes and limits on where they could live. Protection was conditional, and it could vanish overnight.

In Eastern Europe, the situation was even worse. Russia, home to nearly half of world Jewry, confined Jews to the Pale of Settlement, a territory where they could live and work, but only under heavy restrictions. Most Jews crowded into shtetls, small market towns where poverty was the norm and hunger common. And then there were the pogroms—organized riots where mobs tore through Jewish neighborhoods, destroying homes and businesses, beating and killing anyone they found. Local authorities did little to stop them. Sometimes they helped start them.

This was the world Jews faced everywhere: nowhere to go and nowhere safe. The Jewish people were still alive, but only barely, like a sick girl lying in bed, weak and pale, struggling just to breathe.[228]

But weakness is not death. A few Jews had had enough. If Italians, Hungarians, and Poles could demand their own nations, why should we remain powerless minorities in foreign lands? Why wait for someone else to save us?

Born in Sarajevo in 1798, Rabbi Yehuda Alkalai became the rabbi of Semlin, near Belgrade, a region where other peoples were beginning to awaken and demand national independence. If they could claim their freedom, Alkalai asked, why should the Jewish people—God's chosen nation—remain a helpless and subservient minority?

At the end of Deuteronomy, Moses prophesied that Israel's long exile and suffering would eventually end: "And it will be, when all these things come upon you... and you will return to the Lord, your God, with all your heart and with all your soul, and you will listen to His voice... then, the Lord, your God, will bring back your exiles, and He will have mercy upon you. He will once again gather you from all the nations, where the Lord, your God, had dispersed you" (Deuteronomy 30:1–3).

The key word here is the verb "return"—in Hebrew, *v'shavta*. For generations, Jews understood this as repentance—a spiritual return to God through keeping the commandments and living righteously. If the Jews repented (*teshuva*, from the same root), God would miraculously gather them back to Israel. Spiritual devotion was the key to redemption.[229]

Rabbi Alkalai read these verses differently. When Moses said "you will return to the Lord," he wasn't talking about spiritual repentance. He was talking about physical return—return to the land itself. Notice that the very next verse says God "will bring back your exiles." The same root word—return—appears in both verses. First, the people return, and then God brings them back. For Rabbi Alkalai, these weren't two separate events. The people's physical return to the land is itself the *teshuva* that triggers redemption.

"Individual teshuva means a sinner turns from his sin... The graver his transgression, the weightier his *teshuva*. General *teshuva*, on the other hand, means that the entire Jewish people returns to the Lord our God, to the land of our forefathers' inheritance. For 'one who lives outside of the Land is considered as someone who has no God,'[230] and Jews [while living] outside of the Land, are unwitting idolaters... The Torah promises that the Jews are destined to do *teshuva* at the end of their exile, and immediately they will be redeemed. This refers to general *teshuva*—that the Jewish people will return to the Holy Land."[231]

In Rabbi Alkalai's view, exile itself is the sin. Redemption can only come when the Jewish people take responsibility and return—physically, en masse—to the Holy Land.

For nearly two thousand years of exile, Jews waited for God to take the initiative. But as Jeremiah prophesied, it is Israel—the "woman"—who must make the first move: "Return, Virgin Israel... How long will you turn about, faithless daughter? For the Lord has created a new thing in the earth: a woman shall court a man" (Jeremiah 31:20–22).

The people themselves must reach out and seek God by returning to the land. Like a sickly girl who lies waiting for someone else to lift her from her bed, Israel cannot be healed until she stretches out her hands, tests her strength, and takes her first hesitant steps.[232]

A contemporary of Alkalai, Rabbi Zvi Hirsch Kalischer also argued that the Jewish people must act to restore their national life in Israel. Watching the revolutions and nationalist movements that swept across Europe, he was astonished by Jewish indifference to their own fate.

"Why are we any worse than the Italians, Hungarians, and Poles, all of whom are ready to lay down their lives for their country? How much more should we be ready to sacrifice our all for a country which is deemed holy by the whole world? Should we stand afar as if we lacked manhood and the elementary feelings of self-respect?"[233]

Rabbi Kalischer drew a sharp parallel between the Israelites at the Red Sea and the emancipated Jews of his own day. On the eve of their miraculous deliverance, the Israelites said to Moses, "Better for us to serve the Egyptians" (Exodus 14:12), preferring the comfort of slavery to the risk and responsibility of independence. He saw the same spiritual paralysis among the Jews of Berlin and Paris: having obtained equal rights and a seat at the table, they looked around at their elegant drawing rooms and declared, "Here is the land of Israel." Reform Jews reduced the Messiah to a symbol of human progress, abandoning the divine promise of national redemption. Orthodox leaders were no better, waiting passively for a miracle instead of taking action. Both had forgotten that Israel is meant to be an independent, holy nation, and that true redemption could only begin when the Jewish people themselves took the first steps to return.[234]

Both rabbis advocated concrete steps to reclaim the land of Israel. Rabbi Kalischer corresponded with philanthropists like Moses Montefiore, urging the founding of colonies and the purchase and cultivation of farmland in Israel. Rabbi Alkalai outlined a detailed plan for collective *teshuva*, calling for a "General Assembly" to coordinate settlement, negotiate with governments, and organize the return. He even envisioned Britain as a guardian power to facilitate this process, stressing that the historical window of opportunity—from 1840 to 1939—had to be seized, or the moment for redemption might pass. Although their efforts had little immediate impact, Alkalai and Kalischer laid the religious foundations of modern Zionism and awakened a national consciousness that would guide future generations back to the land.

Moses Hess, a radical secular thinker in Germany, arrived at the same conclusion from a very different perspective. Born in Bonn in 1812 to an Orthodox family, Hess rejected Jewish religious life as a young man, immersing himself in philosophy and socialism. He chose total assimilation. When he married Sibylle Pesch, a poor Catholic seamstress, he crossed the Jewish people's most absolute red line. Marrying out meant you were no longer part of the community—and that was exactly the point. He would be German, not Jewish.

Yet the Damascus Affair of 1840 and the rising tide of antisemitism across Europe pulled him back to reality. He saw clearly that Jews could never truly belong in Europe. In his prescient book, *Rome and Jerusalem: The Last National Question*, he rejected everything he once believed: "The Jews will always remain strangers among the European peoples... so long as the Jews place their own great national memories in the background and hold to the principle, 'Ubi bene, ibi patria.'"[235] Jews who traded their historic homeland for comfort and civil rights abroad weren't integrating — they were surrendering. Real belonging required attachment to the collective memory and mission of Israel. Everything else was self-deception.

For Hess, Judaism and Jewish nationality were inseparable. "There is no Judaism without Jews, and no Jews without Judaism. Judaism and Jewish nationality are one and the same, as the body and the soul are one, and as they cannot exist apart from each other."[236] Emancipation in Europe was a lie. Jews could never truly belong in foreign nations. The only real security, the only real home, was the land of Israel itself.

Like Rabbis Alkalai and Kalischer, Hess tried to awaken his fellow Jews to action. "Judaism is not a passive religion, but an active life factor which has coalesced with the national consciousness into one organic whole... the Jews are a nation which...is destined to be resurrected with the rest of civilized nations."[237]

Rome and Jerusalem was largely ignored when it was published in 1862. Most German Jews, eager to assimilate and integrate into European society, dismissed his calls for Jewish nationhood. His warnings about rising antisemitism and the dangers of abandoning Jewish identity went unheeded, and the book stirred little public or political response. Only decades later, as the Zionist movement took shape, was Hess recognized as a prophetic forerunner. His ideas would have to wait nearly forty years before Theodor Herzl would arrive to carry them forward onto the political stage. The sick girl was stirring—but she had yet to stand up.

16

The Man Who Ignited a Nation

When Dr. Max Nordau arrived at the First World Zionist Congress in August 1897, he was wearing a riding jacket. Theodor Herzl took one look at him and ordered him back to his hotel room to change. The Congress was meeting in the grand Stadtcasino hall in Basel, Switzerland, and Herzl had planned every detail: green carpet on the floor, a felt-covered platform, nearly two hundred delegates from seventeen countries dressed in formal frock coats, white bow ties, and top hats. Some had rented their attire. It didn't matter. The Congress, Herzl explained, must look like a parliament of a proper nation. "We must show ourselves to be a people among the peoples."[238]

But who was this man, this assimilated Viennese playwright and journalist, who now staged the rebirth of a nation?

Theodor Herzl was born in Budapest in 1860 into a wealthy, German-speaking Jewish family. He read literature and philosophy, attended theaters and salons, and was convinced the Jewish future lay in assimilation—in the universities and concert halls of Vienna, not in some distant, improbable homeland.

Herzl knew the outline of the Dreyfus case before he arrived in Paris to cover it. What he was not prepared for was witnessing it in person. Dreyfus was tried in secret, denied the right to communicate with his family, and ultimately convicted of high treason. On January 5, 1895, he was subjected to a brutal public "degradation" ceremony at the École Militaire in Paris. His military rank was stripped, his sword broken, and the hostile crowd outside shouted insults and jeers. Two months later he was deported to Devil's Island, a remote penal colony off the coast of French Guiana, where he languished under harsh, isolating conditions for four years.

The French press was looking for blood. The newspaper *La Libre Parole*, run by the notorious Édouard Drumont, warned that Jews were secretly undermining France. "Dreyfus, the Jew, betrays the fatherland!"[239] Drumont blamed all Jews collectively, circulating lurid conspiracy theories that painted them as inherently disloyal or part of an "international Jewish plot." Posters, caricatures, and even board games depicted Jews as grotesque, subhuman hybrids. Antisemitic riots erupted in cities across the country.

This was not a sudden development. Before the Dreyfus affair, Drumont spent nearly a decade building the case against French Jewry—his massive two-volume *La France Juive* blamed Jews for every misfortune since the French Revolution, alleged an "invisible Jewish empire" within France, and named thousands of supposed conspirators. It became a runaway bestseller, reprinted hundreds of times.

Herzl, then a journalist for the Viennese *Neue Freie Presse*, covered the trial and witnessed the degradation ceremony firsthand. He watched Dreyfus stripped of his rank, mocked by the crowd, isolated and alone.

As a cultured European Jew and proud product of Emancipation, Herzl had believed that education, refinement, and loyalty could win Jewish acceptance. Dreyfus embodied everything assimilated Jews aspired to be—a decorated French officer, a patriot. And France destroyed him anyway.

Standing in Paris watching mobs scream for Dreyfus's blood, Herzl now understood that assimilation was a lie. This wasn't just a French problem. Back in Vienna, Karl Lueger made a political career out of Jew hatred. Jews who tried to be "more French than the French" or "more German than the Germans"[240] would always remain outsiders. The answer wasn't trying harder to fit in. It was a Jewish state.

Herzl began to articulate his conclusions publicly. In January, 1896, he published an article in the *Jewish Chronicle* of London titled "A Solution to the Jewish Question," his first open declaration that emancipation was a failure. "Everywhere we have sincerely endeavored to merge with the national communities surrounding us and to preserve only the faith of our fathers. In vain are we loyal patriots, in some places even extravagantly so; in vain do we make the same sacrifices of life and property as our fellow-citizens; in vain do we strive to enhance the fame of our native countries in the arts and sciences. In our native lands, where we too have lived for centuries, we are decried as aliens, often by people whose ancestors had not yet come to the country when our fathers' sighs were already heard in the land."[241]

Less than a month later, he published *Der Judenstaat* (*The Jewish State*), a political manifesto that immediately electrified the Jewish masses. In only 52 pages, he systematically made the case that the only answer to Jewish persecution was national independence in the land of Israel. Herzl's argument was simple: The Jews were a nation, not a religion, and nations need land, sovereignty, and the ability to defend themselves.

"The distinctive nationality of Jews neither can, will, nor must be destroyed. It cannot be destroyed, because external enemies consolidate it. It will not be destroyed; this is shown during two thousand years of appalling suffering. It must not be destroyed, and that, as a descendant of numberless Jews who refused to despair, I am trying once more to prove in this pamphlet. Whole branches of Judaism may wither and fall, but the trunk will remain."[242]

With this clarity, Herzl threw himself into action. He organized the First Zionist Congress within months and spent the rest of his life meeting with kings, ministers, and diplomats. The practical results were disappointing. He failed to secure a charter from the Ottomans and scored very few political victories.

Six months before his death, Herzl entered the Vatican for an audience no Jew had ever been granted. He came as the representative of his people, asking Pope Pius X to recognize the Jewish right to return to their land. He had been briefed carefully on Vatican protocol—every visitor knelt, every visitor kissed the papal ring—and he did none of it. He walked into the room, stood straight, and held his head high.

The Pope was not impressed. "The Jews have not recognized our Lord. Therefore we cannot recognize the Jewish people." He left nothing ambiguous: "Gerusalemme must not get into the hands of the Jews. "[243] Herzl walked out empty-handed. Chaim Weizmann later wrote that Herzl's bearing in such meetings "bordered on arrogance and often seemed inappropriate in light of the political insignificance of the movement he represented."[244]

Weizmann meant it as a criticism. He was wrong. What Herzl displayed in that room wasn't arrogance—it was *komemiyut*, the posture God invoked when He described the Exodus itself: "I am the Lord your God, who brought you out of the land of Egypt... and I broke the pegs of your yoke and led you upright (*komemiyut*)" (Leviticus 26:13). The word appears nowhere else in the Torah. Rashi explains it simply: upright posture, head held high, with dignity.[245]

For two thousand years, Jews had entered rooms like that one and bent their knees. Herzl refused. He stood before the Pope not as a private individual begging a favor from a more powerful man, but as the representative of a nation that had endured twenty centuries of humiliation and was now, at last, rising to its feet. He carried his people on his shoulders—and he carried them upright.

He left Rome with nothing. But the practical results were never really the point. Herzl accomplished something far harder than securing a charter: he convinced a people scattered across a dozen countries that they were a single nation, and that their nation could live again. A few days after the first Congress ended, he wrote in his diary: "At Basel I founded the Jewish State."[246]

Years later, Rabbi Abraham Eliyahu Kaplan captured what Herzl accomplished: "He taught Jews to say two simple words aloud, without apology or hesitation: '*Ani Yehudi*', 'I am a Jew!'"[247]

And he united them. Herzl insisted that Zionism belonged to no single faction: "That Zionism enables consistent freethinkers to join forces with consistent Orthodox Jews will escape only those who do not know what Zionism is. Zionism embraces all the members of the

Jewish nation." Secular and religious Jews, modernists and traditionalists—all were part of the same national movement.[248]

The force Herzl unleashed couldn't be stopped, even after his premature death in 1904. By 1908, Vladimir Jabotinsky, once a thoroughly assimilated Russian intellectual, was writing in an Odessan newspaper on New Year's Day to tell his Russian readers he was no longer one of them: "I have no season's greetings for you, because I no longer care about your future. The only tomorrow that matters to me is my own breaking dawn, which I believe in with every fiber of my being."[249]

The sick girl had risen from her bed. She was walking.

17

The Jews Who Could Not See

In 1917, Britain was bleeding. The Great War was in its third year, an entire generation was decimated, and victory over Germany was far from certain. The British government needed every advantage it could get—and they thought the Jews might provide one.

Prime Minister David Lloyd George and Foreign Secretary Arthur Balfour believed that publicly supporting a Jewish homeland in Palestine could sway Jewish opinion in America and Russia toward the Allied cause. It would also give Britain a foothold in the Middle East and help secure the Suez Canal, the vital artery connecting Britain to its empire in India. The proposed declaration would commit Britain to facilitating Jewish immigration and settlement in Palestine, giving the Zionist movement its first major political backing from a world power. It was the breakthrough that Herzl and his followers dreamed of.

And yet the only Jew in the British cabinet was working to kill it. Edwin Montagu fought harder than anyone to prevent what would become the Balfour Declaration. There was no Jewish nation, he insisted. His family had lived in England for generations, and they had nothing in common with Jews in Poland or Morocco beyond sharing a religion. He was not an English Jew. He was a Jewish Englishman.

In a memorandum to the British government, Montagu laid out his case with words that are still disturbing to any self-respecting Jew: "I assert that there is not a Jewish nation. The members of my family... have no sort or kind of community of view or of desire with any Jewish family in any other country beyond the fact that they profess to a greater or less degree the same religion. It is no more true to say that a Jewish Englishman and a Jewish Moor are of the same nation than it is to say that a Christian Englishman and a Christian Frenchman are of the same nation... I claim that the lives that British Jews have led, that the aims that they have had before them, that the part that they have played in our public life and our public institutions, have entitled them to be regarded, not as British Jews, but as Jewish Britons."[250]

For Montagu, this was personal. Zionism threatened his carefully cultivated status as a British gentleman and government official. The idea that Jews owed loyalty to one another was a direct threat to his own standing in British society. Accepting the ancient Jewish claim to the Holy Land would undermine his own claim to English identity. "I deny that Palestine is today associated with the Jews or properly to be regarded as a fit place for them to live in."[251]

Montagu was not alone. Rabbi Shimon Glitzenstein recalled the angry resistance Zionists encountered in London from wealthy, influential Jews who shared Montagu's views: "The intensive campaign that was conducted in London... encountered a stubborn and bold reaction from a group of extreme assimilationist Jews, 'Englishmen of the Mosaic faith'... They declared that this people [the Jewish nation] no longer exists in the world, it has already passed away, and that only the Jewish religion remains; citizens of England and citizens of other countries are counted among it."[252]

Even Herzl's own son opposed his father's mission. Hans converted to Christianity and rejected the idea that Jews needed a homeland, portraying Judaism as a spiritual tradition that could thrive anywhere. Only near the end of his life did Hans admit that his father had been right. "A Jew remains a Jew, no matter how eagerly he may submit himself to the disciplines of his new religion, how humbly he may place the redeeming cross upon his shoulders for the sake of his former coreligionists, to save them from eternal damnation: a Jew remains a Jew."[253]

Montagu and wealthy assimilationists weren't the only Jews who opposed Zionism. From the very start, Herzl had encountered an even stranger opposition: Orthodox rabbis.

Herzl could understand why assimilationist Jews opposed him. They saw Judaism as a religion, nothing more, and considered themselves fully English or French or German. But what he didn't expect was opposition from the Orthodox rabbis.

"We meet with hostility even from certain so-called official circles within Jewry," Herzl wrote. "This phenomenon was particularly conspicuous in the protests voiced by some rabbis. It will always be one of the great curiosities of our period that these gentlemen should be praying for Zion and working against it at the same time."[254]

Herzl's question was a good one. Why were rabbis fighting against the very thing they prayed for?

The Sages called rabbis like this "*ketanei emunah,*" "those who are small of faith."[255] They were not describing skeptics or secularists but genuine believers, religious Jews who kept the commandments yet suffered from a smallness of faith. Despite their commitment to the Torah, they could not recognize God's hand when it moved through history. As the prophet Jeremiah put it: "They have eyes and do not see, they have ears and do not hear" (Jeremiah 5:21).

Rabbi Zvi Yehuda Kook used a similar term, describing "*tzaddikim she'einam ma'aminim*," "righteous people who do not believe." It sounds like a paradox, but it describes something real, something that the Orthodox opponents of Zionism embodied without realizing it. These men were not hypocrites; they longed for the ingathering of the exiles with genuine feeling. What they suffered from was something more insidious: a complete rupture between their observance and their faith, between the words they recited and their capacity to recognize those words coming true. In the *Amidah*, the central Jewish prayer recited three times daily, we say "May our eyes behold Your return to Zion." The prayer is not asking God to return to Zion. It is asking Him to open our eyes wide enough to recognize the redemption when it unfolds in front of us — because the greatest danger is not that God will fail to redeem us, but that we will watch it happening and not see it.[256]

Why was it so difficult for the rabbis of Herzl's era to see God's hand in the Zionist movement? Many Orthodox rabbis were troubled that most of the movement's leaders were secular. Several were passionate atheists and socialists. How could a movement led by men who didn't observe the Torah bring Jews back to Israel? Others believed that only God could bring redemption. Reclaiming the land through human initiative was presumptuous, an attempt to force God's hand.

But the rabbis were wrong. According to the Sages, living in Israel is a supreme Jewish value—one that applies even to Jews who are far from observant. Rabbi Shmuel Mohilever, an early Religious Zionist leader, pointed this out: "Almost all the decisors of Jewish law... agreed that the obligation to ascend to the land of Israel remains in our time... The Holy One, Blessed be He, desires more that His children dwell in His land even if they do not observe the Torah properly, than that they dwell outside the land and observe it properly."[257]

The sources are clear. The Sages taught: "The Holy One, Blessed be He, said, 'Would that the children of My people were in the land of Israel even though they defile it.'"[258] God's presence rests with Israel even in imperfection: "The Holy One, Blessed be He, causes His Divine Presence to dwell upon Israel even though they are impure, as it is said—'when you dwell among them in their impurity' (Leviticus 15:31)."[259]

Returning to the land is itself repentance. Isaiah called out to Israel: "The watchman said: The morning comes, also the night: if you seek, seek: return, come" (Isaiah 21:12). Rabbi Bachya ben Asher explained: "'If you seek, seek' means that if you wish to be redeemed, seek mercy before Him and return from exile and come to Jerusalem."[260] The call to return to Israel was not a secular invention of Herzl and the modern Zionists; it came from God Himself.

But what about the secular, even atheist, leadership of the movement? Rabbi David Kimche, the 12th-century Bible commentator, addressed this directly. The physical return would come first, spiritual awakening later: "For most of the children of Israel will return in repentance after they see the signs of redemption, and... they will not return in repentance until they first see the beginning of salvation."

The fact that Herzl and his followers didn't keep the Torah didn't disqualify them. They were fulfilling the first stage.[261]

Herzl's Orthodox opponents got it backwards. They thought human initiative threatened God's plan. But reclaiming the land, rebuilding the nation, establishing sovereignty—this was the redemption they prayed for. Zionism wasn't defying God's will. It was God's will in action.

18

Ashkenazic Amnesia, Sephardic Memory

In 1911, a Yemenite Jewish family tore down their own house—not because it was condemned or because they needed building materials, but because they needed fast cash to pay for passage to the land of Israel. The Jews were finally returning home, the Messiah was coming, and they refused to be left behind. When no one would buy the house fast enough, they dismantled it themselves and sold the wood piece by piece. With the money in hand, they boarded a ship and left Yemen—where their family had lived for two thousand years, longer than any Jewish community had lived anywhere in the diaspora. They walked away without hesitation. Yemen meant nothing; it was never home.[262]

This was not a family fleeing persecution. The pogroms and expulsions that eventually ended the Yemenite diaspora entirely only came thirty years later. These Jews left because they heard that the Jewish people were returning home, and they desperately wanted to be a part of it. In that year alone, over 1,500 Yemenite Jews made the journey to Ottoman Palestine. They traded comfort for misery. Ottoman Palestine in 1911 meant swamps and deserts, malaria and backbreaking labor in terrible heat, hostile Arabs and a Turkish government that didn't care if they lived or died. The Yemenite Jews knew what they were walking into; they went anyway.

These Yemenite Jews had almost certainly never heard of Herzl. They knew nothing about Zionist Congresses or debates about whether Jews were a religion or a nation. But in 1910, when a young man from the Zionist Organization showed up with a pamphlet saying Jews were returning to build a nation in the land of Israel, they understood immediately that it was time to go home.

The Jewish people's identity crisis is a uniquely European story. The emancipation that began in Western Europe led many Ashkenazic Jews to reimagine themselves as a religion rather than a nation. But the other half of the Jewish people lived an entirely different experience. These were the Sephardim, the Jews of the Muslim Middle East and North Africa. They never lived under Christendom, never experienced emancipation, and never faced the question of whether they could be both Jews and citizens of another nation.

Under Islamic rule, Jews were recognized as a protected but subordinate people—the *dhimmi*, "People of the Book." Throughout the Ottoman Empire, Jews were organized as a distinct *millet*, a legally recognized national community with its own internal governance. When Jews had disputes among themselves, they resolved them in their own courts under their own law. They ran their own schools where children studied Torah in Hebrew, not the Quran in Arabic. When the Ottoman authorities needed to communicate with the Jews, they spoke to Jewish leaders who represented the community as a whole.

The system was designed not to integrate Jews into Ottoman society, but to marginalize them. Baghdadi Jews spoke Arabic fluently and conducted business with Muslim neighbors, but they were not Iraqi. There was no ambiguity about who they were and no expectation that they should feel torn between their Jewish and Iraqi identities. They did not possess citizenship in the modern sense of the word.

Because their identity was never challenged, Sephardic Jews were spared the crisis that tore European Jewry apart. They never felt compelled to redefine Jewish identity as "Judaism" to gain social acceptance. They never had to invent theories about how Judaism was compatible with loyalty to a non-Jewish nation. They never developed a theology of exile that turned powerlessness into a virtue or argued that Jews were meant to remain scattered forever as a "light unto the nations." They lived as Jews—often in hardship, with limited rights and second-class status—but without the confusion and self-doubt that European modernity brought. When they heard Jews were returning to the land of Israel, they recognized what it meant. This wasn't a new idea. It was what they were waiting for.

Rabbi Yehuda Leon Ashkenazi traces this difference between Ashkenazic and Sephardic Jews back more than two millennia, to the Babylonian and Roman exiles. Ashkenazic Jews descend primarily from the Babylonian exile that followed the destruction of the First Temple. Those Jews who remained in Babylon and did not return with Ezra and Nehemiah became the ancestors of the diaspora that eventually spread into Europe and became Ashkenazic Jewry. Their intellectual and religious life developed in Babylon, not Jerusalem.

But Sephardic Jews trace their origins to the exile that followed the destruction of the Second Temple. These were the Jews who returned with Ezra, rebuilt the Temple, fought the Greeks and Romans, and lived as a free nation in their land before Rome's legions finally defeated them. During the centuries following the destruction of the Temple, their descendants made their way into the lands of Islam. In them, Rabbi Ashkenazi saw the continuation of the Jews of Judea—people whose identity was still shaped by direct memory of sovereignty, Temple worship, and national life in the land.[263]

Rabbi Ashkenazi's thesis is not universally accepted by historians, but he was right about this: Sephardic Jews never forgot they were a nation. When Zionism arrived, the poorest Yemenite Jew understood it faster than the wealthiest German Reform rabbi. He didn't need it explained. He didn't need to reconcile it with other beliefs. Jews were returning home, as he knew would happen.

Between 1948 and the early 1970s, roughly 850,000 Sephardic Jews poured into the new state.[264] Expelled en masse from Morocco, Iraq, Yemen, Libya, Tunisia, and Egypt, most arrived with nothing. They filled Israel's frontier towns, raised large families, served in the IDF and enlisted in combat units at above-average rates.

Three generations later, their grandchildren are the backbone of Israeli society—fiercely patriotic, deeply traditional even when not religious, and constitutionally incapable of the hand-wringing ambivalence that afflicts so many of Israel's progressive elites. They don't agonize over whether Israel deserves to exist or whether Jewish nationalism is compatible with liberalism. The question strikes them as strange. They are a nation. This is their land. What is there to agonize over?

That Yemenite family never read *Der Judenstaat*. They never debated whether Jews were a nation or a religion. They already knew. They knew they were in exile, they knew where home was, and when the moment came, they sold their house plank by plank and left. Their grandchildren are still here.

19

VINDICATED AT LAST

When Mark Twain visited the Holy Land in 1867, he found little to admire. Traveling through the parched hills and crumbling villages of Ottoman Palestine, he wrote that it was "a desolate country whose soil is rich enough, but is given over wholly to weeds, a silent mournful expanse... a desolation." He was astonished by its barrenness: "Even the olive and the cactus, those fast friends of a worthless soil, had almost deserted the country."[265]

Twain wasn't alone. For centuries after Rome destroyed Jerusalem and exiled most of the Jews, the land stayed barren. The Byzantines ruled it, then the Arabs, then the Crusaders, then the Ottomans. None of them could make it flourish. Individuals could scratch out a living, but no nation ever successfully or permanently planted roots there. Since the time of Joshua, the land would bloom for only one people. Sir John William Dawson saw this in 1890: "No nation has been able to establish itself as a nation in Palestine up to this day; no national union and no national spirit has prevailed there... [Its occupants were] mere tenants at will, evidently waiting for those entitled to the permanent possession of the soil."[266]

"And your enemies will be desolate upon it" (Leviticus 26:32). Nachmanides explains that the land's barrenness was not a curse but rather a comfort and consolation for the Jewish people. The land would stay barren until the rightful heirs, the people of Israel, returned.[267]

The connection between Israel and its land is organic. The nation can't flourish scattered in exile any more than the land can bloom without its people. Ezekiel described the Jewish people in Babylon as dry bones scattered across a valley, lifeless and waiting to be gathered back together. Rabbi Elijah of Vilna took the image literally: living outside the land of Israel is a form of burial. The bones only come back to life when the people return to their land.[268]

Modern Zionism proved Nachmanides right. The same soil that Twain dismissed as a "desolation" came back to life. Jews drained the swamps, farmed the deserts, and rebuilt ancient cities. After two thousand years, the land finally had its people back. Every empire that ruled it failed to make it flourish. The Jews returned, and it bloomed.

The Holocaust settled the argument between Zionists and assimilationists. German Jews did everything possible to prove their loyalty to the "Fatherland," fighting for the Kaiser's army during the First World War and loyally serving Germany as model citizens. The Nazis gassed them anyway. Herzl warned them decades earlier that Jews needed their own state because the "enlightened" countries of Europe would eventually turn on them. After Auschwitz, no serious person could argue that he was wrong.

On May 14, 1948, David Ben-Gurion stood before a crowd in the Tel Aviv Museum and read the thirteen short paragraphs of Israel's Declaration of Independence. People wept openly. Five Arab armies were already massing at the borders, but Ben-Gurion read every word anyway. Jews would no longer beg for refuge or wait for foreign powers to protect them. For the first time since Rome burned Jerusalem, we were a sovereign nation in our own land.

The Psalmist wrote: "Let this be inscribed for the latest generation, and a newly created people will praise the Lord" (Psalm 102:19). Rabbi David Altschuler explained that "newly created people" isn't referring to a messianic religious revival but to the full restoration of Israel's national life. The birth of the modern State of Israel was the literal fulfillment of this prophecy.[269]

Rabbi Yehuda Leon Ashkenazi was born in Algeria in 1922, the son of the last Chief Rabbi of Algeria. He grew up studying Torah and Kabbalah at home while attending French schools during the day, pulled in two directions from the start. During World War II, he joined the French Foreign Legion and was wounded at the Battle of Strasbourg. The war forced him to confront questions he couldn't dodge: Where did he belong? What did it mean to be a Jew living in France?

The answer came after the war, when he met Jews with radically different backgrounds and ideologies—secular Zionists, religious survivors from Eastern Europe and North African refugees. What held them together was not religion, but nationhood. Years later, he explained: "I discovered for the first time the other branches of the Jewish people, and simultaneously I was exposed to the political identity of the people that grew without any connection to religion... That was the moment when I began to understand that what unites all Jews throughout the world is first and foremost a national belonging rather than a religious belonging... I understood then that the religion of

Israel is the individual's revelation of the unique national identity of Israel, and not a belief system around which individuals with similar personal beliefs unite."[270]

When he worked with secular French Jews after the Holocaust, he didn't push them to become Orthodox Jews or to live a meticulously religious lifestyle. Instead, he encouraged them to identify with the Jewish people. For him, national identity came first, religious practice second—just as Ruth first declared her allegiance to Israel, and only then to the God of Israel.[271] If Jews felt themselves to be part of the people of Israel, they would eventually find their way back to the God of Israel too.

He was still living in France when the Six-Day War broke out. Immediately after the war, he told his wife: "This is the last war that finds us outside the land of Israel." Years later, he recalled: "The certainty grew stronger within me that only madness would cause me not to join this shared destiny of the Jewish people, this messianic hope that had become reality."[272]

In 1968, Rabbi Ashkenazi moved his family to Jerusalem. The Jewish state didn't need to be perfect for him to recognize what it was: the answer to two thousand years of exile.

20

THE POST-ZIONIST REVOLT

A 39-year-old Israeli diplomat had no business challenging Arnold Toynbee to a public debate. Toynbee was 71, one of the most celebrated historians in the world, and the overflow crowd at McGill University's Hillel House on January 31, 1961 knew it. Yaacov Herzog, Israel's ambassador to Canada, had issued the challenge just five days earlier, without consulting his superiors in Jerusalem. Foreign Ministry officials worried he would be overmatched, and local Jewish leaders feared he would be embarrassed. Herzog went ahead anyway.

Toynbee was an arrogant antisemite who worked throughout his career to delegitimize Jewish nationalism. His twelve-volume Study of History made him one of the world's leading historians, which gave his antisemitism an academic veneer. In lectures and essays, he equated Zionism with racism, charging that "the watchword of antisemitism is back to medieval apartheid; the watchword of Zionism is back to the medieval ghetto."[273] He argued that when Jews lost their land and political independence two thousand years ago they ceased to be a nation and survived only as a religious group. Therefore, the rebirth of Israel was not an act of justice but a moral regression—a return to tribalism in an age that should have outgrown it. He called Zionism "demonic" and labeled Judaism an "extinct society," a "fossilized civilization."

Earlier that week, Toynbee lectured McGill students, repeating these arguments and equating Zionism with Nazism. At the debate, broadcast live on radio across Canada, Toynbee explained his view: "The Western gentile races invented nationalism, which I strongly dislike, and the Jews caught this disease from the gentiles, which is very unfortunate." Herzog answered: "Well, it has been a long, long disease with us, and many physicians have tried to cure us down the ages, but we have refused to be cured."[274]

The debate lasted over an hour. Herzog systematically dismantled Toynbee's arguments, forcing the historian to concede that if Israel's actions in 1948 were equivalent to Nazi atrocities, then so were Britain's in Ireland, France's in Syria, and America's throughout its history. By the end, Toynbee's own wife was overheard telling him: "I told you not to take part in this debate."[275]

Herzog won—but Toynbee's ideas didn't die with his defeat.

In 1975, the United Nations General Assembly passed Resolution 3379 declaring that "Zionism is a form of racism and racial discrimination."[276]

The resolution did more than slander Israel. It denied that Jewish nationhood. If Zionism—Jewish national self-determination—is racism, then Jews have no right to sovereignty. The Soviet bloc and Arab states pushed the resolution through, redefining Jewish history in the process. All Jews in Israel were now, in the eyes of the world, effectively branded as "colonialists." Though the UN revoked the resolution sixteen years later, the phrase stuck. "Zionism is racism" is still a mainstay slur of Israel used at pro-Hamas rallies.

Toynbee and the UN attacked Jewish nationalism from the outside. But the greater threat would come from inside Israel, from Jews who reject the idea that Israel should be a Jewish state at all.

Rabbi Abraham Isaac Kook saw this coming decades before Israel was founded. He warned: "There is a brazen force at work, armed with lawlessness and foreign ways, utterly devoid of Israel's true holiness. It hides its emptiness behind a counterfeit nationalism, mere scraps of history and affection for the [Hebrew] language that dress up Jewish life in Israeli garb. But make no mistake: this corrupt force will breed hatred of Israel and the land of Israel. We have already seen this with our own eyes. When this impurity gains strength, the disaster will be beyond measure."[277]

Though it was a dominant force in his own generation, Rabbi Kook recognized the emptiness at the heart of secular Zionism. It celebrated Jewish history and culture and played a critical role in reviving the Hebrew language. But having cut itself off from the deep foundations of the Torah, the entire movement was built on shaky ground. Without God and Torah, secular Zionism was destined to collapse—and would ultimately lead to self-hatred and the rejection of Zionism itself.

Rabbi Kook's prediction proved prophetic. The failure of modern secular Zionism first became apparent in the wake of Israel's miraculous triumph in the 1967 Six-Day War. Israel conquered vast territories, including Jerusalem's Old City, the Golan Heights, Judea and Samaria, and the Sinai Peninsula. Yet Defense Minister Moshe Dayan immediately handed control of the Temple Mount—the holiest place in the world, where the Temple once stood and where it will one day stand again—back to the Jordanian-controlled Waqf. When asked why, Dayan reportedly said, "Why do we need all this Vatican stuff?"[278]

Returning the Temple Mount to the Jordanian Waqf, the very enemy that had just tried to destroy Israel, was a catastrophic blunder. The Temple Mount is not a historical museum. It is the holiest site in the world for the Jewish people, the place where the Temple stood for a thousand years, the place toward which every Jew in the world prays. It is the ancient center of the Jewish nation, the physical and spiritual heart of Jewish sovereignty. And Dayan gave it away.

To this day, the Temple Mount remains under the control of the Waqf, hostile to Israel and committed to denying any Jewish claim to the site. Jews can visit, but until recently were forbidden from even moving their lips in silent prayer. In recent years, religious Jews have made modest progress asserting our rights there, but the fundamental injustice remains: the holiest site for the Jewish people, in the Jewish state, is controlled by Muslims who reject Israel's very existence and seek our destruction. This is the legacy of Dayan's hollow secular Zionism, which treated thousands of years of Jewish history and memory as irrelevant.

Dayan was not the first Jew to be embarrassed by what God gave him. When the Israelites crossed the Jordan and entered the land, they were nearly destroyed—not by foreign enemies, but by one man's theft. After the miraculous conquest of Jericho, they suffered a humiliating defeat at Ai because one of their own, Achan, stole items set aside for God and sought to conceal his sin: "When I saw among the spoils a beautiful cloak from Shinar, and 200 shekels of silver, and a bar of gold weighing 50 shekels, then I coveted them and took them" (Joshua 7:21).

Superficially, it appears Achan was motivated by old-fashioned greed. But the Sages question why Achan stole the cloak, and their answer is eye-opening: "Achan stretched his remaining foreskin in order to conceal the fact that he was circumcised."[279]

In other words, Achan did not take the forbidden loot because he was overcome by temptation. The "beautiful cloak from Shinar" wasn't just loot—it was Canaanite clothing, a way for Achan to erase his Israelite identity and blend in among the local pagans, the people that God commanded the Israelites to drive out of the land.

Even after all the miracles in the wilderness, after all that God did for His people, Achan was embarrassed to be an Israelite. He wanted to look like a Canaanite, to fit in. That embarrassment, that desire to be like everyone else, nearly undermined Israel's conquest of the land from the very start.

Achan's shame and yearning to erase what made him distinctly Israelite became the defining pathology of Israel's intellectual class. In the decades following the 1967 and 1973 wars, the greatest threat to Israel no longer came from the Arab armies surrounding our borders, but from our own intellectual class. Leading Israeli historians, writers, and academics—many funded by the same state whose existence they scorned—began dismantling the very foundations of Zionism from within.

In the 1980s and 1990s, a group of Israeli scholars—Benny Morris, Tom Segev, Ilan Pappé, and Baruch Kimmerling—set out to "revise" Israel's founding story. What was once understood as the prophetic ingathering of an exiled nation, they recast as a modern invention. These post-Zionist scholars argued that "the idea of a unitary Jewish people, with a shared identity and history of persecution, is a myth."[280] The Jews of the Diaspora, they claimed, were not one nation scattered among the nations, but a patchwork of unrelated communities—each with its own history and struggles—until Zionist leaders in the late nineteenth century "partially invented" the notion of a single Jewish people for political purposes.

Baruch Kimmerling went further. He called Zionism's effort to forge a unified Jewish past a "monstrous practice" that exploited the memory of Jewish suffering to manufacture a fake national identity. Kimmerling reframed the 1948 War of Independence, portraying Israel's heroic battle for survival as a colonial war of deception and ethnic cleansing. Israel, he wrote, was "built on the ruins of another society."[281]

Israel's enemies abroad loved this. Finally, Israeli academics were saying what anti-Zionists had claimed for decades: that the Jewish state was illegitimate from the start, that Jewish history was a fabrication, and that Israel was a colonial project with no moral foundation. The post-Zionist historians gave them the intellectual cover they needed.

If modern Zionism has one sacred pillar, it is the Law of Return. Passed in 1950, two years after independence, it states: "Every Jew has the right to come to this country as an oleh."[282] In the 1930s, as the Nazis tightened their grip on Europe, the British sealed the gates of Palestine, trapping hundreds of thousands of Jews who had nowhere else to go. The world watched and did nothing. The State of Israel's answer, once it had the power to give one, was the Law of Return: no

Jew would ever again be stateless, and no foreign power would ever again decide whether Jews could come home.

This is not just a lenient immigration policy. The Law of Return expresses the covenantal idea that the Jewish people are one family with a shared homeland to which every member has an eternal claim. As David Ben-Gurion said, the law was meant to ensure that "Israel is not merely a state of its citizens, but the state of the Jewish people."[283]

For decades, a group of Israeli intellectuals has been trying to dismantle the Law of Return. They are embarrassed of its Jewish particularism and view it as simply ethnic privilege, incompatible with Western democracy and liberalism. Tom Segev called it "a contradiction to equality." The philosopher Haim Ganz argued that Israel should grant "national preference" to all citizens equally, not just to Jews, which would transform the Jewish state into a state like any other. Even novelists like Amos Elon and David Grossman described the Law of Return as "morally indefensible" and an obstacle to peace.[284]

Look past the language about equality and democracy and the argument is simple: the "Jews" are not a people or a nation, and therefore have no unique claim to the land of Israel. If Israel is just a state of all its citizens, no different from France or Canada, then the Law of Return makes no sense. Why should Jews have special rights to immigrate? Ending the Law of Return would end Zionism itself, which is precisely the point.

Israel's schools were supposed to connect Jewish children to their homeland. The State Education Law of 1953 tasked all schools—including secular ones—with instilling "the values of Jewish culture," "love of the homeland," and "loyalty to the Jewish people."[285] This means that even in secular schools, students have to study the Bible, Jewish history, Jewish thought, archaeology, and geography. But the Labor Zionists who designed the curriculum were secular, and their secularism showed. The teachers themselves had no personal connection to what they were teaching; the Torah was a text, not a way of life, and students could tell the difference. Students learned about Torah in the classroom but rarely saw it practiced at home. The next generation of secular Israelis grew up with some abstract knowledge of Jewish history but no spiritual connection to it, making them vulnerable to the post-Zionist assault that followed.

By the 1990s, Rabbi Kook's warning about secular alienation materialized in the schools. Education Minister Shulamit Aloni and the Zimmermann Committee gutted the Jewish curriculum. They removed most Bible teaching from history classes and replaced Jewish history with "universal history." Israeli students in secular public schools no longer begin their studies with the Exodus or the kingdoms of David and Solomon, but with the Greeks and other ancient civilizations, in which the Jewish people appear only as secondary characters reacting to other civilizations. The Exodus, the prophets, the return to Zion—the entire story of Jewish nationhood—was replaced with lessons on global progress and universal moral development.[286]

In February 2024, Knesset Member Galit Distal Atbarian rose to describe how Israel's secular schools had robbed her of her Jewish identity. Her words were raw: "The state education system robbed me of my identity, and what is happening now is a thousand times worse. Judaism is a treasure of embodied knowledge, a diamond. We are forced to ignore this diamond because people do not know what is there. An ignorant generation grew up here... We had the roots cut off from under our feet. I studied [secular] philosophy for 7 years, but it's dust compared to the diamond we sit on and bury."[287]

The impact of Israel's post-Zionist intellectual trends is reflected in a painful demographic shift. In 2025, roughly 79,000 Israelis left the country, while only 25,000 new immigrants arrived and about 21,000 returned, creating a net deficit.[288] The people leaving are not primarily chasing career opportunities or adventure. They are secular Israelis who have lost connection to Israel's national mission and do not see themselves as part of Jewish history and destiny. Raised to see Israel as just another Western democracy, the logic of staying becomes hard to defend: if Israel is just another Western country, why not pick one in a better neighborhood, where Iranian missiles aren't falling on your living room?

The educational and ideological erosion in secular Israeli society inevitably led to political acts of surrender. In 1993, Prime Minister Yitzhak Rabin signed the Oslo Accords, agreeing to create a Palestinian Authority in Judea and Samaria, Israel's biblical heartland. Rather than settling and defending the land God promised to Abraham, Israel's left-wing leadership chose to trade it for promises of peace and international approval. The Arabs, of course, treated the Oslo Accords as a Trojan Horse, using it to advance their long-term goal of destroying Israel. But the deeper problem lay within Israel: a generation of leaders and intellectuals who had abandoned belief in the Jewish national mission.

As Yoel Marcus wrote in 1995, "Our people has long since tired of bearing Zionism on its shoulders generation after generation... While the Arabs have remained faithful to their ideology of the holiness of the land, preferring to forgo peace rather than concede anything of their demands, Israel is ready to withdraw from the lands that were the cradle of Judaism... in exchange for personal safety and a 'normal' life.'"[289] This was the fruit of post-Zionist education.

In 2005, Prime Minister Ariel Sharon unilaterally withdrew from the Gaza Strip, abandoning twenty-one Jewish towns and forcibly evicting over 8,000 Jews from their homes. The move was celebrated by Israel's secular elite as a courageous step toward peace and normalization. In retrospect, it was the tragic culmination of decades of surrender and ideological exhaustion—the kind that produces a Prime Minister who stands before his people and announces that he has lost the will to fight for them. Ehud Olmert said it himself: "We are tired of fighting; we are tired of being courageous; we are tired of winning; we are tired of defeating our enemies."[290] This was the so-called "leader" of the Jewish state.

Hamas, the Palestinian Authority, and other terrorist groups quickly recognized the meaning of this fatigue: Israel's leaders no longer believed in the justice of their cause or the holiness of their mission. The withdrawal paved the way for Hamas's takeover of Gaza and, ultimately, for the October 7, 2023 massacre, when those same terrorists unleashed unprecedented brutality on Israeli communities just across the Gaza border. The Gaza disengagement was not just a tactical mistake; it was the direct result of a spiritual and ideological vacuum at the heart of secular Zionism.

The tragedy of Israel's retreat from Gaza was not just about territory. The disengagement was a betrayal of the families who were encouraged to settle there and then forcibly evicted, and a betrayal of the Torah itself, which commands us to settle, not abandon, the land of Israel. But even worse was the betrayal of Jewish nationhood. The retreat from Gaza effectively announced to the world that we were giving up on our right to the land. If the Jewish state itself was willing to uproot Jewish communities and abandon part of the biblical homeland, then Jewish nationhood was negotiable after all.

Our shameful retreat from Gaza in 2005 signaled weakness to Hamas and to our enemies all across the Middle East. On October 7, 2023, Hamas terrorists crossed the Gaza border and slaughtered over 1,200 Israeli civilians—a direct consequence of the 2005 disengagement. In the aftermath, many Israelis who had believed the government's promises of peace and normalcy began asking questions that secular Zionism could never answer: Who are we? Why are we here? What is this all for?

Rabbi Kook foresaw the collapse of secular Zionism decades before it happened, but also predicted what would rise in its place. In the very same letter in which he warned of the dangers of hollow nationalism, he wrote: "Yet I trust in God that He will not let us fall. All who revere God's word, all who yearn for the redemption of His people and His Holy Land will rally to our cause. We will establish a precious foundation in Zion and breathe new life into our resettlement, built on the bedrock of pure faith joined with the joy of living and the pursuit of righteous aspirations. And God will be with us to rebuild the ruins of our people for all generations."[291]

Those words are proving true. After decades of secular dominance and post-Zionist education that stripped Jewish history from the curriculum, something is changing in Israeli society. Young secular Israelis are returning to faith and national consciousness.

After October 7, students at Ohel Shem, a secular high school in Ramat Gan, began putting on *tefillin*[292] before classes. Oral Malik, an 18-year-old senior, set up a *tefillin* station for his classmates. When he helped a friend wrap the holy straps on his arm for the first time since his bar mitzvah, the student said, "I haven't done this since age 13. And now I'm 17." At Dror High School, a 16-year-old named Afik Ben David spent his own money to set up a similar station. Kids who had never given any of this a second thought started lining up.

School administrators and parents tried to shut it down, arguing that religious observance has no place in secular schools. The irony was lost on them: if these teenagers were smoking pot or cutting class, no one would care. But putting on *tefillin*? That must be stopped! The students kept doing it anyway.[293]

After October 7, thousands of Israeli soldiers—normally described as "secular"—began praying before going into combat. The demand for *tzitzit*[294] in IDF units became so overwhelming that synagogues in Israel and across the diaspora worked around the clock tying thousands of pairs to keep up.[295]

The prophets predicted this day would come. "After that, I will pour out My spirit on all flesh; Your sons and daughters shall prophesy... And your young men shall see visions" (Joel 3:1). "For I have drawn Judah taut, and applied My hand to Efraim as to a bow, and I will arouse your sons, O Zion... And make you like a warrior's sword" (Zechariah 9:13). Joel saw a generation of young people returning to God with spiritual vision. Zechariah saw them rising up as warriors to defend Israel. Both prophecies are being fulfilled now, in the generation fighting this war.

Douglas Murray described what this generation of Israelis has become: "They know that they are fighting for the Jewish people as their forbears have before, but this time with a state, with an army, with an Air Force. And they've stepped up to this moment and they have been extraordinary. People will write books about this generation."[296]

Hamas launched the October 7 attack to destroy Israel. It did the opposite. The war reminded Israelis, secular and religious alike, that we are a people with a purpose. Israel emerged from the war as the region's undisputed military superpower, but also with something deeper: a young generation that now understands why the state exists and what we are fighting for. The secular Zionism that Rabbi Kook warned against is finally giving way to what he predicted would replace it: a nation committed to building a holy society in the land God promised our ancestors.

21

Jews Who Won't Fight

"The State of Israel is an enemy state." "The draft law is consent to genocide." "We will die before we enlist." And the most telling: "Better to die as a Jew than live as a Zionist."

That was the message 200,000 Haredi Jews brought to the streets of Jerusalem in October 2025, shutting down the city for hours in what organizers dubbed the "Million Man March"—a rare display of solidarity in a community that usually can't agree on anything. They were there to protest the shocking notion that they, like every other Israeli, might be required to join the Israel Defense Forces and fight to protect the State of Israel.[297]

For two years after October 7, 2023, hundreds of thousands of Israeli reservists were called back again and again, serving for many months at a time. They sacrificed their businesses and wrecked their families. Many put their education on hold for two years, came home injured, or developed PTSD from what they experienced.

Israel desperately needed more soldiers. There was an obvious pool: roughly 80,000 young Haredi men between 18 and 24, all eligible for service.

The Haredi community refused. Haredim make up 18% of Israel's Jewish population—growing fast, with birth rates averaging 6.4 children per woman—and for two years of the most brutal war in Israel's history, they carried on as usual. As IDF reservists sacrificed everything to defend the people of Israel, Haredi men studied in yeshivas, collected their stipends and took their normal vacations. There were notable exceptions,[298] but they were few and far between.

The rest of the country was furious. Over 80% of non-Haredi Jews now support forcibly drafting Haredim. The government responded by cutting benefits and subsidies, arresting hundreds of draft dodgers, and threatening financial penalties for families whose sons refused to serve.

That's what brought 200,000 Haredim into the streets of Jerusalem. They came not to protest against Hamas or Hezbollah, but against their own government's demand that they share the burden of defending the Jewish state.

After the demonstration, Haggai Luber—whose son Yehonatan was killed fighting Hamas in Gaza—expressed the pain many Israelis felt: "After we all saw the massacre and horrors on Simchat Torah, we were sure the Haredim would change their ways and join the defense. We tried speaking to their hearts—with proofs from the Torah, with appeals to the Jewish heart of kindness, with the law of a *milchemet mitzvah,*[299] with 'Do not stand idly by your neighbor's blood'... But we must admit: their leaders, activists, and most of the public closed their ears."[300]

These are not secular Jews indifferent to Torah. These are Haredi Jews—"ultra-Orthodox," as they're often called—who dedicate their entire lives to the most rigorous observance of Jewish law. They spend years in yeshiva studying Torah and structure every moment of their day around Jewish law. They are meticulous about observing Shabbat, the kosher laws, prayer, and every detail of religious observance.

When Moses spoke to the tribes of Reuben, Gad, and Manasseh, who asked to settle on the eastern side of the Jordan instead of crossing into battle, he was quite clear about their obligation to fight: "Shall your brothers go to war while you sit here?" (Numbers 32:6). The Torah establishes collective responsibility—no able-bodied man can remain behind while his brothers put their lives on the line. Deuteronomy 20 outlines the obligation of going to war, and every man is expected to participate in the nation's defense.

Haredim argue that full-time Torah study exempts them from military service, that their learning protects Israel spiritually just as IDF soldiers protect it physically. But nowhere does the Torah grant a categorical exemption for Torah study that nullifies the duty of defense, especially in times of existential threat. So why do these deeply religious people bend over backward to avoid what the Torah clearly commands? Is it simply cowardice dressed up in religious language?

To understand the Haredi refusal to serve, we have to understand what it means to be Haredi in Israel today. Haredim live in an alternative reality. The journalist Menachem Rahat explains: "The average Haredi lives in a sealed capsule, cut off from reality to the point of lacking even basic understanding of the ongoing burden of military service borne by non-Haredim. Anyone who has spoken with a 'classic' Haredi has seen how deep the disconnect really is. Many have shockingly little knowledge of basic life in the State of Israel. They have no idea where the war took place, why it broke out, or how many soldiers and civilians were lost. Most importantly, they have no grasp of the immense suffering and strain of families whose breadwinners have been serving in reserve duty for 400, 500, even 600 days."[301]

Dr. Yehuda Yifrach conducted research among Haredi *kollel*[302] students and found that these students, who benefit from roughly 5,000 shekels per family in state subsidies—welfare, property tax reductions, education, healthcare—are completely unaware that they are a financial burden on the state. They do not believe that the average non-Haredi Jewish household pays three times more in mandatory taxes than a Haredi household. When confronted with the data, 46% insisted they contribute to the economy just like everyone else. Another 26% claimed they contribute even more. And 20% dismissed the figures entirely, arguing that their spiritual contribution makes economic data meaningless. "It's very hard to engage them in conversation about these issues," Yifrach writes, "because they simply refuse to acknowledge reality."[303]

According to Rabbi Dr. Michael Avraham, "they completely ignore the crushing burden on reservists and the economic and social consequences. They don't understand how a state functions or how it differs from a community. In their minds, they're still living in Warsaw or Vilna."[304] They live in the reborn, sovereign state of Israel. But theologically, Haredim are still living in the shtetls of Eastern Europe. As one of the great Hasidic Rebbes of Gur once said, "The people of Israel will require two redemptions: the first, to bring Israel out of exile; the second, to bring the exile out of Israel. And the second is harder than the first."[305]

Rivka Ravitz, herself from the Haredi world, explains: "Being Haredi in Israel mainly means being different—being separate from other communities, especially from the secular population. People often say that this separation has changed in recent years, and maybe to some extent it has. But from what I see, the sense of separation remains. It's at the very core of what it means to be Haredi. The very word 'Haredi' comes from the idea of fear—of being afraid to get too involved with the secular world. That fear, or perhaps that caution, defines the Haredi community in Israel more than anything else."[306]

Haredim are defined by their separation. They have intentionally walled themselves off from the rest of Israeli society, and that isolation has become central to their way of life.

The community originated in Europe in the 18th and 19th centuries as a conservative reaction to the secularizing forces of modernity and the Jewish Enlightenment. Traditionalist Jews in Eastern Europe resisted assimilation and maintained strict adherence to Torah and Jewish law, creating insular communities focused on religious study, prayer, and observance. They saw themselves—and still see themselves—as the guardians of authentic Judaism, which they believed was under existential threat from secular influences.

The Holocaust devastated European Haredi communities, destroying the yeshivot and institutions that had preserved this way of life for centuries. After World War II, survivors rebuilt these communities, particularly in Israel, re-establishing their institutions and doubling down on the culture of separation.

But what does separation mean in a Jewish state? In Europe, Haredim walled themselves off from gentiles and secular Jews alike. That made sense in exile. But in Israel—the one place on earth where Jews can be Jews without apology—does building walls against other Jews still make sense?

The answer, for the Haredi community, has been to remain separate. As Aharon Rose writes, "What primarily sets this Jewish movement apart from others is its total rejection of modern values, norms, and forms of inquiry. Haredi Judaism, regardless of its particular faction, objects to Jews entering the cultural fray of the modern West, studying in its institutions, revering its leaders, fighting in its wars, or partaking of its cultural bounty."[307] Even when those wars are fought to defend the Jewish people, Haredim included, in the Jewish homeland.

Some Haredim identify with the State of Israel, but most experience their life in the Jewish state as "exile among Jews." Rabbi Yitzchak Yosef, Israel's former Sephardic Chief Rabbi, made this clear when he declared that "if they force us into the army, we'll all move abroad... we'll all buy tickets."[308] Incredible as these words are from a former chief rabbi of Israel, they are revealing: for many in the Haredi world, Israel is not their nation in any ideological sense. It is simply the place where they happen to live.

Ambassador Yechiel Leiter diagnosed the problem in the early 1980s: "We have stopped thinking of ourselves as a nation... We are a society that observes commandments without national purpose. Many give up Israeli nationality entirely, taking on foreign citizenship, while continuing personal religious observance but abandoning their responsibilities to the nation. This is the catastrophe: the negation of the chosenness of the Israeli nation, of the Jewish people, forgetting the foundation of foundations—the divine promise that never ceases to exist."[309]

Rabbi Tzvi Friedman, a leading figure in the extremist Jerusalem Faction—the most hardline anti-draft group in the Haredi world—explained his stance in a meeting with secular Israelis. Friedman is well known for declaring that Haredim who enlist in the IDF "leave religion, and that is worse than death."[310] But in this meeting, he went further, revealing the reasoning beneath that view: "Karl Marx said that dividing humanity into nations is backward. There are only classes... We share the same belief. Judaism is a religious association. It is not a nation at all."[311]

Here's the crux of the matter. The Haredi refusal to serve in the IDF isn't about protecting their way of life or avoiding secular influence. It runs deeper than that. At the core of their theology sits a fundamental error about Jewish identity: they don't believe the Jews are a nation.

As Rabbi Yehoshua Pfeffer writes, "The lack of identification with Israel relates to a strongly parochial Haredi identity rather than a broader Jewish identity... The non-Israeli Haredi belongs to a distinct story and identity that doesn't correspond, at least far from fully, with the story of the Zionist entity." The "Zionist entity"—not the Jewish nation, not the fulfillment of biblical prophecy, not the ingathering of exiles. Just an "entity," a political arrangement that happens to call itself Jewish. "The legitimate fear of secularization has led to the a priori determination that we have no part in the great story of the return of Jews to their homeland. In other words, the story of Israel is not a 'Jewish story' because Judaism is a religion and not a nation."[312]

This fundamental error about Jewish identity explains how Haredi leaders can stand before their community and declare military service "genocide" while their fellow Jews bleed and die defending the country. It explains why 200,000 Haredim can fill the streets of Jerusalem protesting not against Israel's enemies but against Israel itself. It explains why their signs read "Better to die as a Jew than live as a Zionist," as if being Jewish and being part of the Jewish nation were somehow contradictory.

There is much to admire in the Haredi community. Their dedication to Torah is genuine and deep. Their commitment to Jewish law is uncompromising in an age of compromise. Within their own communities, they demonstrate extraordinary kindness, building robust social services and charitable networks that care for their own with impressive devotion. The problem is not their rejection of secular culture, much of which genuinely opposes traditional Torah values and deserves to be rejected. The problem is not even their insularity, which in many ways protects them from corrosive influences. The problem is deeper: the Haredi community has confused community with nation.

The Haredi worldview sees God's purpose as creating a holy elite—a community of the righteous, devoted entirely to Torah study and observance, completely cut off from the messiness of national life and the burden of national defense. In this view, the highest achievement is building thriving yeshivas, supporting families in lifelong Torah learning, and maintaining separation from the corrupting influences of the wider world.

How does this square with the Torah's explicit laws of war and national governance? Haredim have no shortage of answers. Some argue that Torah learning protects Israel more effectively than army service. Others consider the state fundamentally illegitimate. Still others see themselves as a spiritual elite whose separation from national life is itself a sacred duty. That these answers contradict one another is telling, for no coherent theology unites them. The Haredim did not study the Torah and conclude that they should not serve. They decided not to serve, and built their theology around that decision.

But this was never God's plan. The Jewish people are not the Amish or the Mennonites. We are not a tight-knit religious community that shares deeply held beliefs and practices. We are a nation, the descendants of Abraham, Isaac, and Jacob, who God called to build a holy society in the land He promised our ancestors.

God did not call us to become a holy community. The call was to be "A holy *nation*, a *kingdom* of priests" (Exodus 19:6), a nation that would live in its land, govern itself according to Torah, defend its borders, and through its national existence become a light to the world.

Two hundred thousand Haredim filled the streets of Jerusalem to protest that call. Until they answer it, they will remain what they showed themselves to be that day: a separate people living among the nation, sharing the land but not the destiny, benefiting from its blood and sacrifice while refusing to share its burden.

THE AMERICAN RECKONING

"'How long will you waver between two opinions? If the LORD is God, follow Him; but if Baal is God, follow him.' But the people said nothing" (I Kings 18:21)

Israel365

22

SELF-LOATHING, FOR AN HONORARIUM

The flagship synagogue of Reform Judaism paid a man who believes the Jewish state is idolatry to preach from its pulpit.

In 2021, Temple Emanu-El banned Alan Dershowitz from its pulpit. For years, the famous Harvard lawyer had been the synagogue's star attraction, defending Abraham, Moses, David, and Noah in dramatic mock trials that drew standing-room-only crowds of 1,500 people. The audiences loved it. Then Dershowitz was falsely accused of sexual assault by Virginia Giuffre—an accusation she later recanted, and which her own lawyers admitted was wrong. The synagogue board didn't wait for the facts, and banned him anyway—not because they believed the accusations, but because they didn't want the association.[313]

In his place, they invited Peter Beinart—and paid him handsomely to deliver his verdict on the Jewish state.

Beinart isn't just critical of Israeli policy. He believes the Jewish state is idolatry. The very idea of Jewish sovereignty, in his view, is worship of a false god. "A state is human-made. To make its existence sacred is to worship something other than God." For Beinart, the State of Israel isn't the fulfillment of prophecy. It is the golden calf, recast in blue and white.[314] This was the voice Temple Emanu-El chose to amplify from its pulpit.

Dershowitz was stunned. "I offered to speak on how to combat antisemitism and anti-Zionism, but the Temple preferred to hear from Beinart, who advocates the end of Israel as the nation-state of the Jewish people and supports boycotts against Israelis. Temple Emanu-El has silenced my voice while amplifying one of Israel's most toxic detractors. Shame on the Temple."[315]

Beinart is a darling of the anti-Israel left, a regular on the New York Times opinion pages—a modern court Jew.[316] Like the "protected Jews" of 18th-century Prussia or the Soviet regime's "pocket Jews" who sat on the Anti-Zionist Committee, Beinart serves those who seek to weaken or destroy the Jewish people, providing the moral cover they need. When a Jew with impeccable progressive credentials declares that Jewish sovereignty is idolatry, Israel's enemies don't have to make the argument themselves. They can just quote him. The New York Times gives him a platform precisely because he does their work for them.

What does that say about how the leadership of Temple Emanu-El understand Jewish nationhood? What does it say that the flagship institution of American Reform Judaism honored a man who believes Israel's existence is a sin?

It says they don't believe in Jewish nationhood at all.

But Temple Emanu-El is not unique. The confusion runs deeper than one synagogue or one denomination. Millions of American Jews who would never invite Beinart to speak, who consider themselves supporters of Israel and donate to AIPAC—even *they* struggle with the question at the heart of Beinart's accusation.

Is Israel essential to being Jewish, or is it just a political cause, something some Jews support and others reject, like any foreign policy debate?

This is the Blaustein-Ben Gurion debate all over again, updated for a new generation. Blaustein insisted American Jews were "Americans of the Jewish faith," no different from American Catholics. Ben-Gurion called this out as a lie. Jews are a people, and the State of Israel represents that people—including the Jews of America.

That argument was never resolved. It was buried, papered over, made comfortable through deliberate vagueness. For decades, American Jews avoided choosing. They supported Israel generously while building lives in America. They maintained ties to Jewish peoplehood while identifying primarily as Americans. They managed to be both without ever having to decide which one mattered more.

That era is over. More than six million Jews live in the United States today—the last great diaspora of the Jewish world.[317] How they answer this question now will determine not only their own future, but the future of the Jewish people itself.

23

WHO NEEDS JERUSALEM WHEN YOU HAVE PITTSBURGH?

Jacob Henry Schiff, the most powerful Jewish banker in America and the country's leading Jewish philanthropist, had no patience for Zionism. Writing to Dr. Solomon Schechter through the pages of *The American Hebrew* in 1907 and later cited in the New York Times, he made his position clear: a Jew could not be both a true American and an honest Zionist.

"Speaking as an American, I cannot for a moment concede that one can be a true American and an honest adherent of the Zionist movement... If they are honest Zionists—I mean if they believe and hope and labor for an ultimate restoration of Jewish political life and the re-establishment of a Jewish nation—they place a prior lien upon their citizenship."

Schiff was no stranger to Jewish causes. He funded immigrants, supported Jewish institutions, and even encouraged efforts to allow persecuted Jews to settle in Palestine as a safe refuge. Yet for Schiff, America was not exile; it was his promised land. Jews in the United States must embrace it fully as their permanent home, not as a temporary refuge or a stop along the way to a distant homeland. As he put it, "The

Jew should not for a moment feel that he has only found an 'asylum' in this country; he must not feel that he is in exile and that his abode here is only a temporary or passing one."[318]

Schiff was not alone. From the very beginning, many Jews believed their future was not in Zion, btaut in America.

Decades before Herzl ever spoke of a Jewish state, Reform Jews in the United States made the same bargain as their counterparts in Paris and Berlin, formally renouncing Jewish nationhood. In 1841, at the dedication of Kahal Kadosh Beth Elohim in Charleston, South Carolina—the birthplace of American Reform—Reverend Gustavus Poznanski proclaimed from the pulpit: "This country is our Palestine, this city our Jerusalem, this house of God our Temple."[319] America was the Promised Land, and Charleston the new Jerusalem.

By 1885, Reform rabbis made it official. In the Pittsburgh Platform, they announced: "We consider ourselves no longer a nation, but a religious community, and therefore expect neither a return to Palestine, nor a sacrificial worship under the sons of Aaron, nor the restoration of any of the laws concerning the Jewish state."[320] Who needs Jerusalem, the Temple, or the Jewish homeland when you can have... Pittsburgh? With this statement, Reform Judaism didn't just abandon Zionism—it spat on two thousand years of longing for Jewish nationhood, trading it in for American patriotism and the promise of full acceptance.

When Herzl suddenly called for Jewish state a decade later, American Reform rabbis reacted harshly, condemning Zionism outright. Like Schiff, they warned that Zionism would "infinitely harm our Jewish brethren... by confirming the assertion of their enemies that the Jews are foreigners in the countries in which they are at home."[321]

It would take another forty years for the Reform movement to begin softening its anti-Zionist stance. But even then, many individual rabbis were still committed to opposing Jewish nationhood. One of the most vocal was Rabbi Morris Lazaron, who insisted that any form of Jewish national power was inherently immoral. In a 1937 address, Lazaron claimed that Jewish nationalism was "a *hukat hagoyim*," a forbidden imitation of gentile nations, and warned that behind Zionism lurked "the specter of the foul thing which moves Germany and Italy... a chorus of 'Heil!'"[322] For him, a Jewish state was not just unnecessary—it was a Jewish version of fascism. A Jewish democracy, he believed, would somehow morph into Nazism simply the moment Jews held power. He never bothered explaining why.

Lazaron even rewrote Jewish liturgy to fit his ideology. He latched onto the universalist lines at the end of the classic *Aleinu* prayer—"when the world will be perfected under the kingdom of the Almighty"—and pretended that this was the whole prayer. But the *Aleinu* is built in two parts, and the order matters. The first paragraph is unapologetically particularistic: "He has not made us like the nations... nor assigned unto us a portion as unto them." It affirms the Jewish people's distinct identity, its unique role, and its separation from the nations. Only after establishing Jewish nationhood does the prayer move to the second paragraph, which describes the Torah's universal vision of the end times. The structure is deliberate: Israel is able to serve as a model for other countries precisely because it is a distinct nation, not because it assimilates and dissolves itself into humanity. Yet Lazaron ignored the first half of the prayer entirely, because the plain meaning of the *Aleinu*—its sequencing of particularism first and universalism second—undercuts the theological framework he promoted.

In June 1942, while European Jewry was being systematically annihilated, nearly one hundred Reform rabbis gathered in Atlantic City—not to demand Allied intervention, not to organize rescue efforts, and not to call for Jewish self-defense. They met to condemn Zionism.

Led by Lazaron's allies, including six former presidents of the Reform Rabbinic Assembly and the president of Hebrew Union College, they issued a manifesto opposing Jewish sovereignty and rejecting even the formation of a Jewish army to fight alongside the Allies. This "Statement of Principles by Non-Zionist Rabbis" birthed the American Council for Judaism, an organization dedicated to denying that Jews had any collective national rights at all. In the midst of the Holocaust, their priority was condemning other Jews for asserting national identity.[323]

Many of the Reform rabbis who opposed Zionism openly denied that the Jews had ever been a nation at all, dismissing Jewish peoplehood as "a fabrication woven from the thinnest kind of threads." These rabbis shamelessly rewrote Jewish history altogether, insisting the Jews were a faith, not a nation, from the very beginning. Their motive, of course, was protecting their own status. Elmer Berger, another anti-Zionist Reform rabbi, spelled it out: "Those who seek to identify political Zionism with religious Judaism work a profound and dangerous injustice to Americans of all faiths—above all to American Jews."[324]

Their impact was subtle but real. They did not stop Zionism, of course. But they planted something rotten in the soil of American

Jewish life: the idea that Jewish nationalism was not just unnecessary but somehow un-American, even immoral. That seed would keep growing, long after these men were gone.

24

The Parlor Zionists Awaken

Louis Brandeis never observed a Passover Seder, did not pray in a synagogue even on the High Holidays, and gave only perfunctory gifts to Jewish charities. He socialized almost entirely with non-Jews and had little engagement with the Jewish community. And yet, by his fifties, this deeply assimilated Jew became the leading voice of Zionism in the United States.

The first Jewish justice to serve on the Supreme Court joined the Zionist movement in 1912 and quickly assumed its helm in America. He reframed Zionism as an extension of American ideals, not a betrayal of American loyalty. "To be good Americans, we must be better Jews, and to be better Jews, we must be Zionists."[325] By using phrases like "the Jewish pilgrim fathers" and linking Jewish nationhood to democracy, social justice, and liberty, he made Zionism respectable to American Jews who previously saw it as foreign or divisive.[326]

In a letter to his mother-in-law, he wrote that Zionism "has seemed to me, on the whole, the most worthwhile of all I have attempted," describing it as a "movement to give the Jews... the land of their fathers where the Jewish life may be lived normally and naturally, and where the Jews can govern themselves."[327]

Brandeis insisted that multiple loyalties are only a problem when they clash, and that advocating for a Jewish homeland did not conflict with loyalty to the United States—that one could be fully a Jewish nationalist and fully an American patriot at the same time. In doing so, he allowed American Jews to avoid confronting the deep tension of their dual identity, a tension they were eager to sidestep. His framing made it feel natural to embrace both loyalties without reckoning with the hard question of what it meant to be truly Jewish or truly American.

It also did something else: it made supporting Zionism respectable without requiring anyone to actually move to Zion. You could write checks, attend rallies, raise funds—all while remaining safely in America. But Brandeis never addressed the obvious problem lurking beneath this arrangement. If Jews are a nation and the land of Israel is their homeland—if Zionism means the return of the Jewish people to their ancestral land—then what does it mean to support this vision while deliberately choosing to stay thousands of miles away? The question was uncomfortable. American Jews chose not to ask it.

A few years ago, I shared a car ride with a young Orthodox man from New York—meticulous in his observance, proud of his Zionism. We were talking about Israel's political meltdown between 2019 and 2022, when the country lurched through five elections in three years, unable to form a stable government. He laughed and shook his head: "You guys have such a crazy system here!"

"*You* guys."

I couldn't let it go. Yes, Israel's politics are messy and dysfunctional—but they're *our* mess. Israel's chaos belongs to every Jew, wherever he lives. This young man publicly identified as religious and Zionist, yet without realizing it, he had just shown his hand: he was American first, Jew second. Israel's struggles were not his struggles. Its destiny was not his destiny. He was a spectator in the stands, rooting for his team, but never once imagining himself on the field.

That small moment in the car captured something that has plagued American Jewry since Herzl published *The Jewish State*. Golda Meir had a name for it: "Parlor Zionism."[328] She meant the Jews who passionately championed the cause from the comfort of their New York living rooms—who raised money, attended rallies, gave speeches—but never seriously considered moving to the land themselves. They wrote checks. They did not write chapters of history.

Even Louis Brandeis, the man who legitimized Zionism for American Jews, understood the limits. He admitted that Zionism was, for most Americans, a project "for the rescue of the defenseless Jews in Europe, those who have been afflicted by tyranny and persecution. American Jews have found their homes here, and *Aliyah* is not their destiny."[329] Rabbi Meir Bar-Ilan put it more bluntly: "Would significant numbers of Jews make *Aliyah*? Would wealthy Jews move to the land with their assets? Even at its height, American Zionism did not go that far."[330]

As historian Jeffrey Gurock notes, this was no accident. The movement "was dominated by well-to-do Jews who rarely faced the harsh realities of exile, for whom Palestine Zionism was an abstract ideal—a philanthropic project rather than a revolutionary lifestyle."[331] Safe and comfortable in the United States, American Jews became donors rather than settlers, spectators rather than pioneers. Their support for Zionism was generous—but ultimately, it was philanthropy.

This is why Ben-Gurion's visit in the 1950s caused such a stir. He wasn't questioning their commitment to Zionism in theory—he was questioning their practical choices and lifestyle. By staying in the United States while supporting Israel from afar, American Jews were living a comfortable, abstract form of nationalism. Ben-Gurion forced them to confront the truth: if they weren't willing to make Israel their own homeland, their national identity was far less clear than their ideology suggested.

Hillel Halkin saw the same hypocrisy a generation later. After the UN's 1975 resolution declaring that "Zionism is racism," American Jews rushed to show solidarity with Israel. "It's all very kind of Jews in New York or Los Angeles to wish to express their solidarity with us in the face of such a scandal and to find no better way to do so than to wear 'I am a Zionist' buttons like carnations in their lapels. But since a Zionist is precisely what none of them is—for what Zionism happens to involve is the Jewish decision not to live in Los Angeles or New York—they are doing no one any service by confusing the issue even further... From the very inception of the Zionist movement, there has always been a tendency to refer by it to people who approve of other people leading Zionist lives—an attitude of the man who once said that he loved work so much, he could sit and watch it all day."[332]

If Israel is the nation of the Jewish people, but American Jews have no intention of joining that nation, what does that make them? Jews who support the Jewish homeland, but don't see it as their own? Zionism for thee, but not for me?

This contradiction was baked into American Zionism from the beginning. But that didn't stop the movement from growing. American Jews may have been unwilling to move to Palestine themselves, but they were willing to fund those who did. They were willing to fight for diplomatic recognition, to lobby their government, to raise massive sums of money. It was checkbook Zionism, not pioneering Zionism—but it had real impact. And it became a powerful force in American Jewish life.

In 1917, Britain issued the Balfour Declaration, publicly supporting "the establishment in Palestine of a national home for the Jewish people." The statement electrified the Zionist movement. Newspapers across the United States hailed it as "the greatest occurrence in modern Jewish history,"[333] and younger Jews, previously indifferent or hostile, found themselves swept up in a new sense of collective purpose.

Rabbi Stephen S. Wise seized the moment. On December 23, he led a massive rally at Carnegie Hall, attended by 15,000 people. Holding a printed copy of the Declaration, he declared that while it was "a scrap of paper," it was "written in English and signed by the British government, and therefore inviolable."[334] The event was more than a celebration—it was a declaration that Zionism had arrived in the American mainstream.

By 1922, Zionism had become respectable. When the United States Congress unanimously endorsed the Balfour Declaration, supporting a Jewish homeland gained official American approval. Even the Reform movement changed its tune in the 1937 Columbus Platform: "In the rehabilitation of Palestine, the land hallowed by memories and hopes, we behold the promise of renewed life for many of our brethren."[335]

American Jews embraced Zionism between the First and Second World Wars—but the slaughter of six million Jews in the Holocaust made it a matter of survival.

For most American Jews, the Holocaust was personal. The Nazis murdered their families—the siblings, parents, and cousins they'd left behind in Europe—while they themselves walked free in America. The U.S. refused to bomb the train tracks to Auschwitz, and American Jewish leaders, with some heroic exceptions, failed to mobilize the pressure that might have forced Roosevelt to act.[336] Many felt they hadn't done enough. Their families had burned while they argued about baseball and worried about their mortgages. Out of that guilt and grief, American Jews embraced Zionism with a new urgency. Never again would the Jewish people depend on the goodness of others for their survival.[337]

Speaking before the United Nations as chairman of the American Section of the Jewish Agency in November 1947, Rabbi Abba Hillel Silver of Cleveland, Ohio declared: "We are an ancient people and though we have often on the long, hard road which we have traveled, been disillusioned, we have never been disheartened. We have never lost faith in the sovereignty and the ultimate triumph of great moral principles. The Jewish people belongs in this Society of Nations. Surely the Jewish people is no less deserving than other peoples, whose national freedom and independence have been established..."[338] Silver was not asking for permission. He insisted on Jewish statehood. After six million were murdered, the debate was over.

For two decades after the establishment of the State in 1948, American Jewish support for Israel remained strong but distant. Israel was a cause they funded, a country they admired from afar. The struggles seemed real but remote, something happening to other people in another place.

Then came the spring of 1967.

For weeks, Egyptian President Gamal Abdel Nasser tightened the noose. On May 22, he closed the Straits of Tiran, cutting off Israel's southern port. He massed 100,000 troops in Sinai, expelled UN peacekeepers, and formed military alliances with Jordan, Iraq, and Syria. Nasser declared his forces were "ready not only to repulse any aggression, but to initiate the act ourselves"[339] and promised to "drive the Jews into the sea."[340] Syrian Defense Minister Hafez called for a "battle of annihilation" against Israel.[341] Massive rallies in Cairo chanted for Israel's destruction. News reports showed Israelis preparing graves in parks and public spaces, anticipating heavy casualties.[342] American Jews watched in horror as Arab leaders openly planned genocide.

The comparisons to Hitler were impossible to ignore. Once again, a genocidal enemy threatened the Jewish people while the world stood by and did nothing. Jews were on their own.

American Jews responded with a fire that surprised even themselves. Emergency fundraising drives raised $430 million in only a few weeks. At a single New York luncheon, donors pledged $15 million in minutes. One man took out a second mortgage on his house to contribute. Rallies drew 150,000 in New York and 50,000 outside the White H ouse.[343] Thousands of American Jews, seized by the terror that Israel might be destroyed, tried to volunteer for the Israel Defense Forces, swamping airlines with requests despite Israeli pleas to stay home. Jewish leaders lobbied President Johnson relentlessly.

Then the war came—and within six days, it was over. Israeli tanks rolled across the Sinai. Jerusalem was reunified. The tiny Jewish state crushed the armies of three nations. Fear transformed into collective pride almost overnight. Madison Square Garden filled with 20,000 Jews cheering Israel's victory, while Americans watched on television as Israeli soldiers stood at the Western Wall for the first time in two thousand years. Yossi Klein Halevi captured the moment: "There was an emotional trajectory that united Jewish people in a way I don't think we've ever seen since the revelation at Mount Sinai 3,500 years ago."[344]

The war changed something in American Jewish life that would never quite change back. Synagogues began using Israeli pronunciations of Hebrew and incorporating Israeli melodies into prayers. Community centers, schools, and summer camps filled with Israeli songs, dances, and plays. Jewish Federations and local charities reoriented their missions around supporting Israel, and bar mitzvah speeches revolved around the bravery of Israeli soldiers. Israel became the beating heart of American Jewish identity. Jews who once took pains to present themselves as a slightly exotic, less WASP-y version of Protestants now began to see themselves as part of a single Jewish nation. Even from thousands of miles away, they felt that Israel belonged to them—and they to Israel.

25

From Am Yisrael Chai to "My Judaism"

In the spring of 1963, a group of middle-aged Jewish men sat in a small study circle at Beth Israel synagogue in Cleveland, reading Ben Hecht's *Perfidy*. Among them were Lou Rosenblum, a NASA research scientist, and Herb Caron, a clinical psychologist at the VA hospital. The book was a savage indictment of the American Jewish establishment's passivity during the Holocaust, accusing major organizations of timidity while millions died. Caron broke down in tears as he read. Others had similar reactions.

They moved on to Joseph Schechtman's biography of Vladimir Jabotinsky, *Fighter and Prophet.* Jabotinsky spent his final years traveling desperately across Europe, warning the Jews there that catastrophe was coming. In Warsaw in 1938, he told a packed hall: "The catastrophe is coming closer. I become gray and old in these years, my heart bleeds, that you, dear brothers and sisters, do not see the volcano that will soon begin to spit out its all-consuming lava." We must "eliminate the Diaspora or the Diaspora will surely eliminate you."[345] He died of a stroke in the Catskills in August 1940, still trying to sound the alarm. Almost nobody listened.

The men were shaken. Lou Rosenblum, Herb Caron, and the others were teenagers during World War II. They knew the Nazis murdered six million Jews, but they'd never understood the full story of what the American Jewish establishment had done—or failed to do—while it happened. Now, reading Hecht and Schechtman in 1963, they were learning it for the first time. They kept returning to the same question: why had there been so little response to the catastrophe unfolding in Europe—not just from governments, but from American Jews themselves?

For Rosenblum, the sharpest answer came from Chaim Greenberg, a journalist and scholar who published an essay called *Bankrupt* in February 1943. While Jews were being murdered in Europe, American Jewish organizations continued their "normal behavior of in-fighting and advantage-seeking," each jockeying for position rather than unifying to build the political force that might have saved lives.[346] They never got down on their hands and knees and pleaded. They never lay down in the streets and refused to move. Jabotinsky fought until the day he died, but the Jewish establishment negotiated, issued press releases, and stood by as six million were slaughtered.

Rosenblum and Caron vowed not to repeat that mistake. When they discovered that three million Jews were trapped behind the Iron Curtain in Russia, forbidden from teaching their children Hebrew, from living as Jews, or from emigrating to Israel, they promised each other that they would not sit quietly and trust the Jewish establishment to handle it.

That October, they formed the Cleveland Committee on Soviet Anti-Semitism (CCSA), the first grassroots Soviet Jewry organization in America. They convinced the mayor of Cleveland to serve as honorary chairman, built an ecumenical board with a Catholic monsignor and a black city councilman, and began raising hell.

These weren't rabbis or scholars, and neither had any history of activism. Rosenblum was a scientist at NASA's Lewis Research Center; Caron was a clinical psychologist treating veterans at the VA. Regular congregants at a small Conservative synagogue who had never before tried to change anything. But they grasped something that the established Jewish organizations seemed to have forgotten: Jews are a people, not just a religion. When Jews anywhere are threatened, all Jews must respond. The Soviet Jews they were fighting for lived thousands of miles away, spoke a different language, and would likely never know their names. None of that mattered. They were fellow Jews, and that made them family.

In April 1964, the Jewish establishment finally convened a national conference in Washington to address the persecution of Soviet Jewry. Five hundred delegates gathered at the Willard Hotel, including every major leader of American Jewry. Rosenblum and Caron showed up from Cleveland, already convinced the whole thing would be an exercise in hand-wringing.

The proposed resolutions from the Jewish establishment told them everything they needed to know: prayer vigils, educational programs, vaguely defined "awareness" campaigns. These were toothless and symbolic gestures, not sustained action. It was clear that the establishment did not have a plan to mobilize the millions of American Jews who knew nothing about the suffering of Soviet Jewry.

Rosenblum and Caron wrote a blistering letter to the other delegates: "The question is not whether the coming Conference will denounce

Soviet antisemitism in sufficiently strong terms. (They will denounce it and this is known to all in advance.) The crucial question is: Will the Conference provide the mechanism for bringing the information to the millions, now uninformed and silent, so that their outcry can be brought to bear?" They presented a resolution of their own, demanding the creation of a funded, staffed committee to coordinate real action. "Any plan short of the creation of such an 'ad hoc' group is unthinkable."

They got a taste of what was coming before they even reached the hotel. Sharing a taxi from the airport with Rabbi Balfour Brickner, head of the Union of American Hebrew Congregations' Social Action Center, they mentioned their proposed resolution. Brickner was sympathetic in principle—but the organization came first: "I may personally think what you're doing is right, but this is going to cause too many problems for UAHC organizationally."[347] Twenty years after Chaim Greenberg published *Bankrupt*, the American Jewish establishment had learned nothing.

As they predicted, the conference only made symbolic gestures. But Rosenblum, Caron, and their Cleveland allies didn't wait for permission from the establishment. They went home and built the movement themselves. What started in a small study circle in Cleveland would eventually spread across the country, mobilizing hundreds of thousands of American Jews and helping to bring down the Soviet Union itself.[348]

A few months after the Washington conference, across the country in Manhattan, another grassroots organizer was beginning his own campaign. Jacob Birnbaum, a tall and quirky Jew with a British accent and a Russian fur hat, began knocking on dormitory doors at Yeshiva

University. Then in his thirties, Birnbaum had recently arrived from England with a mission that would change American Jewish life: to awaken American Jews to the plight of their silenced brothers and sisters in the Soviet Union. He called it "spiritual genocide"—the slow erasure of Jewish identity behind the Iron Curtain—and he believed only the Jews of America had the freedom and power to stop it.

Birnbaum came from Zionist royalty. His grandfather, Nathan Birnbaum, coined the term "Zionism" and served as secretary general of the first Zionist Congress in Basel in 1897. Jacob grew up hearing that Jewish destiny was collective, not personal. Jews were a people—*Klal Yisrael.*

Within months of arriving in New York, Birnbaum founded the Student Struggle for Soviet Jewry (SSSJ), the first full-time Soviet Jewry organization in America. What began as a few young idealists soon grew into a national movement. They rallied, fasted, and picketed in front of the Soviet embassy. They wrote letters to imprisoned refuseniks.

And they sang. Their protest songs sounded less like folk tunes and more like national anthems:

"There's a fire burning brightly in the sky, and the roar of thunder crashing from on high. I see a nation there awakening; iron chains will soon be breaking."

These young American Jews didn't see themselves as donors or spectators; they saw themselves as part of an awakening Jewish nation, as players in the game.

A year later, Birnbaum wanted a song to rally the activists—a melody that could carry the words *Am Yisrael Chai*—"The People of Israel Live." He reached out to Rabbi Shlomo Carlebach, the magnetic singer whose music was already gaining attention across the Jewish world.

Carlebach was constantly on the move. While traveling through Prague, behind the Iron Curtain, he flushed Birnbaum's letter down an airplane toilet, afraid he might be arrested by the KGB. Yet the idea stayed with him. There, in the Soviet Union, he wrote and first performed *Am Yisrael Chai* before a small group of young Russian Jews.

Just before a major rally that year in New York, Carlebach called Birnbaum. "Yankele, I've got it for you."

Outside the Soviet U.N. Mission, thousands of demonstrators heard the song for the first time. Even the normally skeptical New York Times noted something different in the crowd when they sang. The song caught fire. It became a fixture at rallies and gatherings, spreading through the movement as activists carried it from city to city.[349]

But Carlebach had added something to Birnbaum's request. Alongside *Am Yisrael Chai—the nation of Israel lives*—he introduced three more words drawn from the moment when Joseph reveals himself to his brothers in Egypt: *Od Avinu Chai—our father still lives*. The choice was deliberate. Not "our teacher," not "our faith." Our father—the language of family, of peoplehood, of blood.

The SSSJ grew quickly. Over the next two decades, the Soviet Jewry movement became the largest and most sustained wave of Jewish collective action in American history. The movement was about freeing

Soviet Jews, but it was also about American Jews themselves—a public declaration that Jewish pride was nothing to apologize for, and that Jewish solidarity was not optional. Jews from every denomination and every political stripe marched and rallied for people they had never met and could barely communicate with. They were telling the world: we are a nation.

The scale of the movement became clear in 1987, when roughly 250,000 Jews gathered on the National Mall for Freedom Sunday—the largest Jewish demonstration in American history. They carried signs, sang songs, and chanted slogans that said what everyone already felt: this was a people, a nation, speaking as one.

The movement succeeded. Beginning in the late 1980s, well over a million Jews left the Soviet Union and its successor states. Of those, nearly a million made *Aliyah* to Israel, while several hundred thousand settled in the United States and other Western countries. The Soviet Jewry movement achieved what once seemed impossible: it helped bring down the Soviet Union and freed the Jews trapped behind the Iron Curtain.

The movement succeeded. Soviet Jews were freed. And American Jews lost the cause that made them a people again.

Nati Cantorovich, an Israeli official who worked with Soviet Jews, later called the movement "the last event that united practically all Jews, independent of their political interests and religious views ."[350] He was right. The Soviet Jewry movement was the final time American Jews acted like a nation, the last collective expression of Jewish peoplehood in America.[351]

When the cause disappeared, so did the unity. Without Soviet Jews to rescue, American Jews had no shared national mission. The movement that once mobilized hundreds of thousands left behind a void. Sociologist Charles Liebman, writing in the 1990s, explained that the Soviet Jewry movement was the peak expression of “ethnic Judaism”—built on peoplehood, solidarity, and collective action. Once it ended, it was replaced by "privatized Judaism": personal meaning, individual journeys, and spirituality.[352] With no large, compelling communal struggle to replace it, American Jews turned inward. What they found—or created—was an approach aptly called "My Judaism."

The phrase sounds harmless enough; personal, authentic, even spiritual. You hear it everywhere in American Jewish life: "I'm trying to connect to my Judaism." "I'm exploring my Judaism." "I want to make my Judaism more meaningful." But it reflects a fundamental confusion about what it means to be a Jew. "My Judaism" is the language of religion, not nationhood. It treats being Jewish as a private faith choice, something you tailor to your preferences, like "my Christianity" or "my spirituality."

This shift didn't happen by accident. American Jews live in a religious marketplace shaped by Protestant norms: individual conversion, personal relationship with God, and private faith. In this environment, as Liebman observed, synagogues no longer declare "Here I stand"—they ask "Where would you like me to stand?"[353] Religion in America is a consumer choice.

Studying American religious life, David Campbell and Robert Putnam found that "many Americans—at least one third and rising—nowadays choose their religion rather than simply inheriting it."[354] With brand loyalty low and the marketplace crowded, successful religious denominations act like entrepreneurs, marketing their product to fickle consumers.

If being Jewish is whatever I want it to be—picking the pieces I like and rejecting the parts I don't—that is religion, albeit in its most modern and shallow form. But Jews don't get to opt out of being Jewish. Being part of a nation means there is no "choosing." You are a Jew whether you like it or not. You can be a right-wing Jew or a left-wing Jew, a religious Jew or an atheist Jew, but ultimately, you are a Jew because you were born a Jew. It is who you are and who you will always be.

The constant refrain of "My Judaism" may sound like a harmless turn of phrase, but Pew Research confirms it reflects something real. Today, most American Jews define being Jewish by moral values, culture, or memory—not by peoplehood.[355] Jewish identity has been reduced to a set of personal commitments at best, and nostalgia at worst. To be Jewish has come to mean the social equivalent of being Protestant or Catholic, and to be Orthodox, Conservative, or Reform as analogous to being Baptist, Methodist, or Episcopalian. Judaism has been filed away in the religion drawer, next to all the others.

The consequences have been catastrophic. In Israel, a Jew who stops keeping Shabbat is still an Israeli—still part of a nation, still subject to its draft, still sending his children to Israeli public schools. His Jewish identity doesn't depend on his synagogue attendance. He remains part of the people, and the door back to Torah observance remains open. But in America, Jewish identity rests almost entirely on religious practice. When that goes, everything goes. American Jews who stop going to synagogue don't become secular Jews—they become "nones," generic Americans, indistinguishable from everyone else, lost to the Jewish people within a generation or two.

The damage of "My Judaism" goes beyond assimilation. When Jews themselves speak the language of "My Judaism," they teach the rest of the world how to see them.

Jonathan Jaffe describes how his daughter and several classmates tried to start a Jewish Student Union at their local public high school. Despite a large Jewish population, the school had never hosted a Jewish club. The students submitted a proposal focused on cultural programs and community events—and were promptly rejected on the grounds that religious groups are not authorized to form clubs. When the students pointed out that the school proudly featured Latino, Asian, Pacific Islander, and African American clubs, the administration rejected the comparison. Judaism, they insisted, was a religion, not an ethnicity or culture. Only after lengthy discussion, when the administration finally understood "the civil and cultural underpinnings of Judaism," was the club authorized.[356]

The school administrators didn't invent this idea. They absorbed it from the broader culture—a culture shaped, in no small part, by Jews themselves.

This confusion has become a weapon in the hands of antisemites and anti-Zionists. If Jews are merely a religion, they have no collective claim to national sovereignty in the land of Israel. Religions can be practiced anywhere, and they do not require states of their own. Catholics do not need a state to practice Catholicism, and Buddhists do not need a state to practice Buddhism. If Judaism is only a faith, then Jews have no more right to a state in Israel than Presbyterians have to a state in Scotland. Zionism can then be dismissed as a colonial project: a group of white people who practice a religion suddenly inventing an ethnic identity to justify taking Palestinian land. It matters little that most Israelis are of Middle Eastern or North African descent and do not fit the "white colonizer" label. The narrative has already taken hold.

Assimilated Jews are not the only ones handing this weapon to our enemies. Anti-Israel activists can point to the thriving Orthodox communities of Lakewood and Boro Park and make an even stronger argument: here are Jews who are clearly very religious and serious about their faith—yet they too have chosen America over Israel. If even the most committed Jews on earth are content to remain in exile, the case makes itself: Jews don't need a state. They need a synagogue.[357]

This is the price of redefining a people as a religion. Once Jews accepted that framing, their enemies ran with it. As Rabbi David Gedzelman explains, Jewish peoplehood is now "characterized by a growing number of scholars as a thoroughly modern construct, an invention born of the ideas of modern nationalism, with no real connection to any sense of groupness, national identity in exile, or covenantal connection among the Jews who lived before the modern era."[358] The natural instinct of Jews to remain bound to one another is increasingly treated as illegitimate, even racist—an echo of the UN's infamous declaration that Zionism itself was racism.

"My Judaism" did more than weaken American Jewish life. It provided the intellectual weapon for erasing the Jewish nation itself.

26

SCARLETT JOHANSSON AND THE END OF THE LINE

Scarlett Johansson is one of Hollywood's biggest stars—and she is proudly Jewish. Her mother, Melanie Sloan, is an Ashkenazi Jew from the Bronx whose family came from Poland and Russia. Many of her relatives were murdered in the Warsaw Ghetto. She grew up with Shabbat dinners, Chanukah candles, and Passover seders.

In 2014, she became the global brand ambassador for SodaStream, the Israeli company that makes home carbonation machines. When BDS (Boycott, Divestment, and Sanctions) activists and Oxfam, the left-wing, anti-Israel NGO, came after her because SodaStream had a factory in Ma'ale Adumim, a Jewish town in Judea, Johansson didn't fold. She defended the company, where 500 Arabs and Israelis worked side by side receiving equal pay and benefits, calling it "a bridge to peace." She quit Oxfam rather than drop SodaStream.[359]

By any measure, Scarlett Johansson is a good person and more engaged with her Jewish identity than most American Jews. She is certainly more willing to stand with Israel than Natalie Portman, who was born in Jerusalem to Israeli parents, yet has repeatedly attacked the Jewish state, declined the Genesis Prize to protest Israel's conduct in

Gaza, and made a career out of dressing up hostility to Israel as Jewish values.[360]

And yet. She has been married several times—to Ryan Reynolds, Romain Dauriac, and Colin Jost. Three marriages, but not one Jewish husband. Her children are being raised in non-Jewish homes.

Scarlett herself is the child of an intermarriage. Her Jewish mother observed the Jewish holidays; her father, Karsten, celebrated Christmas and Danish harvest festivals. Both traditions lived side by side—a happy, "blended" childhood in which nothing had to be chosen and nothing had to be given up.

Judaism was present and meaningful in some way, but it was not decisive. It was something to honor and remember, but certainly not something that demanded total commitment or exclusivity.

I am not invoking Scarlett Johansson to attack her. She is more publicly Jewish, more morally serious, and more willing to stand with Israel than most American Jews. But her life illustrates a misunderstanding shared by many good people about being a Jew. For Scarlett, being Jewish is her *heritage*. It's something her ancestors were, something she inherited, like being descended from Irish immigrants or having Italian roots.

Heritage is about the past. It's something you honor, something you remember, maybe even something you're proud of. But it doesn't make demands on your future. It doesn't require you to build your life around it. And most importantly, heritage alone won't keep your children connected to the Jewish people.

Scarlett doesn't understand the difference between being biologically and legally Jewish and being part of the Jewish nation. Yes, her children are Jews—a Jewish mother's children are always Jews. That's the biology, the legal status. But will they live as Jews? Will they identify as part of the Jewish people? Will they marry Jews and raise Jewish children? I pray that they will. The statistics say no. Children raised in intermarried homes, evenc when their mother is Jewish, overwhelmingly do not see themselves as part of the Jewish nation. They might acknowledge some Jewish ancestry, the way someone mentions having a Polish grandmother, but they won't live as Jews or raise their own children as Jews.

Being part of a nation isn't passive. You can't just be born into it and expect your children to inherit it automatically while you do nothing. Nations require transmission. You have to build a Jewish home and raise them as members of the Jewish people, not just as kids who happen to have a Jewish grandma. You have to give them a Jewish education, a Jewish community, a Jewish future. If you don't, the chain breaks.

Born to an intermarriage, married three times to non-Jewish men, raising children who likely won't identify as Jews—Scarlett's story is not unusual. It is the American Jewish story. Not because she failed, but because the community that raised her never gave her the tools to understand what was at stake.

Three thousand years ago, God warned what would happen if Jews intermarried: "You shall not intermarry with them; you shall not give your daughter to his son, and you shall not take his daughter for your son. For he will turn away your son from following Me, and they will worship the gods of others, and the wrath of the Lord will be kindled against you, and He will quickly destroy you" (Deuteronomy 7:3-4).

The Sages explain the words "he will turn away your son" to mean that when a Jewish woman marries a non-Jewish man, it is her son—the grandson—who will be turned away from God. The child is still legally Jewish, but he won't be raised as a Jew. In most cases, he'll be lost to the Jewish people.[361]

The Torah prophesied what the statistics now confirm: intermarriage doesn't just affect one generation. It wipes out entire branches of the family tree. Your grandchildren stop being Jewish—either because their mothers are not Jewish and they are therefore not Jewish according to Torah law, or because they're not raised to live as Jews even though they technically are.

This is the tragic reality for Scarlett Johansson's family. Only two generations after her relatives were slaughtered in the Warsaw Ghetto, the family's Jewish connection is being lost again—this time to assimilation and intermarriage.

In 1990, the National Jewish Population Survey landed like a bomb in the American Jewish establishment. Intermarriage was no longer rare—it was now the norm. The intermarriage rate hit a whopping 52%, up dramatically from only 9% in 1965.[362] Some rabbis called it a "second Holocaust,"[363] and they weren't exaggerating. Most children from those mixed marriages weren't being raised Jewish.[364] Family lines that survived since Sinai, enduring millennia of persecution, were quietly being erased as Jewish sons and daughters nonchalantly abandoned their destiny for the loving embrace of their gentile girlfriends and boyfriends.

But the numbers only got worse. By 2020, nearly three-quarters of non-Orthodox Jews were marrying non-Jews.[365] Given that 90% of American Jews are not Orthodox, this trend threatens the very existence of American Jewry altogether. On paper, America boasts over seven million Jews—but only about 4.4 million are actually considered Jewish according to the Torah and traditional Jewish law.[366] The rest have some Jewish ancestry, but they are not part of the Jewish people. The real Jewish population is disappearing.

What about the children? Among intermarried couples, fewer than one in three are raised with a clear Jewish identity. Most are raised secular, superficially Christian or with a diluted "dual heritage" that severs them from Jewish national identity.

How did we get here? Why are the majority of American Jews intermarrying, effectively severing themselves and their children from the Jewish people?

When you treat Judaism as a religion—a set of beliefs you can take or leave—intermarriage makes perfect sense. It's like a Protestant marrying a Catholic. As long as the couple shares basic religious values, they can work out their differences. By 2012, roughly half of all married Americans were married to someone from a different religious tradition. Vice President J.D. Vance converted to Catholicism in his 30s, while his wife, Usha, raised Hindu, did not. Though some criticize Vance, his marriage is now the norm, not the exception.

For most Americans, this is fine. Religion is personal, faith is individual, and love crosses all boundaries. But for Jews, this logic is catastrophic. When being Jewish is understood as following a religion rather than belonging to a nation, the barrier to intermarriage collapses. I'll be Jewish, my spouse will be Christian or Hindu, and we'll figure it out. We'll have a menorah and a Christmas tree. We'll make it work.

It doesn't.

Or maybe you see being Jewish as ethnic background, like being Italian-American or Irish-American. You eat gefilte fish at the Passover seder and you crack jokes about Jewish mothers-in-law, but it's not something you need to pass on intact. Intermarriage just means you're mixing heritages. Your kids get bagels *and* pasta, Yiddish humor *and* Irish alcoholism.

But this gets it backwards. Being Jewish isn't about what you believe or where your grandparents came from. It's about membership in a nation—the nation of Israel, God's chosen people. When you understand that—when you remember what happened at Sinai—intermarriage is no longer a personal choice about who you love. It becomes a choice to leave your people

The day is soon coming when the ravages of intermarriage will reduce non-Orthodox American Jewry to a small fraction of its current size. What's left will be Orthodox communities with high birthrates and in-marriage, a small core of committed Zionists raising Jewish children, and a much larger group of people with Jewish ancestry who no longer qualify as Jews.

In 1992, the Strategic Planning Committee of the UJA-Federation of New York tried to imagine what the Jewish community would look like in forty years. They wrote a fictional *New York Times* article dated June 2, 2032:

"It was a time for memories and tears yesterday as the United Jewish Federation of New York formally ceased operations. The Federation, once known as UJA-Jewish Federation of New York, and its predecessor organizations had once served a community of more than 2 million Jews. Now that the Jewish community numbers fewer than 200,000 persons..."[367] Sadly, the future collapse of America's largest Jewish community no longer feels like fiction.

When Jewish identity is treated as something optional—personal, flexible, easy to edit—most people eventually opt out. Not because being Jewish is too demanding, but because what's offered is too shallow to matter.

The tragedy is that most of these children will be lost—and it's not their fault. They didn't choose to be raised this way or decide to be disconnected from their people. But they're growing up with no awareness that they belong to God's beloved nation, that He called Israel "My son, My firstborn" (Exodus 4:22). They have no idea what they're losing. And so, through assimilation rather than persecution, their family's Jewish story will end with them.

If nothing changes, non-Orthodox American Jewry will disappear within two generations. Most American Jews know this. They've simply chosen to look away.

27

Self-Hating, and Proud of It

In 2015, while I was still working as a synagogue rabbi in America, I joined a rabbinic mission to Israel—a Jewish establishment trip meant to strengthen ties between American rabbis and Israel. It turned out to be eye-opening in ways I never expected.

The itinerary should have been my first clue. We visited the Druze community of Hurfeish and the Karaite community of Be'er Sheva. It was a trip through the Jewish State seemingly designed to avoid Jews.

But the more revealing part of the trip wasn't the itinerary—it was the other rabbis. Reconstructionist and Reform rabbis told me they were afraid to speak about Israel in their synagogues—the topic, they said, was simply too toxic. Conservative rabbis in their 50s and 60s confided that their congregations were dying, and that they were anxiously hoping their synagogues would hold on just a few more years until they retired, so they wouldn't lose their jobs before they were ready to retire.

But the most disturbing moment came during our visit to the offices of Tag Meir, a far-left organization with a long record of anti-settler activism. We sat and listened as Dr. Gadi Gvaryahu, the organization's founder, smeared Orthodox and nationalist Jews as extremists and racists. His entire presentation focused on the "dangerous" Jewish settlers of Judea and Samaria, whose mere presence in the biblical heartland was, according to him, a provocation to the Arabs. Nobody pushed back—besides me. The trip's organizers presented it all as fact, as the only reasonable way to understand Jewish settlement in Judea and Samaria. There was certainly no mention of Arab violence against Jews, despite the reality that over 95% of violence in Judea and Samaria is perpetrated by Arabs against Jews.

Today, I am one of those Jewish settlers "provoking" Arabs by living in Judea, where King David grew up.

The rabbis I met on that trip—afraid to speak about Israel, watching their congregations shrink toward extinction—were signs of a transformation already well underway across American Jewish life: a slow, deep estrangement from Israel and from Jewish nationhood itself. Their congregants didn't want to hear about Israel because, for a growing number of American Jews, Israel had become an embarrassment—a reminder of a particularist, nationalist identity they had spent decades trying to leave behind.

The generation that lived through the horrors of World War II understood the tenuousness of Jewish survival in exile. Their children absorbed the lesson that without a homeland, Jews are vulnerable. Their grandchildren, who grew up with grandparents who survived the Holocaust, grasped what was at stake. But the generation growing up today has no memory of a world where Jews lacked sovereignty. They have never known Jewish powerlessness. The idea that Jews need their own state to survive strikes them as outdated tribalism.

The numbers tell the story. Among Jews 65 and older, 67% feel connected to Israel, compared to only 42% of those under 30. Older Jews see Israel as essential to being Jewish at a rate of 53%; among younger Jews, that number drops to 33%.[368] When October 7 came and Israel went to war, the divide became impossible to ignore. Among American Jews over 55, 82% believed Israel should defeat Hamas before any ceasefire. Among those aged 18 to 24, only 47% agreed. Incredibly, nearly half of young American Jews couldn't bring themselves to say that Israel should win.[369]

The Reform movement, the largest denomination of American Jewry, set out to make Judaism relevant to modern life. What it produced instead was progressive politics with Jewish trappings. Some of its rabbis now endorse treating brit milah—the covenant of circumcision—as one option among many "equally valid" ways to welcome a child.[370] Others publicly label Israel an "apartheid state" and support BDS against the Jewish state.

The results are predictable. Over 70% of Reform Jews intermarry,[371] and huge numbers of people who identify as Reform are not actually Jewish according to Jewish law. A 2024 study found that the majority of non-Orthodox rabbinical students in America are lesbian.[372] When a movement abandons Jewish continuity as its mission, it shouldn't be surprised by who shows up.

If half of Reform isn't Jewish, and Reform has replaced Torah with progressivism, how many Reform Jews will actually be Jewish in a generation? The movement may have a future, but that future isn't Jewish.

Rabbi Ammiel Hirsch, senior rabbi of Stephen Wise Free Synagogue and former head of the Association of Reform Zionists of America, tried to sound the alarm. The number of non-Zionist and anti-Zionist rabbinical students in Reform seminaries, he said, is "high enough to cause concern." He acknowledged the absurdity: "If we're a Zionist institution we can't be ordaining non- or anti-Zionist rabbis—it doesn't make sense." Then he added, "It's not too late. But it is late."[373]

He's wrong. It is too late. The Reform movement has returned to its anti-Zionist roots. Hirsch himself admitted the core problem: for liberal Jews, "Jewish peoplehood is an impediment to human progress."

Young Jews across all denominations are not simply distant from Israel. They're turning against it. Radical left-wing anti-Israel organizations like Jewish Voice for Peace, IfNotNow, and J Street have gained thousands of members. In December 2023, only weeks after Hamas slaughtered 1,200 innocent men, women and children in southern Israel, over 1,000 Union for Reform Judaism rabbis signed a letter warning of Israel's "grave risk of genocide" in Gaza.[374] Mostly in their 20s and 30s, they were unmoved by the slaughter of their fellow Jews yet deeply concerned for the welfare of Gazans—the very people who participated in and celebrated the massacre on October 7.

In April 2025, Stella Linson asked her daughter what she'd learned at Hebrew school that day. It was Yom Hazikaron, Israel's Remembrance Day, a deeply emotional day when Israelis and Jews worldwide honor the fallen soldiers and terror victims who gave their lives for the Jewish state. That Yom Hazikaron was particularly painful. Israel was locked in a brutal war against Hamas, Hezbollah, and Iran, a war that had already added many hundreds of fresh names to the somber roll call.

Sons and husbands who had kissed their families goodbye just months earlier were now among the fallen being mourned.

Her daughter's response? "Isn't it sad that the poor Palestinians had to leave their land because of Israel?"

Linson, who lives in Pennsylvania, picked her jaw up off the floor and asked her daughter to elaborate. Without consulting the parents, their Conservative synagogue[375] taught the children a lesson titled "Palestinian Perspectives," designed to convince Jewish children of the lie that Palestinian Arabs—not Jews—are indigenous to the Land of Israel and that Jewish colonialist settlers stole Arab land.

When Linson asked the education director for the curriculum from that day, it confirmed her worst fears. The lesson sounded as if it was written by Mahmoud Abbas, the Holocaust denier and terror supporter who has headed the Palestinian Authority for the last twenty years. Palestinians were presented as innocents suffering from intergenerational trauma caused by Jews, while Jews were presented as foreigners who appeared out of nowhere and took control of the land. The curriculum delegitimized Jewish claims to the land by calling it "the land that Jews call Israel"—as if the name of the Jewish state were merely subjective opinion rather than historical fact. The curriculum even showcased a song by an Israeli Arab who falsely accused Israel of ethnic cleansing, and a poem by someone who accused Israel of killing children "for the fun of it" and committing a "holocaust" in Gaza.[376]

This curriculum came from an organization called Moving Traditions, which provides materials to dozens of Reform and Conservative synagogues across the country. Moving Traditions' funders list reads like a who's who of the mainstream Jewish establishment: Hadassah

Foundation; Combined Jewish Philanthropies; the Jim Joseph Foundation; and the Charles and Lynn Schusterman Family P hilanthropies.[377] That such a radical, anti-Zionist organization receives support from the pillars of American Jewish institutional life reveals just how deep the rot goes.

The Chief of Program & Strategy for Moving Traditions is Rabbi Tamara Cohen, who participated in a Purim webinar with anti-Israel journalist Peter Beinart, promoting his rabidly anti-Zionist book, *Being Jewish After the Destruction of Gaza: A Reckoning.* Meanwhile, serving on Moving Traditions' board of directors is Rabbi Noah Arnow, who absolves Hamas of responsibility for its October 7 slaughter of Jews and parrots Hamas lies about starvation in Gaza. These are the Jewish leaders shaping the organization that claims on its website to "embolden Jewish youth to thrive" through "caring relationships" and "a Jewish and feminist vision of equity and justice."[378] Apparently, Moving Traditions' vision of "safe spaces" for Jewish teens includes teaching them to mourn for Hamas while Israel buries hundreds of fallen soldiers—and their idea of wholeness means severing Jewish children from their own people in their hour of greatest need.

The people promoting this ideology are Jews themselves—Jews who grew up with Jewish education, who went to Hebrew school and Jewish day schools—and came to the conclusion that Jewish nationhood is evil. Jewish Voice for Peace was founded by Julie Ivny, who joined Hashomer Hatzair, a Jewish youth group, in third grade. J Street was founded by Jeremy Ben-Ami, who completed Hebrew school at Temple Rodeph Sholom in Manhattan. IfNotNow was founded by Simone Zimmerman, a graduate of two Jewish day schools in Los Angeles. These are not ignorant Jews who never learned about Judai sm.[379] These are Jews who learned, and then turned against their own people. What exactly did they learn that brought them here?

The answer begins with what left-wing Jewish parents and institutions actually teach their children. As Naya Lekht writes, many Jewish day schools in North America practice "woke in content, Jewish in form." They teach a different Bible than the one Moses brought to the people of Israel on Mount Sinai, a Bible whose chief tenets are anti-racist education, climate justice, and gender equity. They teach young Jews that to be a good Jew means to repair the world by jettisoning Jewish nationalism for a "more righteous" stew of progressive ideology and self-hatred mixed with some cherry-picked verses from the actual Bible. The result? An entire generation, taught that social justice requires abandoning Jewish particularism, now believes we must surrender our homeland to Islamic terrorists.

Young American Jews have also absorbed a broader ideology that makes them see Jewish loyalty as shameful. They are embarrassed by the thought that Jews might treat other Jews with special loyalty and concern. Far too many have bought into post-colonial ideology that treats all distinctions between peoples—language, religion, and tribe—as the root of injustice. From this perspective, Jewish peoplehood appears like backwards tribalism, incompatible with social justice.

Jewish charitable giving reflects this discomfort with particularism, with only a small share of Jewish dollars supporting specifically Jewish causes. In 2022, Jews made up nearly half of America's 25 biggest philanthropic donors, giving a collective $27 billion. Yet almost none of them direct their giving to the Jewish community. George Soros gave at least $300 million to so-called "racial justice" and "humanitarian" work. Much of this funding actually supports organizations like Adalah and I'lam, which reject Israel's right to exist and promote the boycott movement against Israel.

But even pro-Israel Jews give the vast majority of their funding to general causes. Michael Bloomberg donated $1.7 billion to charter schools, clean energy, and fighting heart disease. Mark Zuckerberg's charity gave over $900 million, mostly to fund research into artificial intelligence and genomics at universities. Of the twelve Jewish billionaires on the list, only one prioritizes Jewish giving.[380]

Nothing exposes American Jewish discomfort with Jewish nationalism quite like the two-state solution—the belief that Israel must hand over its biblical heartland to the very people obsessed with driving all the Jews of Israel into the Mediterranean Sea. Most American Jews support forcing Israel to accept a Palestinian state, even as Israelis—who would actually have to live with the consequences—overwhelmingly reject it as an act of national suicide.[381] Why? Because for many American Jews, supporting the two-state solution isn't really about strategy or security. It's about identity. It allows them to demonstrate, to their non-Jewish friends and to themselves, that they are enlightened, universalist, moral people who care just as much about Palestinian suffering as they do about Jewish survival. They hate being associated with Israeli Jews—with the ugly complexities of armies, war, and settling the land. The two-state solution lets them keep their distance from all of that while still claiming to care about Israel. But when a Jew feels as much for the Palestinian cause as for Jewish survival, he is not being moral. He is revealing, whether he knows it or not, that he is estranged from his people.

This is what leads people like Jason Isaacson, chief policy and political affairs officer of the American Jewish Committee, to make nonsensical declarations: "The land between the Jordan River and the Mediterranean Sea, indigenous to both Jews and Arabs, cannot be the exclusive domain of one people, but must be shared."[382]

Isaacson is not alone. This is the official position of the American Jewish establishment. But his words lay bare what the two-state solution actually assumes: that the land of the Bible—the land God gave to Abraham—belongs equally to the Arabs. Judea and Samaria, where the patriarchs and matriarchs are buried in Hebron, where the tabernacle stood in Shiloh, where David grew up in Bethlehem—all of this must be "shared" with people who deny any Jewish connection to the land, celebrate the slaughter of Jews, and seek Israel's destruction.

The two-state solution is built on the premise of Israeli original sin—that Israel's very existence is the reason there is no peace, and that Israel must repent by gifting land to Arab terrorists and appeasing every Palestinian demand.[383]

In May 2021, Hamas indiscriminately fired thousands of rockets at Israeli cities, without provocation or warning. Jewish children hid in bomb shelters. Twelve people in Israel were killed, including a five-year-old boy and a sixteen-year-old girl. In the middle of this attack, as Israelis ran to bomb shelters for safety, a group of Jewish employees at Google wrote a letter to their CEO. They demanded that Google issue a statement "recognizing the harm done to Palestinians by Israeli military and gang violence."

But the most telling line in their letter wasn't about Palestinians. It was this one short sentence: "We object to the conflation of Israel with the Jewish people." These self-righteous American Jews felt compelled to announce publicly that they had nothing to do with the Jews of Israel—the very Jews who were defending themselves and acting like a sovereign nation. Supporting their fellow Jews under attack would have marked them as backwards tribalists—and so they stood with the attackers instead.[384]

The Google employees at least tried to sound reasonable. Hannah Einbinder didn't bother. The 30-year-old Jewish actress, whose 2025 Emmy acceptance speech ended with "Go Birds, F*ck ICE, and Free Palestine," later sat down for an interview with Simone Zimmerman—yes, the IfNotNow founder mentioned earlier—where she explained that "Israelism, this fusion of Judaism and Zionism, is a danger to Jewish people around the world and a desecration of our beautiful and ancient tradition." Zionism, she confidently claimed, is "a betrayal on so many levels—a betrayal of our collective humanity, a betrayal of the central tenant of Judaism. It is literally the most grave betrayal of our history."[385]

Appreciate the audacity here. Einbinder invented a new word—"Israelism"—to describe the 3,000-year-old Jewish connection to the Land of Israel, as if loving Zion were some modern corruption of the Torah rather than its beating heart. She accused Jewish nationalists of betraying Jewish history, oblivious to the fact that for two millennia, the Jewish people have prayed for nothing more fervently than to return to the Land of Israel. And she did all this while calling the war in Gaza a "genocide," propagating Hamas propaganda while posturing as the defender of authentic Jewish tradition.

This is where assimilation leads: not just embarrassment about Israel, but the conviction that Jewish peoplehood itself is immoral—that caring more for your own nation than for your enemies is a form of racism that enlightened people reject.

What these Jews have actually embraced is the European Union's brand of universalism—the adamant refusal to care more for your own citizens than for strangers. European elites spent decades erasing borders and abolishing national identities, trying to create a post-national paradise. The result? The EU is collapsing while Muslim immigration erases what's left of European civilization. Europe's experiment in universal love has set it on a path toward self-destruction.

Even as millions of Americans came to understand this viscerally, enraged by globalism and drawn to the America First movement under President Trump, American Jews moved in the opposite direction. Embarrassed by Jewish distinctiveness, they felt ashamed, especially in front of their non-Jewish woke friends, to be associated with the unapologetic nationalism of Israel.

But there is a cruelty in treating all people the same, in refusing to show preferential love for your own nation, your own tribe, your own people. It is the same cold-heartedness that led American elites to outsource working-class jobs to China without any concern for their fellow Americans who were losing their livelihoods.

As Daniel Gordis wrote: "What too many of these students do not understand is that the Jewish tradition makes a bold claim—the claim that we learn caring, and we learn love, from that which is closest to us. To love all of humanity equally is ultimately to love no one. To care about one's enemies as much as one cares about oneself is to be no one. There needs to be priority and specificity in devotion and loyalty.

Without them, we can stand for nothing. And without instinctive loyalty to the Jewish people, Jewry itself cannot survive."[386]

Two generations ago, American Jews risked their comfort and their reputations to stand with their people. Today, their grandchildren risk their comfort and their reputations to stand against them.

28

VOTE MAMDANI!

Less than twenty-five years after Muslim terrorists brought down the Twin Towers, New York City elected a radical Muslim as mayor. A democratic socialist with no executive experience or impressive accomplishments under his belt, Zohran Mamdani built his political career on one clear message: Israel is the problem.

When asked if Israel has the right to exist as a Jewish state, he refused to confirm it. "I'm not comfortable supporting any state that has a hierarchy of citizenship on the basis of religion." On Gaza, he declared Israel was committing "genocide" with "intent." When criticized for promoting "globalize the intifada"—code for "murder the Jews"—he compared Islamic terrorism to Jewish resistance in the Warsaw Ghetto. After October 7, when Hamas murdered over 1,200 Jews, Mamdani immediately attacked Israel, not Hamas, for perpetuating "occupation and apartheid" against the Palestinians.[387]

That roughly one-third of New York's Jews voted for him[388] is depressing but predictable. Young secular progressive Jews, ashamed of Jewish particularism and convinced that Jewish nationalism is oppression, found in Mamdani a politician who validated their moral posturing.

What was not predictable was the Satmar Hasidim.

During Sukkot 2025, just weeks before the election, Rabbi Shalom Landau—a popular rabbi on TikTok—welcomed Zohran Mamdani to his *sukkah* in Williamsburg, surrounded by Satmar Ahronim leadership and Orthodox activists. Pictures circulated everywhere of Mamdani wearing a velvet Hasidic yarmulka, smiling alongside the rabbis. Landau praised Mamdani as a "friend of the Jewish community" and gushed: "Congratulations! Why do we have to waste a few weeks on [you] becoming mayor of New York City? We hope you come back." Mamdani responded, "Absolut ely."[389] Rabbi Moshe Indig, a Satmar community leader, publicly endorsed Mamdani,[390] praising his stances on affordable housing.

There was no mention of Mamdani's call to arrest Prime Minister Netanyahu when he visits New York. No mention of his support for BDS. No mention of his claim that Israel is committing "genocide." No mention of his chanting "globalize the intifada" at anti-Israel protests. Just flattery—public flattery of an antisemitic politician by Orthodox Jews.

Not all Satmar Hasidim supported Mamdani. Some Satmar leaders quickly backed his main rival, Andrew Cuomo, expressing concern about Mamdani's progressive agenda. But the fact that any Satmar leaders could embrace a rabid anti-Israel activist is disturbing. These are not assimilated secular Jews embarrassed by their heritage. These are Hasidim—beards, black hats, Yiddish-speaking, meticulous about every detail of Jewish law. How can they embrace a man who wants to destroy Israel and undermine Jewish life?

The answer lies in Satmar's founding story—and its theological distortion of what it means to be a Jew.

As the Nazis were murdering Hungarian Jews by the hundreds of thousands in 1944, Rabbi Joel Teitelbaum, the founder of Satmar Hasidism, was trapped in Bergen-Belsen concentration camp. He was there as part of a group of 1,684 Jews who had been transported to a special section of the camp with somewhat better conditions than most prisoners. The rescue effort was led by Rudolf Kastner, a Hungarian Zionist, who negotiated with the Nazis to save Jewish lives. Eventually, the group was transported by train to Switzerlan d.[391]

The Zionists saved his life.

After the war, Teitelbaum spent two and a half years in pre-State Israel before arriving in the United States in 1947, where he reestablished the Satmar Hasidic Court in Williamsburg. For the next three decades, he waged war against Zionism. Today, Satmar is the largest Hasidic sect in the world, with approximately 100,000 followers.

Satmar's theology is straightforward: Jews are forbidden to establish a state before the coming of the Messiah. The State of Israel, in their view, is a blasphemous rebellion against God that delays messianic redemption. Any secular Zionist effort to create a Jewish state constitutes a sin against God.[392]

In 2017, Rabbi Aaron Teitelbaum, a grand Rebbe of Satmar, laid out his community's position: "We have no part in Zionism. We have no part in their wars. We have no part in the State of Israel. We'll continue to fight God's war against Zionism and all its aspects."[393]

What this really means is that Satmar treats Judaism as a religion rather than a national identity. In their worldview, the Jewish people's true sovereignty can only be realized through divine intervention with the Messiah's arrival. Until then, Jews must remain a religious community in exile—praying, studying, waiting—not a nation with any claim to land or sovereignty.

But this is magical thinking, not Jewish theology.[394] God did not choose a religion to wait for His intervention. He chose a nation to act within history. David led armies. Solomon built a Temple, forged trade routes, and negotiated with foreign kings. This is what the Bible calls the Jewish people to do. Christianity has its own theology of waiting: for the Rapture, for the Second Coming, and for God to end history on His terms. That is a coherent Christian position. But Jews are not Christians. Satmar's vision of a Third Temple descending from heaven while Jews sit in Brooklyn is not a Jewish idea dressed in rabbinic clothing. It is a category error to apply a religious framework to a people God called to be a nation.

This theology is why some Satmar rabbis believed they could praise Mamdani despite his rabid anti-Israel positions. If Jews are just a religion, then Israel is not our nation—it is a secular political entity that has nothing to do with authentic Judaism. Mamdani's attacks on Israel become irrelevant. What matters is local politics, community relationships, and the practical benefits Mamdani might deliver to the Satmar community in Brooklyn.

Rabbi Indig was explicit about this. "I don't involve myself in foreign affairs and international politics. I'm only interested locally, here in New York, in what is in the best interest of our community now. Bibi knows how to run his own show. He doesn't need to worry about our community in Brooklyn and I don't need to worry about him."[395] Israel was someone else's problem. Brooklyn housing and education—that was his concern.

And so a community whose leader was saved by Zionists now produces leaders who offer public praise to a man whose politics directly endanger Jews worldwide. The community saved by Jewish nationalists now treats Jewish nationalism as irrelevant.

Satmar is the loudest Orthodox voice against Jewish nationhood in America. But the mistake at its core—treating Judaism as a religion rather than a nation—is not unique to Williamsburg. It is the default position of American Jewish life. Satmar just happens to have a Rebbe and a theology to justify it. Everyone else just has excuses.

29

Next Year in Jerusalem. Maybe.

We hadn't seen each other in years, not since I'd moved my family to Israel. Now here we were, both getting off the same El Al flight from Tel Aviv to Newark, waiting for our luggage at the carousel. He asked about my Aliyah experience—but his questions felt off. It wasn't just friendly curiosity. He seemed to be probing for cracks, searching for regrets.

"Were you able to find schools that were religious enough?" "It must have been very hard on your kids." "Most of the rabbis I know who made *Aliyah* aren't so happy."

I answered honestly. The schools in Israel aren't perfect, but neither are the schools in America. My children struggle at times, but they've grown tremendously and loved being in Israel. I love my work—teaching Torah, building friendships with Christians who cherish Israel, connecting people to the Holy Land.

But he kept pushing, trying to deflate my enthusiasm. This wasn't some anti-Zionist Hasidic rabbi. This was a Religious Zionist rabbi who led solidarity missions to Israel after October 7. He wore his

Zionism proudly. So why was he trying to poke holes in my experience? Why did my *Aliyah* make him so uncomfortable?

Then it hit me: My presence in Israel confronted him with a question he'd spent a lifetime avoiding.

America's Orthodox Jewish population numbers about 900,000 people—roughly 15% of American Jewry. Each year, approximately 3,000 to 4,000 Jews make Aliyah from the United States, most of them Orthodox. That's barely half of one percent annually—and with Orthodox birthrates among the highest in America, the community grows faster than it leaves. By any honest accounting, American Orthodox Jews are building their future in the United States, not Israel.

This is the community that recites three times each day the words "Sound the great shofar for our freedom; raise a banner to gather our exiles, and bring us together from the four corners of the earth into our land." This is the community that sends its teenagers to Israeli gap-year programs, whose members fly to Israel multiple times a year for holidays and to tour the land. Yet when it comes to actually moving to Israel, to living what they pray, the overwhelming majority find reasons to stay put.

Modern Orthodox Jews are fully observant of Jewish law while engaging with mainstream American life—college, careers, professional dress. They send their children to Jewish day schools and Israeli gap-year programs and proudly hang Israeli flags in their synagogues. They are, in short, the segment of American Jewry most explicitly committed to the idea that Israel is the Jewish homeland. They make up only 3% of American Jews—but they are the Zionist vanguard of American Jewish life.

And most of them are staying put.

Unlike anti-Zionist Hasidim or non-Orthodox Jews—few of whom seriously consider moving to Israel—Modern Orthodox Jews were raised to believe that *Aliyah* is the ideal. They learned this in day school. They know Jews belong in Israel. Since October 7, some have begun taking it seriously for the first time, rattled by rising antisemitism and the sudden vulnerability of American Jewish life. But the overwhelming majority have chosen, consciously or passively, to remain in America.

There are good reasons, of course: it's hard, it's scary, they're comfortable, elderly parents need care, career concerns, Hebrew is difficult. The list goes on. Fair enough. Not everyone can uproot their life at any given moment.

But what damages American Orthodoxy isn't just the failure to make *Aliyah*—it's refusing to talk about it.

Most American Orthodox Jews—even the most committed Zionists among them—have never been taught why God gave the Jewish people a land in the first place. They know how to keep Shabbat and kosher. They know the laws of prayer and family purity. But the theology of the land—why it matters, what it demands, and the brokenness of Jewish life in its absence—this they were never taught. And what you were never taught, you will never miss.

Most pro-Israel Orthodox rabbis don't openly encourage Aliyah. They are caught in a genuine tension: they know that living in Israel is the fulfillment of everything they teach, yet they have built their lives in America serving communities they love and leading congregations that depend on them. It is easier not to examine that choice too closely.

And their congregants feel the same pressure from the other direction—people who have built their lives in America and have no serious intention of leaving don't want to hear, week after week, that God is calling them home. It implies, uncomfortably, that they are living a second-rate Jewish life. And so both sides collude in silence. When someone actually moves, the community celebrates with speeches and l'chaims. But otherwise, the subject is quietly dropped. Why talk about something that makes you feel guilty?

This silence is more damaging than they realize. Because they avoid the topic, they never internalize the goal of the Torah: to shape a holy nation in the Land of Israel that will serve as a light and model for all nations. Instead, they focus solely on the religious and ritual aspects of the Torah that can be performed by individual Jews anywhere in the world. These become the entirety of their Jewish practice, disconnected from the national mission that is the Torah's ultimate goal.[396]

The Torah contains hundreds of commandments that are generally organized into three categories. Some govern the relationship between man and God—kosher laws, prayer, the holidays. Others govern the relationship between man and his fellow—honoring your parents, giving charity, treating your employees fairly. A third category governs a person's relationship with himself—humility, self-discipline, the ongoing work of building one's own character. For centuries, these three categories appeared to capture the full scope of what God asked of a Jew.[397]

Today, Rabbi Shalom Rosner identifies a fourth category, one that was simply unavailable for nearly two thousand years: commandments that are *bein adam la'amo*, between a person and his nation. Visiting the sick is an act of kindness between two individuals. But moving to Israel, serving in the Israel Defense Forces, defending the Jewish people in the public square, choosing to raise your children inside Jewish history rather than watching it from afar—these carry a different weight entirely. Their impact is national, not personal. No amount of individual piety can substitute for them, and no diaspora community, however Torah-filled, can provide them.[398]

The Jews of the *shtetl* deserved no criticism on this score. They had no way to express this dimension of religious life, so they poured their hearts and souls into Torah study, prayer and acts of kindness. This is not to be belittled; their devotion kept the Jewish people alive throughout generations of exile. But today, for the first time since Bar Kochba's rebellion against Rome, the Jewish nation is reborn. And so God expects something new from this generation: not just personal piety, not just a thriving synagogue and a tight-knit community, but a genuine reckoning with what it means to be part of a nation with a destiny. That reckoning begins by asking ourselves an honest question: Am I living only for myself and my family and my community, or am I living for my people?

By avoiding that question, American Orthodox Jews have unwittingly reduced the Torah to "Judaism"—a religion that can be practiced anywhere, by anyone, disconnected from peoplehood and place. What results is a hollowed-out Jewish life: religiously rigorous but nationally incoherent.

Aliyah is the ultimate test of Jewish nationhood. For two thousand years, we maintained our national identity with the express goal of returning to the land of Israel. We prayed for it incessantly. We yearned for it in every grace after meals. We broke glasses at weddings to remember Jerusalem in ruins. Everything pointed toward return.

Now, after nearly 2,000 years, the opportunity has arrived. The gates are open, and Israel desperately needs her people. The Galilee needs Jewish families. Judea and Samaria need settlers to strengthen our hold on the land. The IDF has a manpower shortage. Yet American Orthodox Jews visit Israel to pray at the Western Wall, celebrate holidays in Jerusalem, and then board planes back "home" to New Jersey or Los Angeles. Israel has become a religious shrine—a holy place to visit and then leave, like any other pilgrimage site.

Many wealthy diaspora Jews spend thousands of dollars on lavish Passover vacations at luxurious hotels in Florida and the Caribbean. Ambassador Yechiel Leiter captures the contradiction: "How is it possible to spend thousands of dollars [on Passover vacations] while neglecting the Torah's most foundational commandment? How is it possible to spend thousands on 'pilgrimage' to luxurious hotels in order to celebrate all the festivals with 'excessive joy,' when the entire essence of the festival is the pilgrimage to Jerusalem with all of Israel? There is something fundamentally flawed here! This is a complete contradiction!"[399]

This is what happens when being Jewish is reduced to religious practice and belief rather than national identity. Living in the land becomes an optional enhancement to religious practice rather than its fulfillment.

Maimonides condemned this attitude in the 12th century: "But those who delude themselves and say they will stay put until the Messiah comes to the Western lands, and only then will they leave and go to Jerusalem—I don't know how this catastrophe will be averted from them! Such people transgress and lead others astray, and about them the prophet said: 'They treat my people's wound as though it were not serious, saying Peace, peace, when there is no peace' (Jeremiah 6:14)."[400]

Maimonides was referring to those who have the means to leave exile and come to Israel, and that includes many of today's great Torah scholars. Being learned doesn't exempt them from this obligation. The spies were among the greatest leaders in Israel, yet they rejected the land and caused weeping for generations.

The spies had real reasons to be afraid. Giants lived in the land, the cities had walls and the Canaanites were armed and ready to fight. Today's excuses sound more sophisticated—careers, schools, quality of life. But the problem is the same: rejecting the land means rejecting Jewish nationhood itself. And a people that rejects its own land, no matter how comfortable the alternative, is a people that has lost its way.

Writing in the 18th century, Rabbi Jacob Emden couldn't understand it: "Indeed, it is puzzling regarding the Jewish people: everywhere they have been stringent with themselves in various detailed observances of commandments that they have upheld, being meticulous about them extensively, spending large sums of money and going to great lengths to fulfill them with complete perfection. Yet why do they treat lightly and act lazily toward this beloved commandment, which is the foundation upon which the entire Torah depends?"[401]

Nothing has changed. Orthodox Jews will spend hundreds of dollars to buy the perfect set of four species for Sukkot. They'll meticulously check lettuce leaves for bugs to ensure the lettuce is clean and kosher. They'll install elaborate systems to automate their homes for Shabbat. But living in Israel—the commandment that Rabbi Emden calls "the foundation upon which the entire Torah depends"—this they treat as optional.

Rabbi Joseph B. Soloveitchik was even less charitable: "Judaism has been very careful about not missing the appointed hour. Any delay is considered sinful. Man may sometimes lose his entire world for but one sin—that of tarrying... Among the Jews of America, Orthodox Jews bear the most blame for the slow pace of the conquest of the land through settlement. It was for us, the loyalists of Judaism, to heed the call of the Beloved more acutely, and to respond immediately with extraordinary effort."[402]

As only Hillel Halkin could put it, "What shall we say of our Orthodox Jew who, like a comic lover in the drama, prefers to yearn like his forefathers for the Holy Land from afar rather than live in it now that this is possible? We might be tempted to judge him less charitably."[403]

Rabbi Ashkenazi offers a more charitable, and more penetrating, answer to Rabbi Emden's question. The obstacle to *Aliyah* is not laziness or comfort, though those challenges are real enough. The challenge goes deeper. Every Jew in the United States is fighting a war inside himself—between the Jew he is and the American he has become. One identity pulls toward Jerusalem; the other pulls him toward the town where he grew up, the synagogue his parents built, and the life he has spent decades constructing. Whichever one wins determines everything.

When the American inside him wins, assimilation follows within a generation or two—first Shabbat slips, then the kosher laws, then one day his grandchild is marrying a non-Jew and the chain is broken forever. When the Jew wins, return becomes possible—but only possible.

For as Rabbi Ashkenazi taught: "*Aliyah* demands of that Jew an effort similar to that of Abraham, who was required to detach himself from the landscape of his childhood. It is difficult. It is not an economic matter as many think. It is a fundamental matter of identity. That is why it is so hard."[404]

This is the most honest answer to Rabbi Emden's puzzle. The Orthodox Jew who spends a small fortune on the details of the ritual commandments but treats *Aliyah* as optional is not simply lazy. He is deeply Jewish in his observance—but American in his bones. When he closes his eyes and pictures home, he sees Teaneck or Flatbush, not Jerusalem. Uprooting from that world demands the same rupture God asked of Abraham: *lech lecha*—go, leave, detach. It is a crisis of identity, and it will be resolved in only one way: by deciding, finally, which man he actually is.

Organizations like Nefesh B'Nefesh do extraordinary work handling the logistics—paperwork, flights, absorption, guidance. They've mastered the *how* of *Aliyah*. But most Jews never get to the *how* stage because they never learned the *why*. If you don't understand the why, you will always find a how-not. You will always have an excuse. You will always feel comfortable staying put.[405]

The American Jewish community is living a tragedy, and the most tragic thing about it is that they don't know it. A man who knows he is in crisis looks for a way out. The American Orthodox Jew doesn't experience exile as a crisis—he experiences it as a life well lived and a future worth investing in. He has no sense that anything is missing.

But watch old men and children sitting and playing in the streets of Jerusalem, just as Zechariah promised[406] they would; squeeze into a tiny bomb shelter on the side of a highway with Jews you've never met but feel like family; sit in a shiva house mourning a fallen soldier you never knew but whose loss you feel in your gut—and you will feel something that no American Jewish community, however vibrant and Torah-filled, can give you: the overwhelming, terrifying, electrifying sense that you are living inside the story of your people, that Jewish history is not something that happened in the Bible but something that is happening to you, right now, and that what you do with your life genuinely matters to God and to the Jewish nation. No amount of synagogue-building in New Jersey can give you that.

The critique here isn't directed at any particular individual. I know the obstacles are real—it took my own family years to make the move to Israel. There are seasons of life when *Aliyah* is simply not possible, and no one should be judged for that. What I am challenging is something different: the communal silence, the rabbinic avoidance, the failure to even hold *Aliyah* up as the only genuine aspiration for a committed Jew. A community can acknowledge that most of its members aren't ready to move while still insisting that moving is the goal. American Orthodoxy adamantly refuses to do so.

Where is the longing? Where is the passion to return? Instead of seeking excuses, why aren't they consumed with finding ways to make it work? Instead of justifying their decisions to stay, why aren't they actively planning their return?

Until *Aliyah* becomes not just an ideal but an urgent aspiration, they'll remain where that rabbi at the airport already was—knowing the truth, and choosing not to face it.

30

Professors of Powerlessness

In August 2025, as Israel fought to rescue over twenty hostages still starving in Hamas tunnels in Gaza, Rabbi Yosef Blau[407]—a long-time rabbi at Yeshiva University, one of America's leading Orthodox institutions—issued a public letter. Titled "A Call for Moral Clarity, Responsibility, and a Jewish Orthodox Response in the Face of the Gaza Humanitarian Crisis," the letter was signed by eighty Orthodox rabbis, nearly all from America and Europe.

The letter made a specific accusation: Israel's "limiting of humanitarian aid, at times completely halting the entry of food and medical supplies, has raised the specter of coming starvation." It charged that "Hamas's sins and crimes do not relieve the government of Israel of its obligations to make whatever efforts are necessary to prevent mass starvation."[408]

The problem is that none of this was true. Charlie Kirk and others had already exposed the propaganda campaign trying to portray Israel as intentionally starving Gaza's population. "This weekend, there was an all-out propaganda campaign trying to make it seem as if Israel is intentionally starving the people of Gaza," Kirk said on his show the month before Rabbi Blau published his letter. "I hate being lied to, especially by the media networks."[409] Israel documented massive amounts of aid entering Gaza, and Hamas's theft and hoarding of humanitarian supplies was well established by that point.[410] But these Orthodox rabbis apparently decided that international NGOs and a press corps with a proven anti-Israel bias throughout the war were more credible sources than the Israeli government itself.

The consequences were exactly what you'd expect. Israel's critics seized the letter immediately: "Look," they said, "even Orthodox rabbis now accuse Israel of inhumanity." Every word was quoted, recycled, and weaponized in campaigns designed to isolate Israel diplomatically and economically. Anti-Israel activists were handed precisely what they needed—religious Jews providing moral cover for accusations of Israeli war crimes.

Rabbi Yechiel Leiter, Israel's ambassador to the United States, demanded that Rabbi Blau and the other signatories issue a public apology. "Your statement not only reflects a severe unfamiliarity with the facts," Leiter wrote, "but also relies on the lies of our worst enemies." He criticized the rabbis for ignoring the reality that "Israel is the one feeding those who are firing on our children."[411]

The credulity here is striking: eighty Orthodox rabbis chose to trust international NGOs and a press corps with a proven anti-Israel bias over the Israeli government itself—and handed Israel's enemies a propaganda gift in the process. But when Rabbi Blau defended the letter, something more than a factual error came into view.

Rabbi Blau defended his letter this way: "My support of Israel and Zionism stems from my commitment to Judaism. A non-critical loyalty is contradictory to the introspection fundamental to Judaism.

When religion is used to justify a worship of power, it distorts basic morality."[412]

His co-signatories were more explicit. Rabbi Yitz Greenberg criticized Israel's war against Hamas by declaring that "The heart of Torah is justice, not revenge."[413] Think about what that means: Israel was fighting a war to rescue hostages, to stop rocket attacks on Israeli cities, and to eliminate the terrorists who murdered 1,200 Jews on October 7—as righteous a defensive war as any nation could ever wage. Yet Rabbi Greenberg characterized it as revenge rather than justice, even while twenty Israeli hostages were still starving in Hamas tunnels. His problem wasn't really with specific Israeli policies but with Jewish strength and military power itself.

Rabbi Dr. Shlomo Zuckier, a young Orthodox rabbi and graduate of Yeshiva University, posted this on social media on April 24, 2024—Yom Hashoah, Holocaust Remembrance Day: "This is your periodic reminder that a version of Judaism addicted to power and Jewish supremacy, that is willing to use terror tactics to get ahead, is no better than any other terrorist, supremacist movement addicted to power."[414]

Zuckier's vague post was almost certainly aimed at Israeli government ministers Bezalel Smotrich and Itamar Ben-Gvir, whose right-wing policies he strongly opposes. Fair enough—these are legitimate political targets for criticism. But look at the language he chose: "addicted to power," "Jewish supremacy," words which equate right-wing Jews with jihadist terrorist movements. This isn't political disagreement. This is the vocabulary Israel's most vicious enemies use to slur the Jewish people, now coming from the mouth of an Orthodox rabbi who considers himself a proud Zionist.

What Zuckier revealed here wasn't a policy critique. It was a deep discomfort with Jews wielding power at all. He chose to say this on Yom Hashoah—the day we commemorate six million Jews murdered precisely because they lacked the power to defend themselves. The irony apparently didn't occur to him.

This is not an isolated case. These rabbis share a common anxiety: that Jewish power—military, political, territorial—corrupts Judaism's moral mission. They prefer Jews as a powerless moral minority, physically weak but morally pure.

That preference is a product of two thousand years of exile. Through expulsions, pogroms, and genocide, Jews survived by cultivating spiritual resilience over physical strength and emphasizing moral authority over political power. We had no choice—we had no power, so we made a virtue of powerlessness.

Many diaspora Jews absorbed this exile theology so deeply that they now confuse weakness with righteousness and strength with corruption. But here's what they miss: religions can survive without political or military power. A religion is a system of beliefs and practices that scattered communities can maintain through faith alone.

But a nation without power will be destroyed.

A nation needs sufficient territory, defensible borders, and the means to defend itself and protect its citizens. Without power—and the will to use it—the Jewish state will not survive. This isn't "worship of power." It's the minimum requirement for national existence.

Yet these rabbis, comfortable in America, idealize the powerlessness of exile Judaism. They long for the days when Jews could maintain moral purity precisely because we lacked the power to make hard choices. They're fine with a Jewish people that suffers nobly and endures persecution with dignity. What they cannot accept is a strong and powerful nation that uses its power to crush its enemies.

All of these rabbis consider themselves Zionists, and I do not question their idealism or intentions. But they don't seem to realize that their rejection of Jewish power and victory is actually a rejection of Jewish nationalism itself. In this, they're echoing arguments made a century ago by another group of Jewish intellectuals who also saw themselves as enlightened critics of misguided Zionism.

In the 1920s and 1930s, a group of German Jewish intellectuals moved to British Mandatory Palestine. They gathered in a transplanted German-speaking "salon," debating whether Zionism was ethical or just another form of corrupt, ethnocentric nationalism. Yoram Hazony describes the scene: "As the desperados of the Labor movement were subjecting themselves to heat, malaria, and hunger in the effort to bring food out of the earth, the German intellectuals in Jerusalem—like their peers in Frankfurt and Berlin with whom they kept up a voluminous correspondence—were wracking their consciences over the question of whether the Arabs in Palestine were being treated as a 'thou.'"[415]

The most prominent voice in this circle was Martin Buber, the renowned German Jewish philosopher. As early as 1916, Buber dismissed the idea of a Jewish state as "bold madness" and accused Zionists of succumbing to the "unholy dogma of the sovereignty of nations." He insisted that Zionism should focus on spiritual renewal, not political power: "For me, just as the state in general is not the determining goal of mankind, so the "Jewish state" is not the determining goal for the Jews... I have seen and heard too much of the results of empty needs for power. Our argument does not concern the Jewish state, that, yes, were it to be founded today would be built upon the same principles as any other modern state. It does not concern the addition of one more trifling power structure."[416]

In 1939, as Hitler's armies marched across Europe and Jews desperately needed refuge, Buber attacked unnamed Zionists who were working "to establish our own national egoism," declaring that "they are performing the acts of Hitler in the land of Israel, for they want us to serve Hitler's god after he has been given a Hebrew name."[417] Yes, you read that correctly. In November 1939, more than a year after Kristallnacht, the Nazi pogrom that destroyed synagogues and Jewish businesses across Germany, and as Nazis were already murdering and expelling Jews across Poland, Martin Buber compared Jewish nationalists to Hitler.

Rabbi Judah Magnes, an American who had moved to Palestine and would become the first chancellor of Hebrew University, was another influential voice in this circle. Magnes shared Buber's deep discomfort with Jewish sovereignty and openly rejected political Zionism, insisting that Jews in Palestine should not aspire to self-determination at all.

"The Congress program of the Zionist Organization is a secure homeland for the Jewish people in Palestine... Have you made it clear to yo urselves... what you mean by a 'secure homeland'?... Can the Ottoman government... be blamed for viewing us with suspicion if... while we want equal rights for the Jews of the world, we want more than equal rights in Palestine? I want equal rights for the Jews, no more and no less, in all lands, including Palestine.... In this the Jewish people in Palestine would be on the same level as the Muslim, the Christian, the

Turkish, the Arabic, the Armenian, and other groups of that empire. All that we have a right to ask is that the Jews be permitted to settle in and develop their Jewish economic and cultural life in Palestine freely, just as other people of the empire have the same right."[418]

Magnes believed that the dream of Jewish sovereignty was dangerous, even immoral. Even after the brutal pogrom of 1929, in which Arabs slaughtered 133 Jews and raped and wounded many more,[419] he refused to support a Jewish state that could defend its people. He favored a precarious minority status, in which Jews had a "right" only to equality—but not the political power or sovereignty necessary to secure it.[420]

As the Zionists moved closer to establishing a Jewish state, Magnes only grew more hostile. In 1947—on the eve of Israel's Independence War, a desperate war for survival—he denounced the vast majority of the *Yishuv*[421] as having "left the Jewish tradition of purity and holiness." Instead, his fellow Jews were embracing "Zionist totalitarianism, which seeks to extend its rule over the entire people... if necessary by means of power and violence." Speaking at the opening of the Hebrew University's academic year, Magnes warned that only the university still resisted this supposedly tyrannical project. In his view, it remained the lone institution that "in spite of all the votes of the majority," continued to stand firm against "the totalitarian idea."

Even as the British Mandate was collapsing and Arab forces were preparing to invade and slaughter the Jews of Israel, Magnes cast Jewish self-defense and Jewish sovereignty as moral corruption. Right up until Israel's birth, he preferred Jewish political powerlessness, no matter the cost in Jewish lives.[422]

Albert Einstein shared this discomfort with Jewish power. "I would much rather see reasonable agreement with the Arabs on the basis of living together in peace than the creation of a Jewish state," he wrote. "Apart from practical considerations, my awareness of the essential nature of Judaism resists the idea of a Jewish state, with borders, an army, and a measure of temporal power, no matter how modest. We are no longer the Jews of the Maccabee period. A return to a nation in the political sense of the word would be the equivalent to turning away from the spiritualization of our community which we owe to the genius of the prophets."

Einstein insisted he was "against nationalism but in favor of Zionism ."[423] He believed passionately that Jews needed to see themselves as a nation: "Not until we dare to regard ourselves as a nation, not until we respect ourselves, can we gain the esteem of others."[424] Yet he refused to accept what building that nation would actually require—the hard, unpleasant work of state-building and the willingness to fight when necessary.

Reality kept intruding on his idealism. After the 1929 pogrom, the prominent British Zionist leader Selig Brodetsky spoke to German Zionists in Berlin. "I told them in the best German I could manage what we demanded of the British Mandatory government, and I said that Arabs who had murdered Jews must be dealt with according to the law. The audience was shocked. Einstein complained to me afterwards that I had spoken like Mussolini. I had shown no spirit of conciliation; I had demanded that Arab murderers should be punis hed."[425]

To Einstein, holding Arabs accountable for murdering Jews was indistinguishable from fascism. His biographer, Ronald Clark, captured the problem: "Positions of power are rarely gained or held by those who believe that all men are not only brothers but innocent ones. A good deal of ruthless wire pulling is required, a good deal of balancing and counterbalancing... All these, the common coin of getting things done, are required even of a statesman with the moral integrity of [Chaim] Weizmann. But to a man of Einstein's temperament this element of wheeling and dealing was repugnant."[426]

For all his scientific genius, Einstein could not, or would not, understand basic human nature. He wanted a Jewish nation built on moral purity alone, as if good intentions could substitute for power.

Even as Arab armies poured across Israel's borders from every direction, Buber worked frantically to undermine the Jewish sovereignty that had just been established. On May 27, 1948, one day before the collapse of Jewish forces under siege in the Jewish Quarter of Jerusalem's Old City, Buber published an article excoriating the Jewish state as a "desecration" of Jewish ideals: "Never in the past have spirit and life been so distant from each other as now, in the period of 'rebirth.' Or perhaps you are willing to give the name 'spirit' to a collective selfishness which acknowledges no higher standard? This 'Zionism' desecrates the name Zion. It is nothing more than one of the crassest nationalisms of our time... We are not obliged to conquer the land, for no danger is in store for our spiritual essence or our way of life from the population of the land. Yet the inclination to power makes only one demand: Sovereignty."[427]

"No danger" from the local Arab population—this while the Arab Legion was systematically destroying the Jewish Quarter block by block. Arab soldiers looted and burned over 300 Jewish homes, synagogues, and yeshivas. The Hurva and Tiferet Yisrael synagogues—landmarks of Jerusalem's Jewish life for centuries—were blown up with explosives, while Torah scrolls were paraded through the streets, desecrated, and burned. Rabbis were marched through jeering crowds carrying white flags. Fifteen hundred Jewish men, women, and children were taken prisoner, and several were tortured. Martin Buber, sitting two and a half kilometers away in his Hebrew University office, was too consumed with the moral dangers of Jewish sovereignty to spare any concern for the fate of his fellow Jews.

David Ben-Gurion, who was fighting to establish a Jewish state, was infuriated by these celebrated academics trying to prevent the fulfillment of Herzl's dream. "We all want to bring Jews today to Palestine," Ben-Gurion told Buber. "I ask you, and I asked Magnes years ago: Did you come to Palestine with the consent of the Arabs or against their wishes? He came against their wishes, and with the force of British bayonets... I say, there is no example in history of a nation opening the gates of its country because the nation that wants to enter has explained its desire to it."[428]

Berl Katznelson, the Labor movement's leading ideologue, initially maintained friendly relations with Buber's circle. As founder and editor of the Labor newspaper Davar, he valued their contributions on economics, literature, and other fields. But the 1929 massacre changed his view. He watched these intellectuals call for a government with an Arab majority while rejecting Jewish nationhood, and concluded that they were driving Jewish Palestine to hysteria and despair. He quickly shifted gears, damning the intellectuals as "*tlushim*"—"the uprooted"—the perfect way to describe Buber and his friends.

These professors lived in their own dream world where Arab terror and brutality did not exist. They were cut off from the painful realities facing the Jewish people. While pioneers drained swamps and defended settlements, these intellectuals debated abstract ethics. As Jews desperately sought a refuge from rising European antisemitism, these professors worried about whether Zionism was sufficiently universal in its moral vision.[429]

This discomfort with power didn't begin with Martin Buber and his friends. It goes back to the very origins of Jewish nationhood—to Jacob himself.

Isaac envisioned a partnership between his sons: Esau would be the powerful leader and man of the world, while Jacob would be the teacher and man of the spirit. Together, they would create a model nation that united material strength with spiritual devotion to God, proving that power and holiness could be integrated rather than opposed. Esau would rule as king while Jacob served as his partner and teacher. But Rebecca understood what Isaac did not—that Esau was corrupted and lost to evil. Jacob would have to build a nation that accomplished both missions on its own. Jacob needed both blessings: not only the spiritual blessing Isaac initially intended for him, but also the blessing of material abundance and power that Isaac had intended for Esau. A nation cannot survive on spirituality alone.

Yet when Rebecca told Jacob to take the material blessing, he resisted. Rabbi Yaakov Tzvi Mecklenburg explains that Jacob's response to his mother—"perhaps my father will feel me" (Genesis 27:12)—is telling. The word "perhaps" gives him away. Jacob was *hoping* his father would catch him so the whole plan would collapse. Why? Not because he was squeamish about deceiving Isaac, but because he did not want the blessing of power itself. He was a man of the spirit, devoted to a life of study. The thought of wielding material power repulsed him. It seemed like a corruption of the spiritual life he'd chosen for himself. He only went through with Rebecca's plan because she forced him to.[430]

But Jacob's education was incomplete. At Laban's house, he learned that pure spirituality without strength just leaves you exploited and vulnerable. Many years later, when he wrestled with the angel and prevailed, he earned a new name: Israel. Jacob had to learn that the righteous must also wield power, in a holy way, or they will be destroyed by evil. Power itself is not darkness; refusing to use it when necessary is the real corruption.[431]

The modern Jewish intellectuals who recoil from Israeli strength are stuck where Jacob started. They still believe that power corrupts, that spiritual purity requires physical weakness. Jews living in exile with no possibility of strength made a virtue of weakness, just like the young Jacob did. But the moment we began returning to our homeland, that attitude became suicidal. The Jewish people have no choice now but to become Israel and embrace the dual blessing Rebecca envisioned for us. Israel must be holy like Jacob, but it must also be powerful like Esau.

The rhetoric is nearly identical, separated by eighty-six years and nothing else. Buber warned against "worshippers of force" in 1939; Zuckier equates Israeli self-defense with terrorism in 2025. Buber compared Jewish nationalists to Hitler; Greenberg calls Israel's war against the murderers of October 7 mere "revenge."

And the dynamic? Exactly the same. While IDF soldiers risk their lives and Israeli families live under constant threat of Hamas rockets and terror attacks, these American Orthodox rabbis agonize over whether the "mean Jewish state" is living up to their Western ethical standards. They live in an academic fantasy world completely disconnected from the brutal realities of national survival.

The Arabs have not changed their murderous plans. From the Hebron massacre of 1929 to the October 7 massacre of 2023, the goal remains the same: the Jewish presence in the land of Israel. Yet many of the Jewish people's brightest minds are just as foolish today as they were a century ago—maybe more so, since they now have a hundred years of evidence proving their critics were right all along.

These modern "*tlushim*" care about Israel and the Jewish people, but they have internalized a theology that sees nationhood itself as a corruption of Judaism. They cannot stand up for the vital interests of Jews as a nation because doing so would require accepting that nations sometimes need to make hard, morally complex choices—and they refuse to grant Israel that permission.

The Jewish state needs power to survive. It needs strong borders, a powerful military, and the steely resolve to defend itself even when that defense looks ugly to those watching from the comfort of American universities. It needs Jews who understand that we are a nation returning to history as actors in our own story, not victims in someone else's.

After the Kishinev pogrom of 1903, in which 45 Jews were murdered and hundreds were wounded and raped, the young Vladimir Jabotinsky spoke to a group of Jewish intellectuals in Odessa. The entire Jewish world was in shock, yet these intellectuals still struggled to confront the reality of Jewish powerlessness. Jabotinsky had no patience for their moralizing: "We are a people [and] you may as well be angry with your parents for having brought you into the world as wish to be excused from belonging to your people. Life is always a war. The weak are treated with contempt."[432] A nation without power is a nation destined to be crushed.

This is the curse of the Jewish intellectual. From Buber's Jerusalem salon to the faculty lounges of American universities, the pattern never changes—brilliant Jewish minds, disconnected from the brutal realities facing their people, insisting that Jewish power is the problem. They theorize while Jews fight and moralize while Jews die. Jabotinsky would have recognized them immediately. A century later, the professors are still moralizing. And the Jews are still paying the price.

31

Jerusalem on the Euphrates

Twenty-six centuries ago in Babylonia, the prophet Ezekiel condemned two groups of Jews. The first condemnation was predictable—the second less so.

Most Jews were living in Babylonia, exiled from Jerusalem and Judea after the destruction of the Temple. The first generation of exiles wept by the rivers of Babylon, dreaming of home. But their children grew comfortable. They wanted what every immigrant generation eventually wants: to fit in, to belong, to stop being different. "Let us be like the nations, like the families of the lands, to serve wood and stone" (Ezekiel 20:32). Rabbi Binyamin Lau explains their mindset: "This is the cry of Jews attempting to escape their old identity, fleeing the land of their origin, and seeking a new identity as immigrants: new names, new dress, new interactions, and gradual assimilation."[433]

To these Jews who wished to be like all the nations, God's response through Ezekiel was harsh: "As I live, says the Lord God, surely with a strong hand and with an outstretched arm and with poured out fury, will I reign over you. And I shall take you out of the peoples, and I shall gather you from the lands in which you were scattered, with a strong hand and with an outstretched arm and with poured out fury"

(Ezekiel 20:33-34). You want to assimilate? God will make sure you come home—even against your will.

But Ezekiel had a second target, and this one is less obvious. These weren't Jews abandoning their faith. These were religiously observant Jews who kept all the commandments, who remained faithful to the Torah of Moses, who maintained their distinct Jewish identity in every detail. They were model Jews by any standard.

Their goals were admirable, yet Ezekiel condemned them just as sharply as the assimilationists. What was their crime?

Rabbi Lau writes: "Within the group of those faithful to the Torah of Moses, the Babylonian Jews who wished to preserve their distinct Jewish identity, there was a desire to realize the ideal of the nation even on Babylonian soil. Even without the Temple, they strived to serve God fully and to shape their Jewish identity in all its details, ignoring the land of Israel."[434]

These religiously observant Jews believed they could build in Babylon what properly belonged to Jerusalem. Ezekiel had prophesied about the divine presence descending from the Temple to accompany them in exile.[435] Perhaps they could create a "miniature Temple" in Babylonia—a fully observant Jewish community that maintained all the commandments even outside the land.

And honestly—who could blame them? The journey back to Jerusalem was dangerous, the city was in ruins, and the land was desolate. Babylonia was prosperous and stable. They could build something beautiful right where they were, without risking everything for a pile of rubble thousands of miles away. Who needs the land when you have faith in God?

Ezekiel had no patience for this argument: "But on My holy mount, on the mountain of the height of Israel, says the Lord God. There all the house of Israel—yea, all of them—will serve Me in the land; there I will accept them, and there I will require your heave offerings and the first of your food with all your hallowed things... And you will know that I am the Lord when I bring you to the land of Israel, to the land that I lifted My hand to give to your forefathers" (Ezekiel 20:40-42).

"*There* you shall serve Me." Not in Babylonia. Not in any exile, no matter how comfortable or how religiously observant the Jewish community may be. Yes, God's presence accompanied the Jewish people into exile, but like a candle in a dark room rather than the sun in an open sky. In the land of Israel, God's presence is fully revealed; in exile, it is hidden, diminished, a flickering light in the darkness. The full expression of Jewish nationhood, the complete fulfillment of the Torah's purpose, can only happen in one place. A "miniature Temple" in Babylonia—or Brooklyn, or Los Angeles—cannot serve as an alternative to the real thing.

Ezekiel condemns two kinds of failure: the Jew who forgets he is a Jew, and the Jew who remembers everything except the part that matters most — that his people belong to a specific land.

The parallels to American Jewry today are uncomfortable but unmistakable.

The secular American Jews who treat Israel as just another country, who reduce being Jewish to bagels and Holocaust memory and regard the Torah's commands as charming relics of the past: these are Ezekiel's assimilationists. They are Americans who happen to be

Jewish, not Jews who happen to live in America. "Let us be like the nations." Three thousand years later, the words are the same.

But what about the Orthodox American Jews? The ones who build elaborate Jewish communities in Lakewood and Flatbush and Teaneck, with beautiful synagogues and excellent schools? The ones who name their shuls 'Young Israel of' some American suburb? The ones who fly to Israel for the holidays but always return "home" to America?

These are Ezekiel's observant Babylonian Jews, trying to build in exile what belongs in Jerusalem.

"There you shall serve Me... there is My holy land for them." Not here. Not in comfortable exile. Not in successful diaspora communities, no matter how vibrant or observant. There—in the land of Israel, where the Jewish nation belongs.

Until American Jews internalize this, they will remain in the same confusion that plagued the exiles of Babylonia. Ezekiel's rebuke still stands.

But Ezekiel didn't just rebuke—he warned what would happen if Jews refused to return willingly. When Jews refuse to come home by choice, history has a way of making the decision for them. The comfortable exile becomes uncomfortable. The welcoming host nation turns hostile. And what seemed like a permanent home reveals itself to be temporary after all.

Few American Jews ever thought it could happen to them, in the land of the free and the home of the brave. Yet Ezekiel saw it coming: God would take the Jews out of the nations "with a strong hand and with an outstretched arm and with poured out fury."

They may be the last generation that gets to leave on their own terms.

32

What Do You Love More?

It was an awesome moment for both the Jewish state and President Trump. After Israel endured two painful years of war and heroic sacrifice, President Trump and Prime Minister Netanyahu achieved a ceasefire deal that would ultimately bring home all of the living hostages held by Hamas. During his historic celebratory speech at the Knesset in Jerusalem, Trump repeatedly declared his love for Israel and the unique friendship between America and Israel. He praised the many people in the room, both American and Israeli, who played key roles in securing the agreement. And then he turned his attention to Dr. Miriam Adelson—the pro-Israel GOP mega-donor and holder of both Israeli and American citizenship.

"Miriam, stand up, please. She really loves this country. She and her husband are so incredible, we miss him dearly."

The president paused, then grinned. "I'm going to get her in trouble with this, but I once asked her, 'Miriam, I know you love Israel. What do you love more, the United States or Israel?' She refused to answer." Another pause. "That might mean Israel." The room stirred uncomfortably. "I must say, we love you. Thank you, darling, for being here. She's a wonderful woman."[436]

In Trumpian style, the President said the quiet part out loud. As the entire world watched, he asked his most important Jewish donor to declare her primary allegiance—and when she wouldn't, he announced to the world what her silence meant: that one of America's most influential pro-Israel Jews loves Israel more than America.

Trump, of course, knows that Miriam is first and foremost an Israeli. In a 2012 interview, Adelson herself said her heart has always remained in Israel, but she got "stuck" in America after meeting Sheldon Adelson—"the love of [her] life"—on a blind date in 1991. She became an American citizen but never renounced her Israeli citizenship.[437]

The awkward exchange was a gift to the conspiracy theorists. Congressman Thomas Massie posted on X: "Israeli citizen Miriam Adelson bought the Dallas Mavericks for $3.5 billion; now she's buying politicians. She's spending millions in Kentucky to buy Ed Gallrein, my primary opponent, a Congressional seat in Kentucky. Why? Because I won't vote to send your tax dollars overseas." When a user replied, "She's an American citizen. Stop lying," Massie shot back: "She's an Israeli citizen first. Even Trump says she probably loves Israel more than America."[438]

Set aside for a moment the inconvenient fact that Miriam grew up in Israel as a full Israeli citizen who served in the IDF and only became a dual citizen after marrying Sheldon Adelson in 1991. She is one of millions of people who hold American citizenship alongside another country's citizenship, who by definition maintain connections to more than one nation. But this controversy was never really about Miriam Adelson. It was an accusation against every American Jew who loves Israel.

In December 2025, Senator Bernie Moreno introduced the Exclusive Citizenship Act of 2025, a bill that would require American citizens to hold exclusive allegiance to the United States. No dual passports or backup plans allowed. One nation, one identity, one loyalty. As Moreno wrote: "Being an American citizen is an honor and a privilege—and if you want to be an American, it's all or nothing. It's time to end dual citizenship for good."[439]

Moreno's bill stalled and is unlikely to pass. But whatever Moreno intended, it sends a clear message to the hundreds of thousands of Jews who hold dual American-Israeli citizenship: your loyalty to the United States is in question.

This accusation has a long pedigree in America. In March 1950, less than two years after the founding of the State of Israel, Dorothy Thompson directed the same argument at American Jews: "The American of Jewish religion has always been, and as long as this nation holds to its basic and Constitutional principles will always be, accepted as a full and equal citizen. But sooner or later the Jewish nationalist, which today means the Israeli nationalist, will have to choose allegiances. 'One cannot,' says an old Jewish proverb, 'sit on one chair at two weddings.' There is no room in American nationality for two citizenships or two nationalities. To say it extremely brutally: no one can be a member of the American nation and of the Jewish nation—in Palestine or out of it—any more than he can be a member of the American nation and the British or German nation."[440]

For decades, the accusation periodically bubbled up from under the surface of American life. In 1986, the leftist novelist Gore Vidal branded Norman Podhoretz and Midge Decter members of an "Israeli Fifth Column" in America while describing Israel as "a predatory people... busy stealing other people's land in the name of an alien theocracy."[441]

The accusation gained academic respectability in 2007 when political scientists John Mearsheimer of the University of Chicago and Stephen Walt of Harvard published *The Israel Lobby and U.S. Foreign Policy*. Their central argument was that a "loose coalition of individuals and organizations" actively works to "shape U.S. foreign policy in a pro-Israel direction" and that this influence "skews US foreign policy in Israel's favor, often at the expense of regional stability in the Middle East."

The real culprits were neoconservatives—most of them Jewish, of course—who manipulated America into the Iraq War to serve Israeli interests. As evidence of this insidious influence, Mearsheimer and Walt cited counterpunch.com, a far-left website, which explicitly invoked "Jewish disloyalty" and condemned "the double allegiance of those myriad officials at high and middle levels who cannot distinguish U.S. interests from Israeli interests."[442]

AIPAC alone, they claimed, gained a stranglehold over Congress and significant leverage over the executive branch, hijacking American foreign policy at the expense of America's own national interests. Jewish lobbying made the United States "willing to set aside its own security in order to advance the interests of another state."[443]

The accusation has been there all along, waiting. What's changed is that it's moved from the fringe to the mainstream. And now it's coming from both left and right simultaneously.

The new woke left revived the dual loyalty charge in 2019 when Rep. Ilhan Omar implied that American Jews and pro-Israel groups put Israel first: "I want to talk about the political influence in this country that says it is O.K. for people to push for allegiance to a foreign country." This came after she tweeted that AIPAC simply buys political support—"It's all about the Benjamins baby." Rep. Rashida Tlaib, another leader of the pro-Hamas faction in Congress, attacked supporters of anti-BDS legislation, saying they "forgot what country they represent."[444]

Both faced bipartisan backlash. The House condemned Omar's remarks, rejecting "the pernicious myth of dual loyalty and foreign allegiance, especially in the context of support for the United States-Israel alliance"—language that recognized what Omar was really saying: that Jews cannot be fully patriotic Americans.[445]

How quaint that era seems now, when more than a handful of politicians were still willing to stand up for American Jews.

It turns out that Omar and Tlaib were not outliers, but simply ahead of their time—antisemitic pioneers who expanded the Overton window of acceptable discourse and opened the floodgates of antisemitism on the American Left.

At Tufts University in November 2020, a Jewish student government leader named Max Price was grilled for over an hour by fellow students about whether his Jewish and Zionist identities compromised his ability to serve on the student judiciary. Was being co-president of Tufts Friends of Israel enough to disqualify him? As Price put it: "The undercurrent of nearly every question was whether my Zionist beliefs, which are a central expression of my Jewish identity, disqualified me from serving on student government."[446]

Jewish students across America have faced similar treatment—and far worse, especially after October 7. At many schools, any Jew willing to publicly support Israel is distrusted and effectively expelled from progressive spaces.

There is a bitter irony here. Progressive Jews built the American left. They built the labor movement. They wrote the New Deal. As Batya Ungar-Sargon said: "The thing that makes this so appalling is that Jews built the left in this country. We built the labor movement. We wrote the New Deal. 70% of the lawyers who worked on civil rights cases were Jews! We've been at the forefront of every liberal and leftist issue in this country! The absolute chutzpah of saying 'you're not welcome here'!"[447] Yet that's exactly what the American Left has said to progressive Jews: "You're not one of us—and you're not welcome here."

During the presidential campaign of 2024, Pennsylvania Governor Josh Shapiro was a leading candidate to be chosen as Kamala Harris' running mate. Shapiro is a moderate Democrat, a two-term governor of a critical swing state, and Jewish. During the vetting process, former White House counsel Dana Remus asked him: "Have you at any time been a double agent for Israel?"[448] Shapiro couldn't believe it. This wasn't some fringe congressman or college activist. This was the Vice President of the United States vetting a Jewish U.S. governor for her ticket, and her team wasn't sure that he could be trusted to serve his own country.

While the Left used the dual loyalty charge as a convenient way to discredit pro-Israel voices, Israel-haters on the right made this argument their cudgel of choice against outspoken Jews.

Though President Trump is no isolationist and is arguably the greatest friend of Israel to ever occupy the White House, his America First movement always included "America Only" voices. After Trump's return to the presidency, and particularly after the assassination of Charlie Kirk, the isolationists made their move to co-opt the movement and brand conservative pro-Israel advocates as disloyal to the United States.

On the night of June 12, 2025, Israeli forces carried out precise and lethal strikes against Iranian nuclear and military sites, as well as senior military leaders, igniting a twelve-day war that both humiliated Iran and stunned the world. Iran retaliated with barrages of ballistic missiles aimed at hospitals and civilian population centers across Israel, killing 28 people and wounding thousands. After witnessing Israel's early success, President Trump decided to join the campaign, striking three key Iranian nuclear facilities with bunker-buster bombs and Tomahawk cruise missiles, shortly before a ceasefire was declared.

While most Republicans supported Israel and military action against Iran, a group of popular right-wing influencers framed U.S. intervention as a betrayal of "America First" and alleged that Trump's decision to bomb Iran was proof of Israeli and Jewish control of American foreign policy.

On the first day of the war—well before President Trump joined the attack on Iran—Candace Owens tweeted: "Our foreign policy is dictated by Israel. Trump will continue to do as he is told by Netanyahu. If you want to know what America will do, spare yourself the fake White House press briefings and start listening to Bibi. We are a colony of Israel. Your politicians are bought and paid for."[449]

From there, it was inevitable that American Jews would be blamed for driving the US into war against Iran to promote Israeli interests. Dr. Simon Goddek, a self-described "Hardcore Libertarian," wrote: "It's especially Jewish Americans pushing hardest to drag the U.S. into a full-blown war with Iran—while being, demographically, the least likely to ever send their own kids to fight it."[450]

Podcaster Darryl Cooper—whom Tucker Carlson has praised as "the best and most honest popular historian in the United States,"[451] and who notoriously blames Winston Churchill for the outbreak of World War II—joined the pile-on. "Now that even the long-time doubters can see that overseas Israelis run U.S. foreign policy, the next pill to swallow is realizing it's no coincidence that nearly every war we've fought this century—Afghanistan only partially excepted—has been against Israel's primary rivals."[452]

At the center of the effort to brand pro-Israel American Jews as disloyal was, of course, Tucker Carlson. In a combative interview with Senator Ted Cruz, Carlson claimed that AIPAC should be registered as a "foreign lobby" under the Foreign Agents Registration Act.[453] A few weeks later, at a Turning Point USA event, Carlson even cited the New Testament to make his case: "I quote the New Testament, but I also refer to common sense when I say that no man can serve two masters. It's not possible. I only have one wife for that reason. You say to your wife, 'I'm going to take another wife, but I'm going to love you just as much. Nothing's going to change.' My wife's going to look at me like, 'No, it's one wife. One wife.' Because you can only really pledge your loyalty to one person or one country. That's a fact."[454]

The charges only grew louder once the joint US-Israel war against Iran began at the end of February 2026. On her SiriusXM show, Megyn

Kelly said: "I don't think those four service members died for the United States. I think they died for Iran or for Israel... This feels very much to me like it is clearly Israel's war. Mark Levin wanted it. It's his war. Ben Shapiro, Lindsey Graham, Miriam Adelson. That's obvious. They're the ones who have been pushing us into this."[455] Lindsey Graham aside, every name Kelly accused is Jewish. The message was unmistakable: American Jews dragged the United States into someone else's war, and American soldiers paid with their lives.

The message from both left and right finally converged: American Jews who care about Israel are suspect. Their loyalties are divided. They cannot be fully American and they don't really belong. Caught between antisemites of the left and antisemites of the right, American Jewry finds itself with nowhere safe to land—what one writer described as being "like a shriveled brown leaf fluttering aimlessly in the wind in the midst of a cold and bitter winter."[456]

American Jews are not the only ethnic group with ties to other countries. Dominican Americans maintain close ties to the Dominican Republic. Filipino Americans support the Philippines. This is considered normal, healthy, even admirable—a sign of cultural richness and strong community bonds. But when Jews express attachment to Israel, suddenly they face interrogation about their true allegiances.

As Gil Troy wrote, "AIPAC became 'the Jewish lobby,' overstuffing into one putrid three-word framing many traditional antisemitic tropes about Jewish power, chicanery and disloyalty. Yet when African Americans fought South Africa's apartheid regime with particular passion, suggesting their deep attachment to the land in southern Africa, I never heard one accused of 'dual loyalty.'... I never heard that slur launched against proud Irish Americans like John F. Kennedy and Ronald Reagan, or proud Italian Americans like Frank Sinatra or Lady Gaga."[457]

American and Israeli interests sometimes diverge—just as American interests diverge from those of Britain, France, or any other ally. When they do, American Jews may find themselves in an uncomfortable position. But when Irish-Americans lobby for Ireland, or when Greek-Americans push policy toward Athens, nobody accuses them of dual loyalty. Israel is a democracy that shares America's core values. Yet American Jews face scrutiny that no other ethnic group endures.

The obsession with Jewish support for Israel—on both the left and the right—is antisemitism, plain and simple.

But are American Jews truly the same as Greek-Americans or Irish-Americans? Or as Gabriel Schoenfeld put it, "Does this pull differ in kind from that which Armenian-Americans feel toward Armenia, or Filipino-Americans toward the Philippines? Does it differ from the pull... that Catholics feel toward the Vatican or Muslims toward Mecca and Medina and their co-religionists abroad?"[458] For Schonfeld, the answer was no. But the reality is less comfortable than that.

Baron Edmond de Rothschild was, by any external measure, a loyal Frenchman. He lived in France, moved in its elite circles, and died in Paris in 1934, where he was buried in French soil. Charles de Gaulle considered him a personal friend and regularly defended his loyalty against skeptics.

And yet Rothschild poured enormous resources into Jewish settlement in the land of Israel—Zichron Yaakov, Rishon LeZion, Hadera, the Carmel Winery, and the early infrastructure that made modern

Israel possible. He never left France. He remained a French aristocrat to the end.

In 1954, six years after Israel's founding, the Rothschild family decided to reinter Baron Edmond and his wife Adelaide's remains in the land he had spent his fortune building. When de Gaulle learned of it, he summoned the Baron's son, Alain, and confronted him directly. Rabbi Joseph B. Soloveitchik, who heard the story from Alain de Rothschild himself, recounted what de Gaulle said:

"A good Frenchman is one who was brought up in French schools, who fights for France in times of danger, who contributes to France and its culture — and who is buried in French soil. I knew your father well and always defended him against those who questioned his loyalty. But now I see they were right. I could forbid the reburial. All I have to do is call the magistrate in Paris. But I do not wish to start a fight with the Jews of France."[459]

De Gaulle was not accusing the Rothschilds of dual loyalty. The Baron had served France faithfully his entire life—and de Gaulle knew it. He was troubled by something else entirely, something he couldn't quite name.

For generations, we Jews have played a dangerous game. To protect our fellow Jews living in Western countries, we told a lie: "We're just a religion. Judaism is like Catholicism or Protestantism—a set of beliefs and practices, nothing more."

It was an understandable survival strategy. If Jews are merely a religious minority, then supporting Israel is no different from American Catholics supporting the Vatican—a matter of religious sentiment, not national loyalty. The dual loyalty accusation loses its force.

Except it hasn't worked. The lie backfired in two catastrophic ways.

First, we fooled ourselves. Millions of American Jews, told for generations that Judaism is merely a religion, internalized the message. This is the "My Judaism" disaster—Jews who believe that being Jewish is a personal spiritual choice, something they can customize, edit, or quietly abandon. They no longer understand that being Jewish means membership in a nation with a collective destiny, a people bound together across time and geography by something far deeper than shared beliefs. The lie we told the world to protect Jews living in exile ended up hollowing them out from within.

Second, the lie no longer protects anyone. The antisemites don't care whether you call yourself a Zionist or an anti-Zionist, whether you support Israel or condemn it. People like Tucker Carlson and Cenk Uygur[460] may claim to distinguish between Israelis and Jews, between Zionists and the rest—but that is pure gaslighting. They hate all Jews: the AIPAC donor and the Jewish Voice for Peace activist alike. To them, we are all complicit. We are all guilty. The "we're just a religion" excuse isn't saving anyone, because it was never Israel that antisemites objected to. It was always the Jews.

There is a third problem we rarely acknowledge, and it is perhaps the most underappreciated: this lack of clarity is deeply unfair to non-Jews.

The nations of the world need to understand why Jewish nationhood matters—not just for Jews, but for them. The Jewish people are called to be "a kingdom of priests and a holy nation" (Exodus 19:6), a priestly nation charged with teaching humanity how to live ethically according to God's will. That mission cannot be fulfilled in exile. It requires the Jewish people to live as a nation in our land, building the society the prophets envisioned. Only then can we become what we were always meant to be: a light to the nations.

Israel is doing that work. But it becomes infinitely harder when forty percent of the world's Jews deny they are part of a nation at all. Step by step, Israel is building what the prophets envisioned, but imagine how much brighter and clearer that light would shine if millions of American Jews stopped pretending they are only a religion and joined the effort.

It is time to stop lying—to ourselves, to America, and to the world. We are not "Jewish-Americans." We are Jews, without hyphenation, members of God's chosen nation. We can be loyal American citizens. We can contribute to American greatness, pray for its welfare, and fight for its security. But we cannot pretend that our deepest identity, our ultimate allegiance, belongs to America. It doesn't. It belongs to the Jewish people.

The world needs to hear this. Not as a confession extracted under pressure, but as a clear declaration of who we are and why it matters. The Jewish people are not a threat to America's future. We are essential to it. Our prophetic return to Israel, our rebuilding of a holy nation, our fulfillment of the prophetic vision—this is not just our redemption. It is the key to redemption for America, and the entire world.

As Zechariah prophesied: "Ten men from every language of the nations shall grasp the garment of a Jewish man, saying, 'Let us go with you, for we have heard that God is with you'" (Zechariah 8:23).

But first, we have to be honest about who that Jewish man is.

The prophets were clear: Jews living among the nations have real obligations to their host countries. In guiding the Jews exiled to Babylon, Jeremiah said, "Seek the peace of the city to which I have exiled you, and pray to God for its sake" (Jeremiah 29:7). In exile, Jews are biblically obligated to actively seek the welfare of their host countries and pray for their success.

How far does this obligation go? "You shall not hold an Egyptian in contempt, for you were resident in his land" (Deuteronomy 23:8). The Egyptians enslaved the people of Israel, worked us to death building Pharaoh's cities, and drowned our baby boys in the Nile. Yet we are forbidden to hold them in contempt because we once lived in their land. If even Egypt—a nation that oppressed our forefathers for hundreds of years—must be honored for "hosting" the people of Israel, how much more so the nations that have welcomed Jews and allowed them to prosper?

The Sages teach: "One should pray for the welfare of the government, for if not for fear of it, each man would swallow his fellow alive."[461] Without government, society descends into chaos and violence, and Jews are usually the first ones to suffer. When Black Lives Matter mobs rioted in American streets, their first targets were synagogues and kosher restaurants.[462] Jews have every reason to support stable governance and public order, and any honest observer must admit that Jews are the least likely group of American citizens to participate in riots and violence.

The Talmud formalized these obligations into Jewish law through the principle of *dina d'malchuta dina*—"the law of the land is the law."[463] This is not a minor technical rule. It means that Jews are religiously obligated to obey the civil laws of their host countries, treating such laws as binding in monetary and civil matters. It means that tax evasion or financial fraud is not only illegal; it is a violation of Jewish law. A Jew is obligated to be a model citizen.

Yet the phrase itself is revealing: *dina d'malchuta dina*—the *law* of the land is the law. Law governs actions, obligations, and public conduct. But law does not govern the heart. The sages who formulated this principle understood that Jews living in exile must strike a delicate balance. On the one hand, they must follow the law and be dedicated citizens who contribute to the welfare of their host nation. But on the other hand, Jews must always remember that exile is not home.[464]

Three times a day, Torah-believing American Jews pray to return to Jerusalem. And at Jewish weddings—even lavish ones at New York City's Plaza Hotel—the groom breaks a glass to remember the destruction of the Temple and declares, "If I forget you, O Jerusalem, let my right hand forget its skill" (Psalm 137:5).

This is not disloyalty to America. A Jew can give his labor to America, his talents to America, even his life to America in defense of the nation. But his heart must remain bound to the Jewish people and to Jerusalem.

Jews are not simply another ethnic group with sentimental ties to their ancestral homeland. We are fundamentally different, and the difference goes back to the very beginning of our history.

Abraham was called *Ha'Ivri*—"the Hebrew" (Genesis 14:13), a title that carries multiple meanings. On the most literal level, it means that Abraham came from the other side (*eiver*) of the Euphrates River. It also identified him as a descendant of Eber, marking him as different from the Canaanites among whom he lived. But it also means something deeper: "The entire world was on one side, and he was willing to be on the other side (*eiver*)."[465]

This was Abraham's destiny, and the destiny of his descendants. Jews stand on one side of the river, the nations of the world stand on the other. The division is not only geographic; it is existential.

The name resurfaces throughout Genesis, always marking this separateness. When Joseph refused Potiphar's wife's advances, she cried out to her household in outrage: "Look, he brought us a *Hebrew man* to mock us. He came to lie with me but I called out loudly" (Genesis 39:14). Like his great-grandfather Abraham, Joseph came from "the other side of the river"—he didn't belong. Later, Joseph told Pharaoh's cupbearer that he was stolen "from the land of the Hebrews," deliberately distinguishing himself from the Canaanites who then lived in Israel (Genesis 40:15), making clear he belonged to a different people entirely.[466]

Abraham articulated the tension when he approached the people of Heth to buy a burial plot for Sarah. "I am a stranger and a resident with you," he told them (Genesis 23:4). The phrase captures the paradox of Jewish existence. Abraham was a resident—living among the people of Heth, contributing to their society, bound by their laws. But he was also a stranger—never fully belonging, never fully absorbed, always separate.

This is not an accident of history or a product of antisemitism. It is fundamental to what it means to be a Jew. A Jew in America must be a loyal citizen, a patriot, a contributor to American greatness. But if he is faithful to his identity as a Jew, he must remain, fundamentally, a stranger. Not out of hostility or lack of gratitude to America, but because his deepest identity is tied to the destiny of the people of Israel.

This is a sensitive point that is easily misunderstood. American Jews genuinely love the United States, arguably more than any group of exile Jews has ever loved their host nation. As Jonathan Sarna notes, "No diaspora community ever identified more strongly with its host nation than American Jews with the United States."[467] Jewish separateness is not an insult to or a rejection of America. And yet the dual loyalty accusation, though it badly misunderstands the nature of Jewish loyalty, still touches a nerve—because the accusers sense something they cannot quite articulate: that a Jew's deepest identity belongs to the Jewish people, not to his host country. That is not disloyalty to America. It is fidelity to what it means to be a Jew.

Which brings us back to Trump's challenge to Miriam Adelson.

Miriam is Trump's largest donor and a close friend, someone he trusts implicitly. Trump—who famously judges everyone he meets based on their loyalty to him—would not maintain such a close relationship with someone whose loyalty to America he genuinely doubted. Miriam has contributed enormously to her adopted country, founding addiction and medical research centers and establishing a foundation to support efforts to prevent and treat life-threatening illnesses.[468] Her support for Israel and her devotion to America coexist without contradiction.

But Trump's question wasn't about loyalty. He wasn't asking whether Miriam obeys American law, pays American taxes, or supports American interests. He was asking something else entirely. He was asking about *identity*. "Who do you love more?" Which nation's story is written in your bones? Where does your deepest sense of self reside? Deep down, which nation is your identity bound up with?

And to that question, there could only be one answer: Israel.

This was the same challenge David Ben-Gurion brought to American Jewish leaders in the 1950s and 1960s. The American Jewish establishment insisted they were "Americans of the Jewish faith," loyal citizens who practiced the religion of "Judaism," no different from American Catholics or American Protestants. A blunt Israeli with no patience for polite fictions, Ben-Gurion saw through the charade and told them they were wrong.

While negotiating reparations with Germany after the Holocaust, Ben-Gurion made clear that the State of Israel represented not only Israeli citizens but the entire Jewish people, wherever they might live around the world. As he wrote in 1960: "The Jewish state, which is called Israel, is heir to the six million. For these millions regarded themselves as the sons of the Jewish people, and only as the sons of the Jewish people. If they had lived, the great majority of them would have come to Israel."[469]

Ben-Gurion was right. In interwar Poland, Jews operated as a separate political nation within the Polish state. They had their own political parties—the General Zionists, the socialist Bund, the Mizrachi Religious Zionists, Agudas Yisroel, and more—all represented in the Polish parliament. In the 1938 municipal elections in Warsaw, the last before the war, Jewish parties won twenty seats on the city council, competing against each other for the Jewish vote. Jews ran their own schools in Yiddish and Hebrew, published over a hundred Jewish newspapers and periodicals, and organized their entire communal life separately from Polish society. By 1931, eighty-seven percent of Polish Jews spoke Yiddish or Hebrew as their native language. They lived in Poland, but they saw themselves as Jews who lived in Poland, not as Poles.[470]

The six million murdered in the Holocaust carried that identity to their deaths. They did not die as Poles or Lithuanians. They died as Jews.

If this was true of European Jews before the Holocaust, what about American Jews today? Can an American Jew claim to be a heart and soul American who simply chooses to practice Judaism—a "Jewish-American"? Or is he, at his core, a part of the Jewish people who is also a loyal American citizen—an "American-Jew"? The distinction is not semantic. It reveals whether Jews see themselves primarily as members of a Jewish nation who live in America, or as Americans whose religion happens to be Judaism.

The answer, for anyone willing to think it through honestly, has always been clear. Ambassador Yechiel Leiter writes: "There is no possibility of dividing between 'religion' and 'nationality.' A Jew is an Israelite even if he doesn't recognize it or doesn't want to be. And an Israelite is a Jew even if he doesn't acknowledge it or doesn't want to be... In whatever country a Jew finds himself, he will indeed need to respect that country and its government and everything involved in the principle of 'the law of the kingdom is the law.' But this doesn't mean he should, God forbid, view himself as an 'American' or a 'Frenchman,' because in doing so he would be denying not only his Israelite nationality but also his Israelite religion."[471]

In early 20th-century Hungary, Hungarian Jewish leaders—both Reform and Orthodox—declared that Jews were "Hungarians of the Mosaic faith," no different from Catholics or Protestants. Rabbi Moshe Shmuel Glazner, the chief rabbi of Klausenburg, would have none of it: "The proclamation that it is possible to belong to the Jewish faith while also belonging to the Hungarian, German, or Slavic nationalities is absolute heresy." He warned that "if we relinquished our nationality, we should cease to be a religious community."[472] The two cannot be separated. Two decades later, the Nazis would demonstrate exactly that. Hungarian Jews who had spent generations insisting they were heart and soul Hungarians died in Auschwitz as Jews.

The same is true of American Jews, whose deepest identity must remain bound to the Jewish people and to Jerusalem. This is not disloyalty. This is simply what it means to be a member of God's chosen nation.

What Jews refuse to see is clear as day to our enemies. Nick Fuentes is, as Ben Shapiro has rightly called him, a "Hitler apologist, Nazi-loving, anti-American piece of refuse."[473] He called Hitler "really fucking cool" and advocated for a death sentence for "perfidious Jews." He is a cancer on society, corrupting and radicalizing young American men. And yet this particular cancer has done a better job than most rabbis at explaining who the Jewish people are.

In a softball interview with Tucker Carlson, Fuentes said: "Israel is unlike every other country... Because the Jewish people are in a diaspora all over the world, they're unassimilable, and they have resisted assimilation for thousands of years... There's a deep religious affection for the State [of Israel]. It's bound up in their identity, the story of the exodus from Egypt, the promise of the land... If you are a Jewish person in America, [you know that] this is not really my home; my ancestral home is in Israel... This religious blood-and-soil conviction, this history of being in the diaspora—stateless, wandering, persecuted... They hate the Romans because the Romans destroyed the Temple. That's why Eric Weinstein goes to the Arch of Titus and gives it the finger and takes a picture. We don't think like that as Americans and white people. We don't think about the Roman Empire 2,000 years ago."[474]

Fuentes is right. A Jew who is faithful to his identity, a Jew who has not abandoned his national heritage and history for the comforts of assimilation, can never forget that he belongs in the land of Israel nor forgive the Roman Empire for destroying the Temple in Jerusalem.

If even a Nazi like Nick Fuentes can see this clearly, how long before the rest of America sees it too?

THE ESTHER MOMENT

"Do not imagine that you will escape... if you remain silent at this time... who knows whether you have attained royalty for such a time as this?" (Esther 4:13-14)

Israel365

33

Toasting Self-Destruction (With Kosher Catering)

We have been here before.

Twenty-five centuries ago, in the Persian Empire, a generation of Jews convinced themselves that exile was home. The Book of Esther records what happened next—and the parallels to American Jewry today are too precise and uncomfortable to ignore.

Nobody forced the Jews of Persia to remain in exile. They were not captives yearning for Zion, forbidden from returning home. Fifty years before the events of the Book of Esther, King Cyrus issued his famous decree allowing Jews to return to the land of Israel. The rebuilt Second Temple already stood in Jerusalem. Yet the vast majority of Jews living in the Persian Empire considered the opportunity to help rebuild Jewish life in their ancestral homeland and said, "No, thank you."[475]

The Sages identify three groups among Persian Jewry during this era.[476] First, the national group: the ancient Zionists who made *Aliyah* to Israel with Cyrus's proclamation, along with others who remained in Persia but financially supported those who made the arduous journey to the Holy Land. Second, the religious group: pious Jews who chose to stay in Persia until God sent an unmistakable divine call summoning them back to Israel. These Jews did not acknowledge the pagan King Cyrus's decree as the word or work of God. And third, by far the largest group, the one that dwarfed the other two: assimilated Jews scattered throughout the empire who no longer remembered the land of Israel and barely remembered the God of Israel.

The assimilated group dominates the landscape of the Book of Esther. These were Jews living ordinary Persian lives, with no connection to Jerusalem or its rebuilding. Their families had lived in Persia for over a century. By now, they were simply Persians of Jewish descent. The religious Jews kept kosher and observed Shabbat, but they too made their peace with exile, waiting for a divine signal to return while feeling no urgency about the land or the people rebuilding it. Religious or secular, the vast majority of Persian Jews were fully integrated into the empire. And nowhere was this more visible than at the feast of King Ahasuerus.

The Sages ask: "Why was Israel in that generation deserving of destruction? Because they enjoyed the feast of that wicked man."[477]

The feast of Ahasuerus lasted seven days, and it included "all the people present in Shushan the capital, from the greatest to the smallest" (Esther 1:5). The Jews were there—both the assimilated and the religious—celebrating together with all the other subjects of Ahasuerus. "And the drinking was according to the law, with no one coercing, for so had the king ordained upon every steward of his house, to do according to every man's wish" (Esther 1:8). The Persians were so tolerant that even kosher food was made available at the feast, so that no one would have to violate Jewish law to attend.[478]

Why was their participation in this feast so terrible? Why were they "deserving of destruction" simply for participating in a royal feast?

Because the feast was not just a party. By attending, the Jews of Shushan were making a public declaration: We are Persians now.

The Sages explain that Ahasuerus' feast was a celebration of Israel's permanent subjugation. Even with a Temple standing in Jerusalem, the Jews remained servants of Persia — and Ahasuerus intended to keep it that way. His feast was a declaration: the rebuilt Temple was a gift from their Persian masters, not a restoration of nationhood. True redemption — Jewish sovereignty, a Davidic king, a people ruling their own land — that dream was dead and buried forever.[479] By attending and enjoying this feast, the Jews were endorsing that message. They were celebrating their own national destruction.[480]

Shushan was a cosmopolitan capital where representatives of 127 provinces lived side by side, and where wealth and advancement mattered more than roots or heritage. The Jews, assimilated and religious alike, were swept into that world, their identity dissolved into "all the people present in Shushan," indistinguishable from their fellow citizens.

"Enjoying the feast of that wicked man" is the Sages' verdict on an entire generation. Some Jews abandoned their identity entirely—they were born in Persia, raised in Persia, and Persian in everything but blood. But even the religious Jews who kept the commandments were content to be Jewish Persians—a comfortable religious community in exile, with no burning desire to return home. They were honored to be Persians.

We usually imagine Mordecai and Esther, the heroes of the story, as righteous Jews who rejected their generation's assimilation from the start. Many among the Sages portray Mordecai as a rabbi, a member of the Great Assembly,[481] one of Israel's great spiritual leaders. Esther frequently appears in rabbinic literature as a deeply religious woman who secretly maintained Torah observance in Ahasuerus's palace.

But other commentators read the text differently. In their reading, Mordecai and Esther were not exceptions to their generation's assimilation. They were its most successful examples.[482]

Their names tell the story. "Mordecai" derives from Marduk, the chief Babylonian god. "Esther"—today considered a quintessentially Jewish and biblical name—derives either from the Persian word for "star" or from Ishtar, the Babylonian fertility goddess.

The author of the Book of Esther intends for us to notice the contrast with their fathers' names. Mordecai's father was Yair and Esther's father was Abihail—both unmistakably Hebrew. Why would Jewish fathers give their children names honoring foreign gods? It is likely that Mordecai and Esther's parents, descendants of Jewish exiles from Jerusalem, established themselves in Persian society and hoped their children would become full-fledged Persians, unencumbered by distinctively Jewish names that might limit their prospects. Mordecai and Esther were names built for advancement in the Persian Empire.

But the Hebrew language has the last word. The Persian name *Esther* sounds like the Hebrew word *hester*—hiddenness. And what exactly is hidden? Her Jewish identity.

Esther also possessed another more traditional Jewish name, Hadassah. It seems she bore both names from birth, carrying a Hebrew name for private Jewish contexts and a Persian name for public life, a practice common among diaspora Jews then and now. But by the time she entered the king's palace, only one name appears. Hadassah has vanished. The woman who stands before Ahasuerus is Esther—and her Jewishness is hidden along with her name.

"Mordecai sat at the king's gate" (Esther 2:19)—not as a doorman, but as a senior official. As Rabbi Meir Wisser explains, Mordecai "was elevated to sit at the king's gate, on seats of judgment, like one of the ministers."[483] You do not reach that position unless you have been shaped by the elite culture of your surroundings, educated in Persian institutions and fluent in Persian politics. When Mordecai uncovered Bigtan and Teresh's plot to assassinate the king, his warnings were taken seriously and acted upon because he was a respected member of the empire's political class. His Jewish heritage seems to have had no bearing on his political views or his career advancement.

Superficially, Esther's rise to queen looks like a success story—a Jewish woman reaching the highest position in the Persian Empire. But what was this success, really? Esther won a beauty contest that was in fact a forced selection for the king's harem, and she got there by hiding who she was. "Esther did not reveal her people or her kindred" (Esther 2:10). Her selection as queen was the fulfillment of an immigrant family's dreams: complete acceptance in Persian society, purchased at the cost of her identity.

The Book of Esther never explains why Mordecai told Esther to conceal her Jewish identity. The simplest explanation reflects a basic experience shared by Jews throughout the generations in foreign lands: survival instinct. Mordecai, concerned for his adopted daughter's safety, urged her not to highlight her Jewishness but instead to present herself as native-born.

Rabbi Abraham ibn Ezra offers a more cynical reading: "Some say that Mordecai did not act properly when he commanded Esther not to reveal her people, for he feared that the king would not take her as a wife if he knew that she was from the [Jewish] exile."[484]

In other words, Esther concealed her identity not for safety but for advancement. She wanted to pass as Persian and belong fully to the kingdom, unencumbered by the embarrassing fact of her Jewish origins. In this, Esther personified the Jews of her generation—Jews who downplayed their identity, who wanted only to be considered good Persian citizens, whose Jewish heritage was at best a private matter and at worst an obstacle to overcome.

This was the price of assimilation. Mordecai and Esther achieved what their fathers hoped for them: success, influence, acceptance. But acceptance came at the cost of their identity. They abandoned their Hebrew names and integrated seamlessly into Persian life, while Esther concealed her identity so completely that nobody knew who she really was. More importantly, they themselves seem to have forgotten who they were.

34

The Day the Music Stopped

For generations, the Jews of Persia had every reason to feel secure. Persia brought law and order to the ancient world, built royal roads, and kept the peace across 127 provinces. The empire was cosmopolitan and tolerant, welcoming to anyone who proved their loyalty to the crown. Jews rose to positions of influence, found favor with sympathetic monarchs, and placed a daughter of Israel on the throne as queen. The relationship seemed stable, even permanent.[485]

Then came Haman.

Haman didn't need a reason to hate Jews. He was an Amalekite,[486] a people without law or morality who emerged from the desert to attack the weak and destroy civilization. Haman needed no reason to want Jews dead. But Ahasuerus needed legal justification, so Haman gave him one.

"There is a certain people scattered and dispersed among the peoples in all the provinces of your kingdom, and their laws are different from every other people, and they do not keep the king's laws; it is not befitting the king to tolerate them" (Esther 3:8).

Haman was not attacking a religion. He was attacking a people. He was accusing the Jews of disloyalty, claiming their ultimate allegiance lay not with the Persian king and empire but with their own nation. The Jews maintained their own distinct legal system, their own communal structure, their own way of life. Despite living scattered across the empire for generations, they remained identifiably Jewish, a separate nation within the empire rather than loyal Persians who happened to practice a minority religion.

Ironically, most Persian Jews were working overtime to prove Haman wrong, abandoning their Hebrew names, concealing their identities and attending the king's feast. Esther herself sat on the throne, and nobody knew she was Jewish. Yet Haman saw through their charade. Despite their desperate efforts to pass themselves off as Persians through and through, the Jews would never be like everyone else.

Haman was not the first enemy to target the Jews as a nation rather than as a faith. The Sages point to the gentile prophet Bilaam as his ancient predecessor, whose very name signalled this same obsession. "Bilaam" derives from "*belo am*"—one who was "part of no nation." His name can also be translated as "one who swallowed up a nation"—a reading that captures his unique hatred for the Israelites as a people.[487] Bilaam had no quarrel with Jewish prayer or belief; he himself was a prophet who believed in the God of Israel. But he hated the nation of Israel as a collective people.

Standing on the hilltop overlooking the Israelite camp, God forced from Bilaam's lips the very blessing he had come to deliver as a curse: "A people that dwells alone, not reckoned among the nations" (Numbers 23:9). The separateness he despised, he could not touch. Eight hundred years later, Haman would try to finish what Bilaam could not.

The terrifying innovation in the story of Esther was not Haman's hatred. There have always been Jew-haters. What was new was his alliance with Ahasuerus. Without the crown behind him, Haman is a fringe lunatic. But Ahasuerus gave Haman his signet ring, and suddenly the Persian Empire belonged to him. Kingdoms are normally constrained by law and morality. But when the guardians of civilization hand their power to lawless hatred, the state becomes a tool for genocide. And just like that, the "tolerant" empire went along with Haman's genocidal plan.

The comfortable life Jews built in exile collapsed overnight. Their safety had always been an illusion, always dependent on who had the king's favor. One antisemite gained Ahasuerus's ear, and overnight, the enlightened Persian Empire became a vehicle for genocide. "Accordingly, written instructions were dispatched by couriers to all the king's provinces to destroy, massacre, and exterminate all the Jews, young and old, children and women, on a single day" (Esther 3:13).

But before the decree, before Haman convinced Ahasuerus to annihilate the Jews, Mordecai woke up.

Haman's rise to power signaled a dangerous new era. Most Jews reacted by keeping their heads down, hoping the threat would pass. They bowed to Haman, demonstrated their obsequiousness, and tried to blend even more thoroughly into Persian society. But not Mordecai.

As a member of the Persian governing class who sat at the king's gate, Mordecai saw Haman up close and understood how dangerous this man was in ways ordinary Jews could not. This was not a political reshuffling—it was an existential threat to the entire Jewish people. Something in Mordecai snapped. He had spent his career as a loyal Persian courtier, navigating the empire's corridors of power, playing the game of assimilation with considerable skill. But now, as a vicious Jew hater rose to power before his eyes, he could no longer do it. And so he made a choice that seemed irrational, even suicidal: he refused to bow.

"All the king's servants who were at the king's gate would kneel and bow down to Haman, for so the king had commanded concerning him. But Mordecai would not kneel or bow down" (Esther 3:2). When asked why, he offered no justification beyond this: "For he had told them that he was a Jew" (Esther 3:4).

Why wouldn't Mordecai bow? The Torah contains no law that forbids bowing to a government official when necessary, particularly when refusing to do so places your life at risk. By refusing to bow to Haman, Mordecai endangered not only himself but all the Jews of Persia. By any normal standard, his defiance was madness.

Some explain that Mordecai refused to bow on religious grounds. According to this reading, Haman embroidered images of idols on his clothing, effectively demanding that Mordecai and the rest of the courtiers bow down to his false gods.[488] Since idol worship is one of the three cardinal sins for which a Jew must accept death rather than transgress, Mordecai had no choice.[489] Read this way, Mordecai's refusal to bow was an act of religious conscience.

Yet the plain meaning of the text points in a different direction. Persia was not a theocracy demanding uniform worship; it prided itself on indulgence and tolerance, on allowing its subjects "to do according to every man's wish" (Esther 1:8). Even the food and wine were kosher. In such an environment, it is hard to imagine that Ahaseuris would force the empire's highest officials to bow to Haman's personal god.

Why, then, did Mordecai refuse to bow?

Rabbi Yaakov Medan explains: "We do not find that the generation of Mordecai was steeped in idol worship, but we do find that it suffered from a deep loss of Jewish self-respect and a readiness to bow before every boastful foreign power. This was the generation that did not go up to their land at the time of Cyrus's proclamation to build the Temple, and knowingly gave up the chance to... strive for national independence in the land of Israel. It was this very generation that sat at the feast of Ahasuerus and acknowledged him as the 'king of the world.' When this same loss of dignity returned in the form of bowing to Haman, Mordecai decided to sacrifice his life and sanctify God's name, in order to stop the moral and national collapse of his generation."[490]

In other words: Mordecai refused to bow as an assertion of Jewish national pride.

Even before the decree, Haman was an open antisemite bent on degrading the Jewish people at every opportunity. He wanted Jews bowing before him, absorbing their humiliation in silence. Mordecai refused to give him that satisfaction. Publicly bowing to the greatest antisemite of the generation would tell every Jewish child in Persia that their people were weak, frightened, and too broken to defend their own dignity—that being Jewish was something to be ashamed of, not proud of.

National pride is not vanity; it is the life force of a people. It is what makes survival worth fighting for. Without it, what stops a Jew from simply looking at his oppressor, then looking at his own scattered, powerless people, and deciding that assimilation is the only rational choice?

The Sages offer a fascinating backstory to Mordecai's heroic stand. According to the *midrash*, Haman challenged Mordecai by pointing to precedent: "Your forefather bowed down to my forefather," referring to Jacob bowing before Esau in fear, afraid of his brother's rage over the stolen blessings. Mordecai responded: "Benjamin, my forefather, was [not yet born and was] in his mother's womb and did not bow down, and I am his descendant. Just as my forefather did not bow down, so I too will not bow down."[491]

The conflict between Mordecai and Haman was not about religion. It was the continuation of an ancient conflict between two nations—Jacob and Esau, Israel and Amalek.[492] God told Rebecca before the twins were born: "Two nations are in your womb, and two kingdoms will separate from your innards, and one kingdom will become mightier than the other kingdom, and the elder will serve the younger" (Genesis 25:23). Mordecai, the assimilated Persian official with the Babylonian god's name, made a long overdue correction to Jacob's fearful submission before Esau. He would never bend his knee before an antisemite again.

When Ahasuerus handed Haman his signet ring to sign the genocidal decree against the Jews, something broke open in Mordecai. The career he built, the influence he accumulated, the careful balancing act he maintained for decades—none of it mattered anymore. He tore off his official garments, wrapped himself in sackcloth and ashes, and stepped into the streets of Shushan, crying out as a Jew with a loud and bitter cry. What changed was not his private religious beliefs but his willingness to be counted publicly as a Jew, regardless of the cost.

The Queen's response reveals how distant she was from Mordecai and the Jewish people. "When Esther's maids and eunuchs came and informed her, the queen was greatly agitated. She sent clothing for Mordecai to wear, so that he might take off his sackcloth; but he refused" (Esther 4:4).

Esther was horrified. Mordecai's outburst endangered everything she worked so hard to accomplish. She spent years hiding who she was, carefully constructing the fiction that she was simply Persian—and now Mordecai was tearing it apart in a single afternoon, wailing in sackcloth through the streets of Shushan for all the empire to see. She sent him clothing—normal Persian clothing—hoping he would come to his senses, compose himself, and return to the palace like a proper courtier. He refused.

Mordecai told Esther's messenger about Haman's plot to slaughter world Jewry. Living in the ivory palace, completely cut off from the Jewish community, Esther knew nothing about the king's decree of annihilation. Mordecai sent her a copy of the decree and told her that she must go to the king and plead for her people's lives.

Terrified, Esther sent word back to Mordecai: anyone who entered the king's inner court uninvited faced a single punishment—death, unless the king chose to extend his golden scepter. Yet thirty days had passed without Ahasuerus calling for her. Their relationship had grown cold. Perhaps he no longer loved her. How could she possibly approach him uninvited, on behalf of the very people she spent years pretending not to belong to? Did Mordecai not remember what happened to the last queen who displeased him?

Mordecai was unmoved. He responded with a challenge that left Esther no room for equivocation or excuses: "Do not imagine to yourself that you will escape in the king's house from among all the Jews. For if you remain silent at this time, relief and rescue will arise for the Jews from elsewhere, and you and your father's house will perish; and who knows whether at a time like this you will attain the kingdom?" (Esther 4:13-14).

This is the most dramatic and most frequently cited moment in the Book of Esther. But too often, students of the Bible miss the deeper meaning of Mordecai's challenge. Mordecai was not only challenging Esther to dig deep and find the courage to risk her life to save the Jewish people from destruction. He was forcing her to answer the most important question of her life.

Who are you? Are you Persian or are you a Jew? Will you hide in the palace while your people are slaughtered? Will you save yourself by abandoning them? Perhaps Esther could escape the decree by keeping silent, by maintaining the fiction that she was just another Persian woman who happened to be queen. But could she live with herself afterward?

Mordechai was challenging Esther, but his question was also meant for every Jew in Persia. Most Jews of that generation identified as Persians first and Jews second, if they identified as Jews at all. They spent generations trying to blend in, to assimilate, to prove they were loyal Persian subjects. They attended Ahasuerus's feast. They adopted Persian names. They concealed their Jewish identity whenever it was advantageous to do so. They believed that if they just kept their heads down and acted Persian enough, they would be safe.

Like Esther, the Jews of Persia could save themselves by disbanding their communities, hiding their identities completely, and melting into Persian society without a trace. And so Mordecai's challenge to Esther was really a challenge to all of them: Will you abandon your people to save yourself? Or will you stand proudly with the Jewish nation, even if it costs you your life?

Mordecai knew Esther might retreat into the palace and deny her people. He knew she might convince herself that she could escape, that her position as queen exempted her from the fate of common Jews. And so he warned her: "Relief and deliverance will surely come [to the Jews] from another place, but you and your father's house will perish."

The salvation of the Jewish people did not depend on Esther alone. God would find another way to rescue His people. Mordecai was certain of that. But what would happen to Esther? Mordecai was not threatening her with physical death. He was warning her about something worse: she and her father's house would perish from the Jewish people. If Esther chose not to stand with her people at this defining moment, she might continue living comfortably in the king's palace. But she would be lost to the Jewish *nation*—absorbed into Persia, erased from Jewish history, and forgotten by her people. She would simply disappear.

Mordecai or Ahasuerus? The Jewish people or the Persian throne?

Esther was shaken. At that moment, she understood that her entire life was built on a lie. The dream of fitting in, of rising in Persian society—it was all a delusion. For the first time, she looked in the mirror and saw herself clearly: I am not like everyone else in this empire. I am a Jew. I am unique. My life is bound to something far greater than myself—to the people of Israel. Whether it leads to salvation or death, I share their fate.

She chose Mordecai. She chose the Jewish people.

35

Found and Lost Again

There are no Jews in the Book of Esther. Not until it's almost too late.

The story revolves around personalities—Ahasuerus, Vashti, Haman, Mordecai, and Esther. These are the heroes and villains. The Jewish people appear only as background, scattered and silent. Mordecai is described as "a Jewish man" (Esther 2:5), as an individual, not a representative of a community or country. Esther's story is hers alone. The Bible tells us nothing about other Jewish girls who may have been swept into the king's harem. "Esther did not reveal her people or her kindred" (Esther 2:10). She is an individual hiding her identity, not part of a collective.

Even Mordecai's refusal to bow to Haman begins as a personal decision. He is one man, acting alone, defying the most powerful man in the empire.

The first person in the Book of Esther to identify the Jews as a people is their archenemy Haman. "There is a certain people scattered and dispersed among the peoples in all the provinces of your kingdom" (Esther 3:8). He saw what the Jews themselves had forgotten: despite all their assimilation, despite abandoning Hebrew names and attending the king's feast and concealing their identities, they remained a nation. Haman's decree forced the Jews to remember what they had tried to forget.

When news of the decree spread, something shifted. "In every province, wherever the king's command and his decree reached, there was great mourning among the Jews, with fasting, weeping, and lamenting; sackcloth and ashes were spread for many" (Esther 4:3). Throughout the empire, the Jews mourned together. In their fear and grief, they rediscovered their peoplehood.

At first, they could only weep. But when Esther called on them—"Go, gather all the Jews who are present in Shushan, and fast for me" (Esther 4:16)—they responded immediately as a united nation with a collective mission.

After Haman fell and Mordecai rose to power, the Jews emerged as a visible force. "The Jews had light and gladness, joy and honor" (Esther 8:16). We are not told that "Mordecai had gladness" or that "Esther had joy." It is the Jews, as a collective nation, who celebrated. And then: "many from among the peoples of the land became Jews, for the fear of the Jews had fallen upon them" (Esther 8:17). The same people Haman described as "scattered and dispersed" became the most feared nation in the empire.

When the day came to execute Haman's decree, the Jews did not hide. "The very day when the enemies of the Jews hoped to gain power over them, the reverse occurred—the Jews gained power over their foes" (Esther 9:1). Unified and disciplined, they worked together to crush their enemies. "The Jews assembled in their cities... and smote all their enemies with the stroke of the sword... and did to their enemies as they wished" (Esther 9:2,5).

Individuals, even great ones like Mordecai and Esther, can only make a symbolic stand. "Mordecai would neither kneel nor prostrate himself" (Esther 3:2). Only a people can wage war. In rising up against their enemies in towns and cities throughout the empire, the Jews revealed themselves to be a cohesive nation even in exile. They were not just a religious group—"Jewish Persians"—with shared beliefs and practices. They were "Persian Jews"—a people who happened to live in Persia, not Persians who happened to be Jewish.

"The Jews ordained and took upon themselves and upon their seed and upon all those who join them... these days of Purim" (Esther 9:27-28). Mordecai and Esther largely acted alone throughout the crisis. But now they needed the Jewish people's consent. The establishment of Purim as a permanent festival required the nation to choose it for themselves. And they did. They chose to commemorate their deliverance not with individual thanksgiving, but by "sending portions one to another, and gifts to the poor" (9:22), emphasizing their collective responsibility for one another. No Jew would be left behind.[493]

The Sages saw the acceptance of Purim as something far more significant than establishing a holiday. It was an act of national rededication. At Mount Sinai, God declared the Jewish people "a kingdom of priests and a holy nation" (Exodus 19:6). The Sages explain that this covenant was imposed against their will. God held the mountain over their heads like a barrel and said, "Accept the Torah or be buried here."[494] The people of Israel had no choice but to agree. But in the time of Esther, scattered across the Persian Empire and on the brink of complete assimilation, the Jews chose freely what their ancestors accepted under compulsion. They reaffirmed their identity as God's nation; not because they had to, but because they wanted to.

This is the real story of the Book of Esther: a nation sleepwalking toward its own extinction woke up. God sent Haman to shake them from their stupor, and they responded by tearing off their Persian masks and embracing the truth they tried to escape: they were God's chosen nation.

No one understood this better than Martin Luther—and no one despised it more.

In his *Table Talk*, the father of the Protestant Reformation was uncharacteristically blunt even by his own standards: "The Book of Es ther... I toss into the Elbe. I am such an enemy to the Book of Esther that I wish it did not exist, for it Judaizes too much and has in it a great deal of heathenish naughtiness."[495]

For Luther, the Hebrew Bible is valuable only insofar as it points toward Jesus—prophecies, miracles, and foreshadowing of the coming Messiah. Every book must justify its place in the canon by serving that story. Esther offers nothing of the kind. It contains no obvious messianic hints, no divine intervention you could reframe as foreshadowing Jesus. Just Jews—Jews in danger, Jews fighting back, and Jews destroying their enemies.

That is the real problem. The Book of Esther doesn't end with spiritual transformation. It ends with Jews picking up swords and slaughtering their enemies. Luther viewed this as carnal nationalism—carnal meaning earthly, fleshly, of this world rather than the next. The book is about the wrong thing entirely: God's people celebrating their survival as a nation as if that were a worthy end in itself, rather than a stepping stone to some higher spiritual purpose.

John Calvin never preached a single sermon on Esther and left it out of his commentaries entirely. He was not alone; in the first seven hundred years of the early church, not one commentary was written on the Book of Esther.[496] For centuries, the church simply ignored Esther, as if the book didn't exist, while continuing to preach from Genesis, Psalms, and Isaiah—books that could be mined for prophecies or signs pointing toward Jesus and the New Testament. Esther couldn't be mined for anything. It was a story about the Jewish people, told entirely on the Jewish people's own terms.

But what Luther missed, and what most Jews miss as well, is that the Book of Esther does not end in Jewish triumph. Yes, the Jews emerge victorious, celebrating, establishing a new festival to commemorate their deliverance. But it also ends with these very same Jews remaining in the voluntary exile of Persia, subject to the whims of the heartless King Ahasuerus. The final chapter ends the book with a subtle jab: "And King Ahasuerus imposed a tribute on the land and on the isles of the sea" (Esther 10:1).

In the years that followed, most Persian Jews chose to remain in exile, never returning to the land of Israel. The national revival sparked by Haman's decree flickered and died. The final books of the Hebrew Bible focus almost exclusively on the Jews who returned to Israel. The Jews of Persia are deliberately left out of the story.

The Sages found a hint to this sadness in the very first verse of the book. The Book of Esther opens: "And it came to pass [*vayehi*] in the days of Ahasuerus" (Esther 1:1). "Rabbi Levi taught a tradition received from the Men of the Great Assembly: wherever the word *vayehi* appears in Scripture, it signals impending grief."[497]

This is a dark reading of the Book of Esther. The story ends in triumph: Haman was hanged, Mordecai rose to power, and the Jews celebrated. The rabbis who preserved this tradition were the same ones who established Purim as a permanent festival—a day of feasting, joy, and gladness. Why would they read grief into the very first word of a story they themselves declared worthy of eternal celebration?

The answer is Esther herself. She saved her people—but remained bound to Ahasuerus for the rest of her life, a Jewish queen locked in a Persian palace, her children raised as Persians and lost to her people forever. The woman who rescued an entire nation could not rescue herself.[498]

Esther's tragedy was not hers alone. She represents the Jews of Persia, who end the story exactly as they began it: subjects of Ahasuerus, dependent on the whims of a gentile king. After the great miracle of salvation and the downfall of Haman and his hordes of antisemites, they celebrated, feasted, and declared a holiday—and then remained in voluntary exile. The Sages read grief into the opening word because they knew how the story really ended: not with the hanging of Haman, but with a people who had been given every reason to go home, and chose not to.

36

The Price of Being American

Twenty-five centuries after Persia, American Jews have convinced themselves that exile is home.

The State of Israel has existed for nearly 80 years. Despite being wildly outnumbered by surrounding Arab nations, it repeatedly and miraculously defeats every enemy that rises against it. The prophetic return to Zion that Jews prayed for across two thousand years of exile suddenly, miraculously, became real. Yet since 1948, most American Jews watched from afar and said, "No, thank you."

Like the Jews of Persia, American Jews can be roughly divided into three groups. First, the Zionists—the idealists who left the comforts of America and made *Aliyah*, along with passionate Zionists who remain in America for one reason or another, but support Israel without ambiguity or apology. Second, the Orthodox—content to remain in America, studying Torah and observing the commandments, waiting for divine intervention to bring them home in some distant messianic future. And third, by far the largest group: assimilated Jews who embrace American identity so thoroughly that being Jewish is at most a private religious preference, and often not even that.

For generations, these assimilated Jews lived as if they had found a new Promised Land. This was not the Pale of Settlement in Russia nor the ghettos of Europe. This was America, the land of the free, where Jews could rise to the very top of society. Jewish senators, CEOs, Supreme Court justices. Invitations to the White House Hanukkah party. Jews achieved success beyond what their ancestors could have imagined. And for a long time, it felt permanent.

But that success came with a price. They sent their children to public schools and handed them over to American culture. A few hours of soulless Hebrew school a week—if that—was no match for what America offered in return. They watched as their children were swept up by progressive ideology and turned against Israel and their own heritage. They intermarried at rates approaching 70 percent. Hebrew and Yiddish names disappeared, and the great-grandchildren of Chaim and Sarah became Oliver and Brittney. Generation after generation attended America's feast and declared themselves delighted to be there.

At most, these Jews view being Jewish as a religious affiliation—and judging by how rarely they set foot in a synagogue, not one they feel particularly bound to. Like Esther and Mordecai before Haman's rise, their Jewish identity is an inconvenient fact of birth, something to be quietly set aside on the way to becoming fully American. They want, more than anything, to fit in.

Like the assimilated Jews of Persia, American Jews suffer from what we might call identity illness—a confusion about who they are that comes from living too long in comfortable exile. In their minds, they're Americans who happen to be Jewish, no different from Americans who happen to be Catholic or Methodist. The illness is so pervasive, the confusion so deep, the notion that they might owe allegiance to the Jewish people never crosses their minds.

American Jews have risen to prominence in every sector of society, including at the "king's gate"—the highest levels of American politics. Yet their success, as always, comes with a cost. Jewish politicians bend over backwards to prove they are not beholden to Israel. Senator Jon Ossoff, a self-described "proud Jew,"[499] voted to block critical U.S. weapons sales to Israel after Hamas slaughtered 1,200 Israelis on October 7, 2023. In the midst of the war that followed, Chuck Schumer—Senate Majority Leader and the highest-ranking Jewish official in the U.S. government—publicly demanded that Israel hold new elections and remove Prime Minister Netanyahu from office. "Prime Minister Netanyahu has lost his way... he has shown zero interest in doing the courageous and visionary work required to pave the way for peace... The Netanyahu coalition no longer fits the needs of Israel after October 7."[500] It was an unprecedented undermining of a US ally that was in the midst of a brutal existential war for survival, and a stunning betrayal of the Jewish state by its most powerful Jewish "friend" in Washington.

This is the current price of admission for Jews in the Democratic Party. And most Jewish politicians are willing to pay it.

Even among those American Jews who remain more connected, who donate to Israel, attend AIPAC conferences, and fly an Israeli flag outside their homes, a careful ambiguity holds things together. They avoid any clear answer to the question that hangs over everything: when it comes down to it, are you American first or Jewish first? That ambiguity allows them to belong to both worlds without ever confronting the tension between them.

But that comfortable arrangement is ending.

37

Who Holds the Ring?

Nothing in the Book of Esther suggests Ahasuerus hated Jews. Quite the opposite. Mordecai sat at the king's gate, a position of undefined but real power. Esther became queen without anyone demanding that she prove her Persian bloodline. This was a ruler presiding over a tolerant empire, one where Jews could rise as high as their abilities took them.

The danger wasn't Ahasuerus's hatred of Jews, but his trust in Haman. Haman wasn't just a powerful official; he was the king's right hand, elevated above every other prince in the empire, the man Ahasuerus relied on most. That relationship is what made Haman so lethal. A Jew-hater with no access to the king is just a bigot. A Jew-hater with the king's ear—and his signet ring—is an existential threat. Ahasuerus didn't need to hate Jews himself. He just needed to trust someone who did.

In modern America, this dynamic is playing out in real time—and it has been building for years.

It began breaking into the open under the Obama administration. Officials like U.N. Ambassador Samantha Power and Deputy National

Security Advisor Ben Rhodes decided that American foreign policy had favored Israel for too long. They wanted "daylight" between the two countries.[501] Obama clashed openly with Prime Minister Netanyahu, treated him with barely concealed contempt,[502] and rammed through the Iran nuclear deal over Israel's explicit objections.[503] The message to American Jews was subtle but unmistakable: your attachment to Israel is a problem.

For decades, Joe Biden's favorite line was "You don't have to be a Jew to be a Zionist." He said it at every opportunity—including at a White House Hanukkah celebration in December 2023, only two months after the slaughter of October 7.[504]

But Biden was only as much of a Zionist as his advisors allowed him to be. Inside the White House, National Security Adviser Jake Sullivan architected a policy of withholding critical weapons shipments to Israel in the middle of a war.[505] Secretary of Defense Lloyd Austin publicly justified halting bombs that Israel needed to fight Hamas, citing civilian casualties in Rafah.[506] Outside, the pressure came from every direction—Bernie Sanders demanding a full aid freeze,[507] Nancy Pelosi and dozens of House Democrats signing letters demanding that weapons be conditioned on Israeli concessions,[508] seventy former American officials and diplomats urging Biden to take a "more stringent approach" toward the Jewish state.[509] Biden didn't share their contempt for Israel—but he gave them the power to act on it anyway. The so-called Zionist in the Oval Office did exactly what Ahasuerus did. He handed Haman the ring.

Many assumed Trump's return would reverse all of this. In some ways, it did. But a new and unexpected danger has taken root inside the MAGA movement itself—and its name is Tucker Carlson.

Carlson is not a fringe figure. Since convincing Trump to put JD Vance on the ticket,[510] he has become arguably the most influential voice on the American right after Trump himself—and Vance has done nothing to create distance between them. Vance employs Carlson's son as his deputy press secretary and shows up on his program regularly, treating him like a trusted friend and mentor.[511] When Carlson praised Holocaust denier Darryl Cooper, Vance said nothin g.[512] When a student at the University of Mississippi asked Vance why America supports Israel given that "their religion doesn't agree with ours," Vance didn't push back.[513]

Carlson no longer bothers with coded language. He calls American Jewish Zionists Israel's "informal employees in the United States." [514] He hosted avowed neo-Nazi Nick Fuentes and nodded along as Fuentes declared that Jews run America and that Hitler was a great leader.[515] He fabricated a story about being detained at Ben Gurion Airport, spreading lies about Israel to millions of followers even after Israeli and American officials publicly debunked him.[516]

He still insists he is not an antisemite, which is precisely what makes him so dangerous. He lends extremist ideology a respectable face, moving it into mainstream conservative conversation while maintaining just enough deniability to feign innocence.

Carlson is Haman. Vance is something else—he has no record of personal antisemitism and there is no evidence he wishes Jews harm. But he is a leading contender for the Republican presidential nomination in 2028, he owes his position to Carlson, and he has refused to distance himself from Carlson's antisemitic associations. A man who may soon occupy the Oval Office has done nothing to push back against the ideology spreading through the movement that put him where he is.

He is Ahasuerus—a ruler who may harbor no hatred himself, but who sits atop a court he no longer fully controls, with a Haman whispering in his ear. And so far, he has shown no inclination to take back the ring.

The charge that Carlson and his followers level at American Jews is always the same: dual loyalty.[517] American Jews who support Israel cannot be trusted, their allegiances are divided and they serve a foreign master.

The dual loyalty accusation is now coming from every direction—left and right, campus activists and prime-time commentators, progressive faculty lounges and MAGA podcasts. Ideological enemies who agree on nothing else agree on this.

Why this particular accusation? Why now?

38

Under the Vine and Fig Tree

When President George Washington visited Newport, Rhode Island in the summer of 1790, the tiny Jewish community there was on its last legs. Most Jews had fled when the British occupied the city during the Revolution, and by the time Washington arrived, the synagogue had no rabbi, no cantor, not even anyone qualified to read from the Torah. Yet the lay leader, Moses Seixas, felt it was his responsibility to greet the president on behalf of what remained of Newport's Jews, and really, on behalf of all American Jews.

The letter Seixas delivered to Washington that summer expressed something unprecedented in Jewish history: gratitude for a government that treated Jews not as tolerated aliens, but as full and equal citizens. "Deprived as we heretofore have been of the invaluable rights of free Citizens, we now behold a Government, erected by the Majesty of the People—a Government, which to bigotry gives no sanction, to persecution no assistance—but generously affording to All liberty of conscience, and immunities of Citizenship."[518]

Washington understood what this meant. In his response, he deliberately used Seixas's language and then went further: "It is now no more that toleration is spoken of, as if it was by the indulgence of one class of people, that another enjoyed the exercise of their inherent natural rights."[519] This was revolutionary. In Europe, philosophers like John Locke argued for religious toleration—the idea that the state should refrain from persecuting people for their beliefs. But for Washington, mere toleration was insufficient. America would not be a nation that grudgingly tolerates the presence of Jews. Washington was declaring that Jews belonged in America just as much as anyone else and that their rights were inherent, not granted as a favor that could be revo ked.[520]

Washington concluded his letter by quoting his favorite biblical verse, from the prophet Micah: "May the Children of the Stock of Abraham, who dwell in this land, continue to merit and enjoy the good will of the other Inhabitants; while every one shall sit in safety under his own vine and fig tree, and there shall be none to make him afraid."[521]

It is hard to overstate how extraordinary this was. At the time Washington wrote these words, perhaps a thousand Jews lived in the entire United States. They were a small and politically powerless community that Washington could easily have ignored. Instead, he took the time to respond personally, quoting the Bible to assure this tiny, scattered population that they had found a permanent home in America.

American Jews took him at his word. For generations, they believed that Washington's vision had come true, that America was genuinely different from every other diaspora in Jewish history. They could assimilate completely, become full Americans in every sense, and still remain Jews. They could sit safely under their vine and fig tree, and there would be none to make them afraid. If Jews gave their heart and soul to America, then America would accept them fully in return.

Perhaps exile itself had finally been overcome; not through return to the land of Israel, but through acceptance in the land of the free.

Yet Washington's favorite verse, read in the context of Micah's full prophecy, tells a different story.

Don Isaac Abarbanel is explicit about when and where this prophecy will be fulfilled: "It is without doubt referring to the days of the Messiah, which are the days following the wrath and the end of Israel's exile."[522] Why is Abarbanel so certain? Because Micah places this promise of peace and security "immediately after he prophesied good concerning Jerusalem, Zion, and the Temple Mount." The sequence is deliberate. The vine and fig tree will not be found in Newport, New York or Los Angeles. The prophetic promise of Jews living in safety and peace belongs to one time and one place alone: the messianic era, in the land of Israel, after the ingathering of the exiles.

The Torah itself said as much. In the great rebuke of Deuteronomy, Moses warned the Jewish people what awaited them in exile: "And the Lord will scatter you among all the nations, from one end of the earth to the other... And among those nations, you will not be calm, nor will your foot find rest. There, the Lord will give you a trembling heart, dashed hopes, and a depressed soul" (Deuteronomy 28:64-65).

Jews can live peacefully in exile for a time. Throughout history, Jews have found periods of relative security in foreign lands. But the complete fulfillment of Micah's promise, the permanent security where "none shall make him afraid," belongs only to the messianic era and the Promised Land.

Washington was both a great man and a genuine friend to the Jewish people. His letter to the Jews of Newport stands as one of the most eloquent expressions of American equality ever written. But could his vision overcome the prophetic reality that permanent Jewish security belongs only in the land of Israel? Has Washington's blessing—"May the Children of the Stock of Abraham continue to merit and enjoy the good will of the other Inhabitants"—come true?

Today, the answer is clear. The promise he made—that Jews could find permanent safety and acceptance in America—was a promise he had no power to keep. Jews are beaten in the streets of New York City. Jewish students are harassed on America's elite campuses. American synagogues require armed security. Despite two centuries of American Jews working desperately to assimilate and to prove their loyalty to their neighbors, the 'good will' Washington prayed they would receive flickered for a time—and then vanished.

Why? What makes the Jewish experience in America different from every other immigrant group? When Rome conquered Greece, the Greeks gradually adopted Roman customs and were eventually accepted as full Roman citizens. When the Mongols conquered China, they assimilated within a few generations. When the Normans conquered England, they intermarried with the Anglo-Saxons and became English. Irish-Americans, Italian-Americans, Polish-Americans—all faced discrimination when they first arrived, and all eventually became simply Americans. The pattern is consistent across history and cultures: conform to the dominant society, and over time you find acceptance.

But Jews are different.

Rabbi Naftali Zvi Yehuda Berlin explains the uniqueness of the Jewish people through Bilaam's prophecy. Most English translations render it: "There is a people that dwells apart, not reckoned among the nations" (Numbers 23:9). Even this simple reading is powerful. God is declaring that Jews will always be distinct, never fully absorbed into the world around them.

But the original Hebrew orders the verse differently: "They are a lonely people that dwells; among the nations they are not reckoned." The slight difference in sequence changes everything. The verse is making two distinct statements, not one.

The first—"They are a lonely people that dwells"—reveals the secret of Jewish survival. When Israel maintains its distinct national identity, when it recognizes that exile is temporary and that its true home lies elsewhere, it "dwells." It lives securely. The second half delivers the warning: "among the nations they are not reckoned." When Jews begin to treat exile as permanent, when they stop recognizing themselves as a nation in exile and start behaving as if they have simply joined another nation, the peoples of the world are disgusted and recoil from them.

This is the opposite of how it works for every other people. Whereas most peoples gain respect and acceptance by conforming, Israel gains it only by remaining true to itself, by remembering that exile is temporary. Security does not come from imitation, but neither does it come from simply maintaining Jewish practices while treating diaspora as permanent. It comes from fidelity to Jewish practice *and* Jewish destiny.

The assimilated Jew who says "I am an American who happens to be Jewish" has abandoned his identity. But the Orthodox Jew who says "I am building a permanent Jewish life in America, with great yeshivas and thriving communities" has made a different mistake. He maintains his identity but treats exile as his destination.

The Sages teach that when Joseph died, the Israelites in Egypt abandoned the practice of circumcision, declaring, "Let us be like the Egyptians."[523] Rabbi Berlin explains: "They thought that since they were in exile, it was proper not to remain separate from them. But the opposite happened: the Egyptians separated themselves from Israel." God's response was to make Egypt unbearable—"He turned the hearts of the Egyptians to hate His people" (Psalms 105:25)—forcing them to remember that they did not belong there.

The opposite error is equally dangerous. The generation of the ten spies maintained their Israelite identity in the wilderness. They kept the commandments, followed Moses, and remained distinct from the nations around them. But they wanted to stay in the wilderness rather than face the challenges of nationhood in the land. God condemned them for it—and an entire generation died in the wilderness, never seeing the land they were meant to inherit.

Assimilation or permanent exile—God will not accept either. When Jews remember who they are, when they live in exile as a temporary condition, He allows them to live in relative peace even in foreign lands. When they forget, He sends enemies to remind them.[524]

And now the pattern repeats itself in America. Assimilated Jews abandon their identity, while Orthodox Jews maintain theirs but build permanent lives in exile. Both believed America would be different—that Washington's promise would hold. It hasn't. And despite everything that divides them, they now face the same accusation: dual loyalty.

This is not a coincidence. Through the dual loyalty accusation, God is forcing American Jews—assimilated and Orthodox alike—to answer the question they spent generations avoiding: Do you belong to America, or to the Jewish people? Where is your true home?

Washington's vine and fig tree were never meant to grow in Newport. Through the mouths of antisemites, God is making that clear.

39

THE DAY MICHAEL BECAME MORDECAI

Michael Rapaport skipped Hebrew school for pickup basketball.

The New York actor and comedian—known for True Romance, Friends, and a podcast whose primary distinguishing feature is profanity—was Jewish the way millions of American Jews are Jewish. He was ethnically and culturally Jewish, but no one ever accused him of taking it seriously. He'd toss a "Shabbat Shalom" on Instagram between expletive-laced NBA rants. When he saw Chabad Hasidim wrapping tefillin on New York streets, outside bagel shops, in the park, he thought it looked weird.[525] He was, as he later described himself, a "very classic New York lox and bagels Jew."[526]

This was Michael Rapaport's entire relationship with Judaism for the first fifty-three years of his life. But then came October 7.

Rapaport watched the massacre unfold on the news. And then, the morning after, he watched hundreds of New Yorkers pour into the streets to celebrate the slaughter. Something snapped. He had spent his whole life building a persona—the street-tough New York celebrity, the foul-mouthed comedian with a podcast and a brand. None of it felt like the most important thing about him anymore. The most important thing about him was that he was a Jew, and now Jews were being slaughtered while people danced in the streets outside his window.

The comedian became a warrior. He started posting daily videos demanding the hostages be released, counting the days of their captivity, tearing into campus antisemites, the cowardly media, and the Hollywood actors whose silence made him sick. He lost acting jobs over it and didn't care. "I've lost acting jobs over my Israel advocacy but I don't have the slightest regret because it was not a choice. Being supportive of Jews, of Israel, of our people was not a choice."[527]

He visited Israel for the first time in December 2023. He walked through Kibbutz Be'eri while the blood was barely dry, stood at the Nova Festival site where 364 young people were murdered at a party, and sat in bomb shelters with former hostages. At Hostage Square in Tel Aviv he told the crowd: "Stick together, smile at each other, stand tall, stand proud." He hosted comedy nights for hostage families and began wearing a Magen David necklace. And at fifty-three years old, he had a bar mitzvah in Israel—the one he never had as a kid too busy shooting hoops to bother.

Two years after October 7, Rapaport began wrapping *tefillin* every morning. The man who once watched Jews do this on the street and thought it looked weird now couldn't start his day without it. "It hits me in my chest. It centers me. It charges me. It makes me feel focused, grounded, and armed—not with weapons, but with purpose, discipline, and identity. It's not just a ritual. It's how I talk to God. It's how I talk to my people. It's how I talk to myself. And I love it. I really love it."[528]

Rapaport hasn't become Orthodox. He is not Shabbat observant and still eats at non-kosher restaurants. But every morning he wraps *tefillin*, and every post ends with the same three words: "*Am Yisrael Chai,*" "the nation of Israel lives." *Tefillin*, for Rapaport, is not about fulfilling Jewish law. It is about strapping himself to his people every single morning before he faces the world.

Mordecai was not a rabbi or a communal leader. He was a diplomat sitting at the king's gate, busy promoting his own political career. He was part of the Shushan elite, a man more likely to be found at a royal party than a synagogue. When he refused to bow to Haman, it had nothing to do with religious law or piety. It was an act of national pride—the refusal of a man who suddenly remembered that his people had dignity worth defending.

Mordecai stood alone. The Book of Esther records no other Jews standing up alongside him—just one man refusing to bow while everyone around him kept their heads down and hoped the problem would go away. The same is true today. For every Michael Rapaport, there are hundreds of Jewish celebrities who said nothing.

Ben Shapiro said something, and paid a price for it. In the years before October 7, Shapiro built the Daily Wire into a massive media empire, but he was known more for his conservative commentary than Jewish leadership. October 7 changed that. He became one of Israel's most ferocious public defenders, and like Mordecai, his refusal to stay quiet put him in the crosshairs of antisemites on both left and right. Death threats poured in against his family, bomb threats forced evacuations of his home and office, and weekly swatting calls brought armed police to his door, all because he dared to defend Israel.[529] Nick Fuentes and other influencers branded him a "Zionist shill" and a "traitor to Ame rica."[530] He fired Candace Owens after she minimized the Holocaust, and publicly called out Tucker Carlson and Megyn Kelly at TP USA's Amfest.[531] He didn't back down from any of it.

A handful of others stood up too. Montana Tucker and Lizzy Savetsky, social media influencers with careers to protect, stepped forward when it cost something. Bill Ackman, a billionaire investor with no history of Jewish activism, used his platform to expose antisemitism on elite campuses and refused to back down when the backlash came.

None of these people were sitting in yeshiva waiting for their moment. They were living secular, assimilated, comfortable American lives—exactly like Mordecai before Haman showed up. The crisis found them; but unlike most of their peers, they didn't look away.

The modern Mordecais were the ones nobody expected. Nobody saw Mordecai coming either.

40

The Coming Decree

Imagine this America: Orthodox synagogues are full on Saturday morning, just as they are today. Jews can attend services freely, observe their holidays, celebrate bar mitzvahs, hold Passover seders. Nobody is stopping you from being a religious Jew.

But something else has changed.

The Israeli flag that used to fly from your porch comes down after the third anonymous threatening note from the Homeowners Association. You take it down, because the alternative—a formal complaint, a fine, a neighborhood feud—isn't worth it. Your daughter comes home from school and tells you a classmate called her a "baby killer" because she's a Jew and Israel murders Palestinian babies. You sit with that for a moment, then tell her to keep her head down.

Your synagogue board has voted, after months of tense meetings, to remove the Israeli flag from the sanctuary. The arguments were practical: an Israeli flag is a political statement that could jeopardize the synagogue's tax-exempt status, and in the current climate, rabbis and congregants who display one risk being reported to the FBI as foreign agents. Better to be safe. The rabbi hasn't mentioned Israel from the pulpit in over a year. He is well aware of the dangers, and he can't be flippant about them. He has a mortgage, a congregation to protect, and a board that isn't looking for trouble.

At work, the calculus is even simpler. Your colleague noticed the photo on your desk—you and your family at the Western Wall in Jerusalem, the same photo millions of Jews have taken over the years—and said nothing. But you noticed him noticing. Your promotion review is coming up, and so the photo goes in the drawer.

In Washington, a law has finally passed designating AIPAC a foreign lobby operating in the interests of a foreign government. Its offices are shuttered, and its former leaders are currently under investigation. Jewish members of Congress who once wore their support for Israel as a badge of honor now answer every question about the Middle East with elaborate statements of balance and neutrality.

And then comes the citizenship law. Dual citizenship is finished. Every American who holds citizenship in another country must choose—one passport, one loyalty, one nation. For most Americans, the new law is a bureaucratic inconvenience. For American Jews who also hold Israeli citizenship, it is a moment of reckoning. Choose. You can be American, you can be Israeli, but you cannot be both. Thousands of American Jews quietly and sadly renounce their Israeli citizenship online, because going to the Israeli embassy in person would expose that they held it in the first place.

You can keep Shabbat, and kosher restaurants are still plentiful. You can teach your children about the Holocaust and cry while watching Schindler's List. You can do all of it—so long as you accept the fiction of "Judaism," that being a Jew is a religious identity, like being Baptist or Methodist, a private matter between you and God that has nothing to do with nationhood or land or collective destiny. The moment you reject that fiction, the moment you openly declare your allegiance to Jewish peoplehood, you have crossed a line. That is where the costs begin and the doors begin to close. That is where you discover that America's tolerance for Jews always had a condition attached, and the bill has finally come due.

This is not a fantasy. We have seen it before—in the Soviet Union.

Soviet Jews could attend synagogue. They could observe Yom Kippur and celebrate bar mitzvahs, so long as everything stayed indoors and apolitical. Rabbis could lead services, provided they registered with local authorities and stayed far away from Hebrew education, youth groups, or anything that resembled Jewish national consciousness. Zionism was treason. "*Am Yisrael Chai,*" the nation of Israel lives, was a subversive slogan. Pray quietly and keep your holidays, but nothing more.

America is not the Soviet Union—yet. But a future that once seemed dystopian is far more realistic than most American Jews want to admit.

In 1977, the American-Israeli writer Hillel Halkin predicted this moment would come.

The issue [of dual identity] has always been there latently; it has surfaced now and again in minor ways—not only in the antisemitic rumblings of the disrespectable fringes, but in the occasional veiled warnings of influential columnists and politicians not known for their friendliness to Israel... Yet it has been held in check by the assumption, common to most Jews and non-Jews alike, that American and Israeli interests were close enough to prevent it from taking practical form.

Already, however, this distinction has lost its fine edge... Yet such innuendos are but a shadow of what might come should the American Jewish community be forced into a posture not of temporary opposition to the diplomacy of one presidential administration, but of permanent confrontation with a long-term foreign policy enjoying bipartisan support and popularity with the American electorate.

One need not invoke the improbable specter of politically inspired mass antisemitism in its classical European manifestation. Yet it is not difficult to imagine a subtly orchestrated campaign against Jewish support for Israel—feeding off and reinforcing a general mood of resentment against a foreign state that seeks to enlist the aid of American citizens and their money to help frustrate American aims abroad...

At the very least, it would threaten to tear the American Jewish community apart into two rival camps. Simply suppose a situation in which each American Jew had to decide for himself, in the most practical political terms, which meant more to him: the welfare of America or the welfare of Israel.

The divisiveness of such a conflict would be enormous... It would plunge the American Jewish community into a degree of discord within itself and with its surroundings that seems unthinkable now...

It is American Jewry's good fortune that such a moment has not yet arrived for it, as it has, for example, for Russian Jewry. But this is hardly a safe assurance that it never can or will."[532]

Fifty years later, I believe that moment is coming soon.

Most American Jews are not blind to what is happening. They see the mobs on the campuses, the synagogues that need armed guards, the politicians who no longer bother to hide their contempt for Israel. They know things have gotten worse. But still they tell themselves what Jews have always told themselves in the late afternoon of a comfortable exile: that this is a passing storm, that America is different, that it will not come to that.

The sons of Jacob could have returned to Israel on several occasions: after the death of Jacob or after the death of Joseph. Had they done so, perhaps they could have been spared the enslavement of Egypt.How did they not notice the impending disaster? Did they not see the cultural revolution unfolding around them, the first signs of hatred creeping into public life? "Now there arose a new king over Egypt who did not know Joseph" (Exodus 1:8). Egypt had changed; its toleration of the Hebrew was replaced by suspicion and hatred. How did they not see it?[533]

American Jews today are no different. They see the warning signs and tell themselves it will pass. But if history is any guide, it won't.

The Talmud preserves a debate between two rabbis about how the final redemption of the Jewish people will unfold. Rabbi Eliezer believed redemption depends entirely on repentance: "If the Jewish people repent, they are redeemed; if not, they are not redeemed." Rabbi Yehoshua challenged him: "If they do not repent, will they not be redeemed at all? Rather, the Holy One, Blessed be He, will establish a king for them whose decrees are as harsh as those issued by Haman, and the Jewish people will have no choice but to repent, and this will restore them to the right path."[534]

As Rabbi Abraham Isaac Kook wrote: "God has made a covenant with the entire congregation of Israel, so that it can never become completely defiled. Impurity may act upon it and leave blemishes, but it can never fully sever it from the source of divine life."[535] When we drift too far from our identity, when assimilation threatens to sever us entirely from the source of divine life, God sends a Haman. Not to destroy us, but to save us from something worse than destruction: from losing ourselves completely.

But we must not mistake what this means. God is not an angry judge dispatching Haman as punishment. He is a father whose children have decided they want nothing to do with Him. Yet he loves his children too much to accept their answer. He will do everything in his power to win back their love.

The Jews of Shushan were deeply assimilated, deeply comfortable, with no interest in what God was asking of them. Cyrus opened the gates, Jewish pioneers rebuilt the Temple, and Persian Jews responded with a yawn. They were done with Jewish chosenness, done with the demanding mission God expected of His people. They had made their choice, and it wasn't Him. God could have accepted that. He could have turned away and found another path to redemption that didn't run through the Jews of Persia. Instead He sent Haman—because a father who truly loves his children does not let them walk away without doing everything in his power to bring them home.

The same love is at work today. Tucker Carlson and Nick Fuentes are not a sign that God has abandoned American Jews. They are a sign that He hasn't. Every day, thousands of Jews drift a little further—another intermarriage, another child lost to the Jewish people. God is not a judge keeping score. He is a father who loves every one of his children, no matter how far they have strayed, too much to let them go without a fight. And so He does what He has always done when

His people drift too far—He sends a Haman. Not to punish them, but to wake them up. Not out of anger, but out of love.

Redemption is inevitable, for God will not allow His people to disappear. As He promised through the prophet Jeremiah: "Thus says the Lord, who gives the sun for light by day and the fixed order of the moon and the stars by night... 'If this fixed order departs from before Me...'then shall the offspring of Israel cease from being a nation before Me forever'" (Jeremiah 31:35–37). As long as the sun rises and the moon governs the night, the Jewish people will endure.

The decree that is coming will not call for genocide. It will demand something else: that American Jews publicly distance themselves from Israel and renounce Jewish nationalism. You can practice Judaism as a private religion. But you cannot identify with the Jewish people or support their state. Choose one: America or Israel. You cannot have both.

The question is not whether Jews will survive, but how. If we do not choose redemption willingly, God will force the question through persecution. He will send a king whose decrees are as harsh as Haman's—not to remove our free will, but to awaken it. Faced with a Haman, every Jew will finally be forced to answer the question many spent their whole life avoiding: Do you belong to the Jewish people, or don't you? Some will say yes. Others, as when Israel left Egypt, will not.

Esther faced this question in the palace of Ahasuerus. She chose her people—and saved them. Sooner or later, our moment will come too. The only question is whether we will be ready.

41

Written In, or Written Out?

When the decree arrives, many American Jews will take the easy path.

They will publicly distance themselves from Israel, renounce Jewish nationalism, and declare exclusive loyalty to the United States. They will become "Bernie Sanders Jews"—Jews who pass the loyalty test by rejecting any ties to the Jewish state. Even some Orthodox communities will explicitly disavow Israel to protect their own insular communities. They will save themselves from ostracism, from damaged careers, perhaps from worse. But in abandoning Jewish peoplehood, they will lose everything that makes them Jews.

We have already seen glimpses of this future—Jewish anti-Zionists wearing tallitot and blowing shofars at pro-Hamas rallies, using the symbols of Judaism to oppose the Jewish people. Strip a Jew of his connection to the Jewish nation and this is what you get: someone who wraps himself in a prayer shawl to march against his own people.

Some will refuse. Like the modern Mordecais who have already refused to bow, they will choose the Jewish people even if it costs them everything. Some will leave for Israel. Others will stay in America but no longer pretend it is home. They will become permanent outsiders, suspected of disloyalty, perhaps facing hostility or worse. Like Mordecai in Shushan, they will pay a heavy price for standing with our people. But they will possess something the others have lost: the deep joy and strength of those who refuse to lie to themselves. They will know, in their bones, that they are God's chosen nation—and no accusation from their enemies can take that away. Like the Russian refuseniks who held firm against the full weight of the communist regime, they will only grow stronger and prouder with every insult thrown their way.

When Persian Jews faced this choice, something extraordinary happened. Mordecai and Esther chose their people. Miraculously, huge numbers of assimilated Jews of Persia woke up and recommitted themselves to Jewish nationhood. They fought, they prayed, and their fate was "reversed for them from grief to joy" (Esther 9:22). They survived, and established Purim to commemorate their deliverance forever.

But in the end, most of them stayed in Persia. They thanked God for their deliverance, then ignored His call to return home.

After the story of Esther, the Torah goes silent on the Jews of Persia. The books written afterward—Ezra, Nehemiah, Malachi—focus exclusively on the Jews who chose nationhood and returned to the land. They tell the stories of Nehemiah's rebuilding of the walls of Jerusalem and how Ezra brought the people of Israel back to God and renewed the covenant.

The Book of Esther is the last call, the final opportunity for the Jews of exile to wake up, remember who they are, and reenter the glorious story of the nation of Israel. Those who answered the call and joined Ezra and Nehemiah in returning to Jerusalem remained part of the story. Those who chose to stay in Persia were lost to history. The Bible intentionally forgets them.

This is the tragedy the Book of Esther does not say aloud but cannot hide. After coming together, after reidentifying as a nation, after defeating their enemies—they did not take the next step. They let the opportunity go to waste. They ignored the obvious lessons of their near-death experience and fell back into a false sense of security.

The Sages taught that if the Jews had "risen up like a wall"—if they had returned en masse to Israel after the salvation from Haman—the Second Temple would never have been destroyed. It would have been the final Temple. Complete redemption would have arrived then and there, 2,500 years ago. But because only Ezra and a small remnant returned while the majority stayed comfortable in Persia, the foundations were too weak. The opportunity for redemption was lost. The Second Temple was eventually destroyed, and the exile began anew for another two thousand years.[536]

Jews are commanded to begin studying the laws of Passover thirty days before the holiday arrives. By the Jewish calendar, this means we begin our Passover study on Purim itself.[537] Still groggy, perhaps a little drunk from the day's celebration, Jews are commanded to pull out their Passover books and begin studying the story of the Exodus from Egypt.

This timing is not accidental. Purim without Passover is incomplete. The Jews of Persia survived Haman's decree, celebrated their deliverance, and remained in Persia. The awakening was real—but it went nowhere. They were saved, and they stayed.

Passover is what Purim was supposed to become. Passover doesn't end with Jews celebrating survival in Egypt—it ends with them leaving. The holiday moves from recognizing Jewish identity to acting on it, from living as a precarious minority to building Jewish sovereignty, from slavery and exile to freedom in the land of Israel. The law requiring us to move immediately from Purim to Passover study corrects what that generation failed to do. Realizing you're part of the Jewish people is only the beginning. The story is incomplete until it leads to an Exodus.

"I will redeem you with an outstretched arm and with great judgments" (Exodus 6:6). God redeemed the people of Israel from Egypt. He redeemed them again in Persia from Haman's decree. "And I will take you to Me as a people, and I will be a God to you" (Exodus 6:7). God took Israel as His people at Sinai. The Jews of Persia renewed that covenant when they reaccepted the Torah after their salvation.[538] But the third promise—"I will bring you to the land... and I will give it to you as a heritage" (Exodus 6:8)—they refused. In Moses' generation, Israel followed God from Egypt through the desert to the land of Israel. In Esther's generation, they stayed in Persia.

Two promises fulfilled, the third rejected. The redemption remained incomplete.

Will American Jews make the same mistake as the Jews of Esther's generation? Will they wake up, fight back, celebrate their survival—and then settle back into comfortable exile? Or will they seize the opportunity that the Jews of Persia let slip away?

42

The Countdown has Begun

The great Jewish communities of exile are disappearing, one by one. The legendary communities of Eastern Europe are gone, destroyed or diminished beyond recovery. The Jews of the Arab world have already returned home. The few remaining diaspora communities are collapsing before our eyes. French Jews, regularly attacked by Muslims in the streets of Paris, are leaving France for Israel by the thousands.[539] The Australian government abandoned its Jews, paving the way for the Bondi massacre of December 2025.[540] The survivors know that their tiny community has no future in Australia. British Jews watch their government pander to pro-Hamas extremists while Muslims grow into an overwhelming voting bloc that will soon dominate national British politics.

American Jews are the last great diaspora.

Israeli Jews have always known we are a nation. But what so many Israelis discovered in the war that followed October 7 was something deeper: that we are not a nation like any other. In bomb shelters and on reserve duty, while defending our borders and burying our friends, Israelis viscerally felt that we are God's chosen people, fighting for God's land, living the destiny that began with Abraham. Secular students who never before opened a Bible or kept Shabbat suddenly demanded *tzitzit*. Soldiers who couldn't recite the *Shema* began asking for prayer books and reciting Psalms before battle

American Jews watched from a distance. Some began to sense, perhaps for the first time, that they are part of a nation. But the confusion remains. They still struggle with dual identity, with uncertainty about what it means to be a Jew, why God set us apart, and whether Jewish peoplehood is compatible with their American identity. While Israel is living the redemption in real time, American Jews are still trying to figure out who they are.

The clock is running out—from two directions at once. America is turning against its Jews. And American Jewry itself is in demographic freefall, hemorrhaging its children through intermarriage and assimilation at rates that make the community's long-term survival in exile a mathematical impossibility.

The dual loyalty accusations are not just ideological attacks. History teaches that when such accusations gain mainstream acceptance, they don't stay rhetorical for long. First comes the accusation of disloyalty, then exclusion, then something worse. We have seen this many times before. As the Sages taught, "It is a well-known law that Esau hates Jacob."[541]

This hatred is not new. What is new is that God is withdrawing the divine protection that kept Jews alive through two thousand years of wandering.

When Jacob left the land of Israel for exile, God made him a promise: "Behold, I am with you and will guard you wherever you go." But embedded in that same promise was its own expiration date: "I will bring you back to this land; for I will not leave you until I have done what I have promised you" (Genesis 28:15). God would protect Jacob in exile—but only until the moment He determined it was time for Jacob to return home.

Jacob's story is our story. What God promised Jacob, He promised to Jacob's children, the people of Israel. "Come and see how beloved Israel is before the Holy One, blessed be He. For in every place to which they were exiled, God's presence went with them."[542] God was with the Jewish people wherever they wandered throughout the world, from Babylonia to America. But the terms were identical: God's protection in exile only lasts until the time comes to return to the land. Not a day longer.

When the time for redemption arrives, God's presence returns to Zion. It does not stay behind to watch over the Jews who refused to follow His command. When the period of exile ends, the people of Israel must return to the land without delay. Every delay, every lingering, is dangerous.

That time has come. The majority of world Jewry now lives in the Holy Land. Three generations after the founding of the State of Israel, the Jewish state is an emerging power in the Middle East. The era of exile is over; the era of redemption has begun. Jews who insist on remaining outside are no longer under the same divine protection that shielded our ancestors in Babylon, Spain, and Poland. The trap can close at any moment.

There is an old story about a husband and wife from Minsk who were sharply divided over the question of *Aliyah* to Israel. Unable to reach an understanding, they agreed to bring the matter before their town's leading rabbi. To everyone's surprise, he ruled against the proposed move. When asked how he could reconcile his ruling with his consistent support for the Zionist cause, he answered simply: it is better to dwell in Minsk and yearn for Jerusalem than to dwell in Jerusalem and yearn for Minsk.[543]

Perhaps he was right—in his generation. Today, it is better to dwell in Jerusalem and yearn for Minsk than to be hunted by antisemites in Minsk and yearn for Jerusalem. The guarantees are gone.

Nearly half a century ago, Rabbi Ashkenazi already feared for the future of American Jews: "Even today I am deeply troubled about the fate of American Jewry. They do not understand that the trap could close on them. Who can guarantee otherwise? Have their rabbis not learned?... Have they not studied our recent history? Not telling their Jews that the time has come to return to the land is absolute irresponsibility. What are they waiting for?"[544]

But do not mistake what this means. God withdrawing His protective hand from exile is not rejection—it is the most urgent expression of His love.

"With everlasting love have I loved you; therefore have I drawn you to Me with loving-kindness" (Jeremiah 31:2).[545] God does not drag His people home by force. He draws us. When a Jewish student is physically blocked from entering her own campus or passed over for an internship because she is a Zionist—this is not an expression of God's anger or disdain. It is God reaching out His hand. The antisemite who makes a Jew feel that he does not belong in America is delivering God's message: "My beloved children, you were not made for this place. Please come back to Me!"

"For the mountains shall depart and the hillside will fade away, but My kindness shall not depart from you" (Isaiah 54:10). Two thousand years of wandering, forgetting, and assimilation have not exhausted His love. The invitation has never been rescinded.

Yet for all His love, God will not make the choice for us. He will send messages. He will make exile more and more uncomfortable. But He will not force our hand. He wants us to choose Him freely; He will not conscript us into His service. The love that has sustained the Jewish people through two thousand years of wandering is precisely the love that refuses to compel, because compelled love is no love at all. God can only do what a loving father does: leave the door open, keep the light on, and pray that His children find their way home.

When Abraham left Ur of the Chaldees, nobody thought it mattered. He wasn't the only person leaving town that day; nothing about his departure looked significant. One man, one family, heading to an unknown destination. Yet that single act—hearing God's call and choosing to follow it—changed all of human history. The entire story of the Jewish people, and through them the story of humanity, was forever changed by Abraham's courageous choice to leave.[546]

American Jews face the same choice today. God is calling them home. Will they hear that call? Will they recognize this moment for what it is? Or will they, like so many Jewish communities before them, assume this is just another passing storm?

Throughout Jewish history, God has used crisis to create windows of opportunity—moments when His people can see clearly who they are and what they must do. But these windows do not stay open forever. When Mordecai called on Esther to act, he warned her: "If you remain silent at this time, relief and deliverance will arise for the Jews from another place" (Esther 4:14). Esther had a choice, but she also had a deadline. The window would close.

American Jews face the same deadline today. The countdown has begun.

God did not choose the Jewish people to become just another nation with its own faith and customs. From the beginning, He promised Abraham: "All the families of the earth will be blessed through you" (Genesis 12:3). But *how* will Israel bless all the families of the earth? The answer is not mystical but rather real and concrete: by teaching them how to build a holy society.

Zechariah prophesied the day when "ten men from every language of the nations shall grasp the garment of a Jewish man, saying, 'Let us go with you, for we have heard that God is with you'" (Zechariah 8:23). The nations will not be forced to follow Israel. They will choose to, drawn by the light of a society that proves holiness and justice can guide the exercise of national power.

But this vision cannot be realized in America. A Jew can study Torah or pray in New York or Los Angeles, but he cannot fulfill his mission there. An American Jew can attend synagogue and write a check to his local Jewish Federation, but he cannot teach the world how a nation—with all its complexities, divisions, and struggles—can live according to God's will.

In America, a Jew is a guest in someone else's home, adapting to rules he did not set and a system not his own. It is like trying to build a skyscraper without a foundation, or trying to conduct a symphony when most of the instruments belong to another orchestra. American

Jews can build communities, businesses, and institutions, but they cannot build a society in which holiness shapes law, power, and public life. “For out of Zion shall the Torah go forth, and the word of the Lord from Jerusalem” (Isaiah 2:3). Torah does not go forth from exile. It never has. It can only go forth from Zion.

And so God will bring His people home. "When you return to the Lord your God... then the Lord your God will bring back your captivity and have compassion upon you, and He will return and gather you from all the nations" (Deuteronomy 30:2-3). Isaiah describes the same promise: "And it shall come to pass on that day that the Lord shall set His hand again the second time to recover the remnant of His people... And He shall raise a banner for the nations, and shall assemble the outcasts of Israel, and gather together the dispersed of Judah from the four corners of the earth" (Isaiah 11:11-12).

These are not conditional prophecies. The ingathering of Israel will happen. But they do not guarantee that every Jew in America will be among those gathered.

When God redeemed Israel from Egypt, He kept every promise He made to Abraham. He split the sea, gave Israel the Torah and brought the people into the Holy Land. Yet four out of every five Israelites missed all of it—because they chose to identify as Egyptians and were left behind.

The final ingathering of Israel will be no different. God will bring His people home. The only question is which Jews will be among them.

The Sages point out a contradiction between two depictions of the coming of the Messiah. Daniel describes it arriving with overwhelming divine glory—"with the clouds of heaven" (Daniel 7:13). But the prophet Zechariah describes the very same redemption with Israel's king arriving "lowly and riding upon a donkey" (Zechariah 9:9). Which one is it? Will the redemption arrive gloriously or humbly?

The answer is simple: it depends on us. If the people of Israel merits it, redemption will come with the clouds of heaven; if not, it will still come, but it will arrive on a donkey. The final destination is guaranteed, but how we get there is not.[547]

"I the Lord in its time I will hasten it" (Isaiah 60:22). How can God both keep redemption to its appointed time and also hasten it? The answer is that both are true, but they describe different realities. "In its time" means God has set a final date by which redemption must arrive, whether we deserve it or not. But "I will hasten it" means that if Israel awakens to its mission and returns to the Holy Land of its own volition, God will bring redemption earlier, with less suffering, and with greater divine glory.[548]

"'Will I bring to the birth stool and not cause to give birth?' says the Lord. 'Am I not He who causes to give birth, now should I shut the womb?' says your God" (Isaiah 66:9). A woman in labor will give birth—the baby that must be born will be born. But how long will the labor last? How much pain will the mother endure? That is not predetermined.

Today we are living through "the birth pangs of the Messiah." We are in the throes of redemption, but we do not know how long it will take for the Messiah to arrive. The suffering that precedes his arrival is not etched in stone. If Israel awakens and returns to our homeland, the labor will be shortened. If we bury our heads in the sand and refuse to hear God's voice, the delivery will be delayed—and far more painful.

American Jews are the most accomplished Jewish community in the history of exile. For over two hundred years, they thrived as an essential part of the most powerful civilization on earth. They built great companies, won Nobel prizes, and shaped American law, medicine, and technology—many while also establishing communities of extraordinary generosity and love for Torah.

If they come home to Israel in great numbers, they will bring all of this with them. Imagine what they could do for their own people, for the State of Israel! American Jews hold the key to hastening the redemption, to shortening the labor and minimizing the pain. If they find the courage to return home now, while the choice is still theirs to make, they hold in their hands the power to speed the arrival of the Messiah himself.

Joseph was the most successful Jew in the history of exile—viceroy of Egypt, savior of nations, the ultimate diaspora triumph. Yet even Joseph, with his Egyptian name, Egyptian wife, and Egyptian palace, found the clarity and the strength to point his children home: "God will surely remember you and bring you up out of this land to the land that He swore to Abraham, to Isaac, and to Jacob" (Genesis 50:24). His success in Egypt never became his identity. In the end, Joseph knew exactly where he belonged—and he made sure his children knew too.

My brothers and sisters in America: However deep your roots have grown, however comfortable your exile has become, let Joseph's words give you strength. The hour is late—but not yet too late.[549]

On his Egyptian deathbed, Jacob gathered his sons for a final blessing. "Gather and listen, sons of Jacob, and listen to Israel, your father" (Genesis 49:2). In one short verse, he refers to himself by both names—first Jacob, then Israel. Why? At the end of his life, having seen everything, having wrestled with God and men and prevailed, why does he still call himself Jacob at all?

Because Jacob sees all of Jewish history stretched out before him. He sees the long exile coming, the centuries of wandering, the confusion of identity. He sees his children losing their home and losing themselves along with it. And so he issues his final challenge to his sons, and to every generation after them: You will be born sons of Jacob—raised in foreign lands, mistaking your nation for a religion, scattered among the nations. But that will not be your destiny. Your destiny will be to become Israel—the nation that God always intended you to be.[550]

Every Jew must ask himself the question Jacob poses with his very name: will I remain Jacob—rooted in exile, mistaking my nation for a religion, waiting for a redemption I am unwilling to hasten? Or will I become Israel—taking my place among my people, in my own land, fulfilling the destiny God has called us to since the day He first spoke to Abraham?

The land is waiting. Your people are waiting. The whole world is waiting. God Himself is waiting.

It's time to come home.

Afterword

For two thousand years, our people lived in a strange form of limbo.

In Hebrew, the word for "Hebrew"—*ivri*—shares its three-letter root with the word for fetus—*ubar*. Like a fetus, a Hebrew is one who lives between: between an origin that is not quite home and a destination not yet reached.

Egypt was our first womb. It is there that Jacob's family grew into the nation of Israel. The pregnancy was agonizing; the people endured centuries of slavery, backbreaking labor and sadistic persecution. But when the birth finally came, Jacob's descendants emerged from Egypt as God's beloved nation. They left the womb, and set off through the wilderness toward their beloved.

Egypt was only our first womb. Every exile that followed repeated the pattern. The nations to which we wandered gave us shelter, language, and livelihood. At times, the warmth was real. But as every generation of Jews in exile eventually discovered, the womb of the nations could never be our permanent home.

A fetus knows by instinct that it must leave the womb, that its warm and familiar surrounding is not its destination. As the moment of birth draws closer, it kicks harder, straining toward a world it has never seen. And yet it also wants to stay, for the womb is all it has ever known, and the world beyond is frightening. It wants to leave and it wants to remain, all at once.

Every Jew in exile knows this tension. Deep down, beneath the comfort and the career and the community he has built, he knows he is somewhere he was not quite meant to be. He cannot escape that feeling, but he is also afraid to act on it. Like a fetus, the Hebrew lives between.

When other peoples speak of their homeland, they call it a motherland. Like a mother, the land gives them their language and customs, their national identity. The relationship is one of mother and child: unearned, instinctive, unconditional.

But the Jewish people have always been different. Babylon, Spain, Poland, and America are the wombs that formed us, sustained us, yet were never truly ours. We do not belong to the land of Israel the way a child belongs to his mother. We belong to it the way a man belongs to his wife.

A child loves his mother, but a man separated from the woman he loves is consumed by it. Other peoples have lost their homelands and, within a generation or two, moved on. We could not. Twenty centuries passed and our yearning for Jerusalem never left us. The longing never faded to mere nostalgia. Every generation felt it anew.

"Therefore, a man shall leave his father and his mother, and cleave to his wife, and they shall become one flesh" (Genesis 2:24). For the Jewish people, that time is now.

Jews and Jerusalem—like two lovers betrothed to be married, separated before their wedding day. Though the years passed and the marriage was never consummated, we remained faithful to one another.

The land refused to bear fruit for other peoples, growing ever more desolate with each passing year. Hard as they might try, no one else could plant roots in God's chosen land. She was pledged to one nation, and one nation only.

The Jews, too, remained faithful. Even as the centuries passed and memories of our homeland grew hazy, we never forgot Jerusalem. At the holiest moments of our year—at the end of the Passover seder and Yom Kippur—we cried out with all our hearts: "Next year in Jerusalem!"

And then, miraculously, the gates opened. After two millennia of separation, the long engagement was over. The wedding could finally proceed as planned.

But something strange happened. Separated for so long, many Jews became addicted to longing. Millions chose to remain in America, the newer and wealthier "chosen land." Like a bride who longs for her wedding day but secretly hopes it never comes, they continue to cry out, "Next year in Jerusalem!"—so long as it's not today.[551] We put our suitcases away in the attic—and did our best to forget where we put them.

Reading the Song of Songs, Rabbi Joseph B. Soloveitchik asked: "What is the essence of this story, if not the description of a paradoxical and tragic hesitation on the part of the lover, when the opportunity presented itself? What is it, if not the deferral of a great and sublime opportunity—one she dreamed of, fought for, sought, and searched for with all the fervor of her soul? Did we get out of our beds and immediately open the door, or did we continue to rest—too lazy to rise? 'I have washed my feet, how shall I soil them?'"[552]

It's the perfect plot for a romantic comedy: the woman who has finally found her true love, the man she's waited her whole life for—but she keeps finding reasons to delay.

Except the hour is getting late. Eventually, the engagement must end, one way or the other. The day is coming when American Jews must make a choice, or the choice will be made for them.

It's time to tie the knot. The God who called Abraham to leave his birthplace for a land He would show him is calling Abraham's children to do the same. "The day is short, the work is vast, the workers are lazy, the reward is vast, and the Master of the house grows impatient."[553] The groom, the Master of the universe, is growing impatient—and He will not wait forever.

It's time to thank America for all its blessings. It's time to stop yearning and start moving. After two thousand years of "next year," it's time to finally come home.

"Then will you dwell in the land that I gave your fathers, and you will be a nation to Me, and I will be to you as a God" (Ezekiel 36:28)

The betrothal is over. The wedding is about to begin. There is only one question left: Will you be there?

"For the Lord delights in His people" (Psalm 149:4)

ENDNOTES

Preface

1. Rabbi Yehuda Leon Ashkenazi, *Sod Midrash HaToldot* (2005), 7:258.

2. Ibid, 259.

3. Rashi, Deuteronomy 33:9.

4. Rabbi Abraham Isaac Kook, letter to Rabbi Avraham Dov Bernstein, *Igrot HaRe'iyah*, Letter 926, February 12, 1916.

Introduction

5. Bernard Lewis, *Notes on a Century: Reflections of a Middle East Historian* (2012), 55–58.

6. Cited in Daniel Gordis, Israel's closing the skies to American Jews—violating a sacred relationship?, January 4, 2022, https://danielgordis.substack.com/p/are-american-jews-somehow-israeli.

7. David Ben-Gurion and Jacob Blaustein Agree that American Jewry's Prime Loyalty Is to the United States, August 23, 1950, in *The Jew in the American World: A Sourcebook*, ed. Jacob R. Marcus (1996).

8. Saul Jay Singer, The Theology Of David Ben-Gurion, March 10, 2021, *Jewish Press*, https://jewishpress.com/sections/features/features-on-jewish-world/the-theology-of-david-ben-gurion/2021/03/10/. Ben Gurion is reported to have said, "Since I invoke Torah so often, let me state that I don't personally believe in the God it postulates...I am not religious, nor were the majority of the early builders of Israel believers. Yet, their passion for this land stemmed from the Book of Books...[and the Bible is] the single most important book in my life."

9. I'm 'fighting Jews, not Zionism,' Ahed Tamimi declares, *JNS*, August 26, 2025, www.jns.org/im-fighting-jews-not-zionism-ahed-tamimi-declares/.

10. Tucker Carlson: Ben Shapiro, pro-Israel voices don't care about America, *Jerusalem Post*, December 21, 2023, www.jpost.com/diaspora/antisemitism/article-780172.

11. Ashleigh Fields, Megyn Kelly, Ben Shapiro spar over Epstein theories, DOJ response, *The Hill*, July 15, 2025, https://thehill.com/media/5401881-megyn-kelly-ben-shapiro-jeffrey-epstein/.

When God Fired the Preacher

12. *Genesis Rabbah* 38:13.

13. *Genesis Rabbah* 39:14.

14. Nahor, like Abraham, descended from Eber—the ancestor whose name gives us the word "Hebrew." Yet the Torah never calls Nahor or his descendants Hebrews. Instead, they are identified as Arameans: "Bethuel the Aramean," "Laban the Aramean" (Genesis 25:20, 28:5). Rabbi Yehuda Leon Ashkenazi explains that from a genealogical

standpoint, they remained descendants of Eber, but "they chose to become Arameans, and as part of this identity decision, they did not wish to return to the Land." This was "a conscious decision, opposite to that of his brother Abram, who returned to his Hebrew identity." Nahor believed he could preserve what mattered while permanently settling among the nations, that his descendants could maintain their essential heritage while adopting Aramean identity. But the Torah reveals the consequence: Nahor's grandson Laban became not merely assimilated but actively hostile to those who remained Hebrew. When Jacob came to Haran, Laban exploited him for twenty years, and when Jacob fled back toward the Land of Israel, Laban pursued him with murderous intent. As the Passover Haggadah teaches: "Laban sought to uproot everything." The Hebrew who chose to become Aramean raised a grandson who tried to annihilate the Hebrew nation entirely (Ashkenazi, *Sod Midrash HaToldot* 7:84).

15. Rabbi Oury Cherki, *De'ah Tzelulah: Olam ve-Adam be-Mishnat ha-Rav Kook* [Clear Thought: World and Man in Rav Kook's Teachings] (2015), 103.

16. Gavriela Ben Shmuel, *Min HaAyin el HaAni: Kri'ot Kabbaliyot be-Mishnato ha-Historiosofit shel Rabbi Yehuda Leon Ashkenazi (Manitou)* [From the Nothing to the I: Kabbalistic Readings in the Historiosophical Teachings of Rabbi Yehuda Leon Ashkenazi] (2020), 347.

17. Rashi, Genesis 21:9.

18. Rabbi Yehuda Leon Ashkenazi, *Sod Midrash HaToldot* 2:281.

19. Genesis 21:22–32.

20. Rashbam, Genesis 22:1–2. "Rashbam" is a Hebrew acronym for RAbbi SHmuel Ben Meir. He was a leading French Tosafist and grandson of Shlomo Yitzhaki, "Rashi."

21. Rabbi Yehuda Leon Ashkenazi, *Sod Midrash HaToldot*, 5:156.

Meek Men Don't Build Nations

22. Rashi, Genesis 25:27.

23. *Genesis Rabbah* 63:10.

24. Rabbi Ezra Bick, Toldot: Dividing the Berakhot, Torat Har Etzion, March 29, 2017, https://etzion.org.il/en/tanakh/torah/sefer-bereishit/parashat-toldot/toldot-dividing-berakhot.

25. Rashi, Genesis 28:12.

26. Rashi, Genesis 32:2.

27. Rabbi Yehuda Leon Ashkenazi, *Sod Midrash HaToldot*, 7:160.

28. Rashi, Genesis 29:12.

29. Babylonian Talmud, Berachot 4a. "Rabbi Jacob bar Idi posed a contradiction: It is written 'Behold, I am with you and will guard you wherever you go,' and yet it is written 'And Jacob was very afraid.' He said: Perhaps sin will cause [the promise to be void]. As it is taught: 'Until Your people cross over, O Lord, until the people You have acquired cross over'—'until Your people cross over, O Lord' refers to the first entry [into the Land, in the time of Joshua]; 'until the people You have acquired cross over' refers to the second entry [in the time of Ezra]. From here the Sages said: Israel was worthy of having a miracle

performed for them in the days of Ezra, just as was done for them in the days of Joshua son of Nun—but sin caused [it not to happen]."

30. Rashi, Genesis 32:5.

31. Babylonian Talmud, Berachot 13a.

32. Rabbi Oury Cherki, *Clear Thought: World and Man in Rav Kook's Teachings*, 135.

33. Rabbi Shlomo Aviner, *Kol HaBakha: Peirush al Megillat Eicha* [The Voice of Weeping: Commentary to the Scroll of Lamentations] (2004), 24.

34. Rabbi Yehuda Leon Ashkenazi, *Sod Midrash HaToldot* 7:226.

Would You Have Left?

35. *Exodus Rabbah* 14:3.

36. *Zohar*, Beshalach 170a.

37. Rabbi Ashkenazi insists that the one-fifth who left Egypt is not necessarily a prophecy about our own redemption: "Does the Midrash seek to present this statement as a necessary law of Jewish history? Does it mean that at the end of the current exile, history will repeat itself and only one-fifth of the Jewish people will return to the Land of Israel?... A person has free choice whether to return or not. A person has the ability to overcome what appears to be determinism, fatalism, or innate tendencies. What concerns me is that in recent generations the Jewish people have relinquished their free choice... The Jews could have left the exile, but they did not do so. The merit of the Zionist movement is that it sought to save the Jewish people from

that fatalism—that only one-fifth would leave the exile." *Sod Midrash HaToldot*, 2:148–149.

38. *Numbers Rabbah* 13:20.

39. Jewish law does not contain an explicit prohibition against giving children non-Jewish names, nor is there any religious obligation to speak Hebrew.

40. Rabbi Yehuda Leon Ashkenazi, *Sod Midrash HaToldot* 8.

41. Ginnifer Goodwin, interview on "Being Jewish with Jonah Platt," January 14, 2025, www.youtube.com/watch?v=sqmGPW82Ih8.

42. *Exodus Rabbah* 1:27.

43. Rabbi Naftali Zvi Yehuda Berlin, *HaEmek Davar* (1880), Exodus 2:11.

44. Attributed to Rabbi Menachem Mendel of Kotzk.

45. Rabbi Reuven Feuerman, Heresy: A New Look at the Evil Son, *Olam Katan*, Passover 2025.

46. Rabbi Abraham Isaac Kook, *Ein Ayah on Ein Yaakov*, Tractate Berachot (1995), [composed 1885–1902], 26. See also Rabbi Reuven Sasson, *One Nation in the Land*: "In the deeper sense, it is impossible for a Jew to separate and sever himself from the Jewish people. The depth of the matter lies in understanding that the soul of the individual is a spark of the collective soul, and that severance from the people is severance from the source of life itself. Just as a leaf cannot survive without its connection to the trunk and the roots, so a Jew cannot be full of vitality and light without being connected to the Jewish

people. It is no accident that the punishment of karet — excision — is described in the Torah as a cutting off from the people: 'and he shall be cut off from his people.' The Jewish people is the Tree of Life, in which all our souls flower and find their existence. Therefore, when a person severs himself from the Jewish people, from the collective vision of the nation, he becomes a withered limb, drained of vitality."

47. Maimonides, *Laws of Repentance* 3:11.

48. Rabbi Yehuda Leon Ashkenazi, *Sod Midrash HaToldot* 7:265.

49. Babylonian Talmud, Berachot 12b.

50. Rabbi Judah Loew of Prague, *Chiddushei Aggadot*, 25.

Why God Passed Over Abraham

51. "Without recognizing our identity as a people, we couldn't properly fulfill any of our religious duties, whether they involve the community or are personal practices. The entire basis for following these religious laws depends on our connection to the Jewish people as a whole, and when we observe them, we do so as part of and on behalf of all Israel." Rabbi Yaakov Moshe Charlop, *MiMaayanei HaYeshua* (1998), 325.

52. Rabbi Yehuda Leon Ashkenazi, *Sod Midrash HaToldot*, 7:362.

53. Rabbi Zvi Yisrael Thau, *L'Emunat Iteinu*, vol. 2: *HaBocher b'Yisrael b'Ahavah* [The One Who Chooses Israel with Love], (2005).

54. Rabbi Yaakov Moshe Charlop, *Mei Marom*, vol. 6 (1986), 325.

55. Os Guinness, *The Magna Carta of Humanity: Sinai's Revolutionary Faith and the Future of Freedom* (2021), 45–46.

56. Rabbi Yehuda Leon Ashkenazi, *Sod Midrash HaToldot*, 5:247–248.

57. Rabbi Moshe Avigdor Amiel, *Ezer El Ami* (2000, originally composed c. 1930s), 17–18.

58. Rashi on Exodus 32:10, citing the Babylonian Talmud, Berachot 32a. The Talmud notes that God's words "let Me alone" imply that Moses' prayer could actually restrain Him—like someone grasping hold of another person. But if God truly intended to destroy Israel, why would He need to tell Moses to "let Him alone"? The very phrasing reveals that God was opening a door for Moses to intercede, not closing one. God was inviting Moses to fight for the people, testing whether he would defend them even when they seemed indefensible.

59. Babylonian Talmud, Sanhedrin 44a.

60. The Hebrew letters tzadi, bet, and resh form the word tzibbur.

61. Rabbi Yehuda Leon Ashkenazi, *Sod Midrash HaToldot*, 2:238.

62. Rabbi Shlomo Aviner, *Nesichei Adam*, vol. 3 (2005), 212.

63. "The Torah's central innovation is its emphasis on the holiness of the collective... Holiness is not meant to be achieved only by exceptional individuals; the community as a whole must rise to a level of sanctity. This begins with the people of Israel as a collective, described as 'a kingdom of priests and a holy nation.' The Torah's demand to build a human society in which all character traits and all values are fully realized together, in complete harmony—even when they appear to contradict one another—is truly radical. This is humanity's task: not the mission of this or that individual, but of humanity itself. And it is Israel's task, as expressed in the verse, 'You are My flock,

the flock of My pasture; you are human, and I am your God, says the Lord God' (Ezekiel 34:31), and in the command, 'Speak to the entire congregation of the children of Israel and say to them: You shall be holy, for I, the Lord your God, am holy.' Israel as a whole must demonstrate to all of humanity that it is possible to establish such a society. Through this, the true human being—one who aligns with the purpose of creation and the Creator's design—can come into being." Rabbi Yehuda Leon Ashkenazi, *Sod Midrash HaToldot*, Volume 3, "You Shall Be Holy."

64. Jews firmly believe in the World to Come (Olam HaBa) and personal reward and punishment, yet strikingly, the Torah never explicitly discusses heaven or any sort of afterlife, focusing instead on the nation's fate in this world. The doctrine appears only in hints, most definitively in Daniel: "Many of those who sleep in the dust of the earth shall awake, some to everlasting life, and some to shame and everlasting contempt" (Daniel 12:2). Maimonides codifies this belief, explaining that while the Torah speaks of earthly blessings, the ultimate reward is spiritual: "The reward for the mitzvot and the good which we will merit if we observe the path of God as prescribed by the Torah is the World to Come... Also, the retribution which is exacted from the wicked who abandon the paths of righteousness prescribed by the Torah is karet (spiritual excision from the afterlife)... A person merits a portion of the World to Come according to the magnitude of his deeds and the extent of his knowledge" (*Mishneh Torah*, Laws of Repentance 9:1).

65. Rabbi Abraham Isaac Kook, Le-Mahalakh ha-Ide'ot be-Yisrael [The Development of Ideas in Israel], *Ha-Ivri* 1, no. 6–7 (1912); reprinted in *Igrot HaRe'iyah*, vol. 1 (1961).

66. Rabbi Abraham Isaac Kook, *Orot HaTeshuva* 4:7 (1955), composed 1914–1924; available at www.sefaria.org/Orot_HaTeshuvah.4.7.

67. Rabbi Shlomo Aviner, *Nesichei Adam*, 212.

68. *Sifrei*, Deuteronomy 43:34.

69. Rabbi Abraham Isaac Kook, *Igrot HaRe'iyah*, Letter #96.

70. It is useful to compare the Torah's approach to war with its approach to prayer. Instructions for individual prayer are virtually non-existent in the Written Torah. Maimonides derives the obligation to pray from the verse "and you shall serve Him with all your heart" (Deuteronomy 11:13), which the Sages interpreted as prayer — "Which is the service of the heart? This is prayer" (*Mishneh Torah*, Laws of Prayer 1:1). The Written Torah gives no explicit command regarding the text, frequency, or times of prayer; these details were instituted later by rabbinic tradition.

71. Deuteronomy 20:2–4: "When you draw near to battle, the priest shall come forward and speak to the people. He shall say to them, 'Hear, O Israel: you are drawing near today to battle against your enemies. Let not your heart faint; do not fear or panic or be in dread of them. For the Lord your God is He who goes with you, to fight for you against your enemies, to save you.'"

72. When Jacob died in Egypt, his sons carried his body back to Canaan to bury him in the Cave of Machpelah—the ancient burial ground of Abraham, Sarah, Isaac, Rebecca, and Leah. Esau appeared and blocked the entrance, claiming the last remaining burial plot as his own. As the lengthy legal dispute dragged on, Hushim son of

Dan—Jacob's grandson, who was deaf and could not follow the argument—suddenly grasped the simple moral outrage: his grandfather lay unburied. He immediately acted: "Hushim son of Dan was impaired in his hearing and his speech. He said to them: 'Why are we sitting here?' They pointed to him with a finger and said: 'Because of this man, who will not allow us to bury our father Jacob.' Immediately he drew his sword, struck off his head, and it rolled into the Cave of Machpelah" (*Pirkei d'Rabbi Eliezer* 39). Only Esau's head entered the Cave of Machpelah; no other part of him was worthy of resting alongside the patriarchs. Through this fanciful story, the Sages are saying something profound: Esau's gift to civilization was his intellect—his logic, legal reasoning, and capacity for abstract thought. That was a true contribution to civilization, from which the people of Israel benefited greatly. But Esau's body—his values, his appetites, his vision of power—was forbidden from burial in that sacred place (Rabbi Yehuda Leon Ashkenazi, *Sod Midrash HaToldot* 7:392).

73. Thucydides, *History of the Peloponnesian War*, "Melian Dialogue," where Athenian envoys declare that "the strong do what they can and the weak suffer what they must"; and Thomas Hobbes, *Leviathan*, ch. 13, describing the natural condition of humanity as "nasty, brutish, and short."

74. Aristotle, *Nicomachean Ethics*, esp. I.1–2 (1094a–1094b), where ethics is defined as the inquiry into the good life and the formation of individual virtue; and Aristotle, *Politics*, I.1–2 (1252a–1253a), which presents politics as the "master science" concerned with the organization and flourishing of the polis. Aristotle treats ethics and politics as related but distinct domains with different immediate aims—personal virtue on the one hand, and the stability and welfare of the state on the other.

75. Niccolò Machiavelli, *The Prince*, trans. Harvey C. Mansfield, chapters 17–18. On the preference for fear over love, see ch. 17 ("it is much safer to be feared than loved, if one must lack one of the two"). On the need for the ruler to be both "fox and lion," see ch. 18. On the necessity of appearing virtuous while being prepared to act ruthlessly, see ch. 18, including the statement: "it is not necessary for a prince to have all the above-mentioned qualities... but it is very necessary to appear to have them."

76. Rabbi Yitzchak Nissenbaum, *Kinyanei Kedem* (1939), Leviticus 36.

77. William Smith, Roman Agrarian Laws, in *A Dictionary of Greek and Roman Antiquities* (1875).

78. Rabbi Yehuda Leon Ashkenazi, *Sod Midrash HaToldot* 5:122–128.

79. Rabbi Joseph B. Soloveitchik, Jewish Sovereignty and the Redemption of the Shekhina, *Tradition* 53, no. 1 (Winter 2021): 7–34, https://traditiononline.org/jewishsovereignty/. This essay is the English translation of a Yiddish sermon delivered by Rabbi Soloveitchik at the 28th national convention of the Mizrachi Organization of America in June 1948, just one month after the establishment of the State of Israel.

80. Rabbi Ovadiah Seforno, Exodus 19:6.

81. Yoram Hazony, *The Virtue of Nationalism* (2018), 233.

82. Ibid, 19–20.

83. Ibid, 137.

84. Bernard M. Levinson, The Origins of Constitutional Thought—Found in Deuteronomy, *TheTorah.com* (Aug. 26, 2025), www.thetorah.com/article/the-origins-of-constitutional-thought-found-in-deuteronomy and Joshua Berman, Did Human Rights Begin With Torah?, www.chabad.org/library/article_cdo/aid/1125703/jewish/Did-Human-Rights-Begin-With-Torah.htm.

85. IDF strikes Syrian regime military HQ over threat to Druze in Sweida, *JNS*, July 16, 2025, www.jns.org/israel-warns-syria-over-threats-to-druze-in-sweida/.

86. Maimonides, *Mishneh Torah*, Laws of Kings 10:12.

87. Maimonides, *Mishneh Torah*, Laws of Kings 12:1.

88. Rabbi Abraham Isaac Kook, *Orot* (1961) [composed 1913–1920], 14.

89. *Zohar*, Genesis 4.

90. Israel Eldad, *Pirkei HaGeulah*, "Segulat Yisrael" (1950).

91. Rabbi Yehuda Leon Ashkenazi, *Sod Midrash HaToldot*, 7:89–90.

92. Rabbi Abraham Isaac Kook, *Orot HaMilchama* 9 (1961).

93. Rabbi Chaim ben Attar (1696–1743), *Or HaChaim*, Exodus 19:7.

No Going Back

94. *Mishnah* Kiddushin 66b.

95. According to Jewish law, Jewish status follows the mother, who is the definitive source of Jewish identity. This principle is clearly stated in the *Mishnah* (Kiddushin 66b), which teaches that a child is Jewish if the mother is Jewish, regardless of the father's identity. The Talmud derives this from Deuteronomy 7:3–4, where only the phrase "he (the non-Jewish father) will turn your son away" is mentioned, implying that a child from a Jewish mother remains Jewish even if the father is not. This maternal lineage basis was codified in later legal works like the *Shulchan Aruch* (Even HaEzer 8:5) and has been universally accepted in Orthodox Judaism since the giving of the Torah. This rule also reflects practical and historical considerations: the mother is always known with certainty, while paternity can be ambiguous, and it serves to preserve the continuity and identity of the Jewish people across generations.

96. Rabbi Meir Soloveitchik, The Jewish Mother—a Theology, *Azure*, Spring 5765 / 2005, no. 20, https://azure.org.il/article.php?id=187.

97. Exodus 12:38. "And also, a great mixed multitude went up with them, and flocks and cattle, very much livestock." See Rashi there: "a great mixed multitude. A mixture of nations of gerim."

98. Exodus 18:1–27. See Rashi on Exodus 18:27: "And he went away to his land": L'gayer (to convert) the members of his family.

99. Andrew Lapin, Why Tucker Carlson pushed for Jewish DNA tests, and the Khazar theory touted by antisemites, *Times of Israel*, February 28, 2026, www.timesofisrael.com/why-tucker-carlson-pushed-for-jewish-dna-tests-and-the-khazar-theory-touted-by-antisemites/.

100. *Ruth Rabbah* 2:20.

101. Rabbi Moshe Miller, *Rising Moon: Unraveling the Book of Ruth* (2015), 95.

102. Babylonian Talmud, Bava Batra 91a.

103. Babylonian Talmud, Yevamot 47a.

104. Rabbi Moshe Miller, *Rising Moon: Unraveling the Book of Ruth* (2015), 95.

105. The Talmudic sequence describes the logic of conversion, not its timeline. In principle, a candidate needs to demonstrate only one thing before being accepted: genuine commitment to joining the Jewish people. Religious instruction comes after. In practice, today's rabbinic courts require months or even years of study before the conversion is finalized—but this is not a departure from the Talmudic principle. Modern rabbis lengthen the process to ensure that the candidate's commitment to joining the Jewish people is sincere and lasting, and not the product of a passing impulse.

106. Michael Wyschogrod, *The Body of Faith: God in the People Israel* (1983), 57.

107. Rabbi Joseph B. Soloveitchik, *Kol Dodi Dofek*, The Covenants of Sinai and Egypt (1957), www.sefaria.org.il/Kol_Dodi_Dofek %2C_The_Covenants_of_Sinai_and_Egypt.8-13?lang=en.

108. Rabbi Aharon Lichtenstein, Conversion: Birth and Law, in *Leaves of Faith*, vol. 2, 145.

109. Cited in Gavriela Ben Shmuel, *Min HaAyin el HaAni*, 353.

110. Jewish law regards conversion as permanent membership in the nation. A convert becomes fully Jewish—like a child born into the family—with no possibility of reversal, even if they later abandon observance or reject the community entirely. This reflects the Jewish people's national character: once you join Israel as a people, the bond is irrevocable, like family ties that cannot be undone. A resentful son remains a son; an apostate Jew remains Jewish under Jewish law (Babylonian Talmud, Yevamot 47b; Maimonides, *Laws of Forbidden Relations* 13:4; *Shulchan Aruch*, Yoreh De'ah 268:12).

The Land that Devours

111. *Numbers Rabbah* 16:5.

112. Rabbi Menachem Mendel Schneerson, *Torat Menachem* 14:155 (1989) [discourse delivered July 23, 1989].

113. See Babylonian Talmud, Sotah 35a: the rabbis explain that when the spies said, "they are stronger than us," it can be read as "stronger than Him," meaning they claimed even God could not defeat the Canaanites—interpreted as a moment of heresy in doubting divine power within the natural order.

114. Rabbi Schneur Zalman of Liadi, *Likkutei Torah*, Shelach, "U'Lekachtem"; see also the Lubavitcher Rebbe, *Likkutei Sichot*, vol. 4, Shelach, sicha 2.

115. Rabbi Yitzchak Nissenbaum, *Kinyanei Kedem*, The Meraglim and the Ma'apilim.

The Unmarked Grave

116. *Deuteronomy Rabbah*, Chapter 2, Section 8.

The Seduction of Normalcy

117. Rabbi Moshe Isserles, Glosses to *Shulchan Aruch*, Yoreh De'ah 178:1.

118. Nachmanides, Leviticus 19:2.

119. Babylonian Talmud, Sanhedrin 103b.

120. The Bible does not explicitly describe the destruction of Shiloh or the Tabernacle, but rabbinic tradition infers it from the events of I Samuel 4 and Jeremiah 7:12 ("Go now to My place which was in Shiloh... see what I did to it because of the evil of My people Israel"). The Sages state that after the Philistines captured the Ark at Aphek (I Samuel 4:11), Shiloh was attacked and the Tabernacle destroyed shortly thereafter (Babylonian Talmud, Zevachim 112b & Sotah 9b; Jerusalem Talmud Megillah 1:7).

121. Babylonian Talmud, Sanhedrin 20b.

122. Rabbi Meir Wisser explains that the people's request for a king was not a personal rejection of Samuel but a rejection of Torah law itself: "They did not want the Torah's laws nor the judgment of a judge according to its statutes. This was rebellion against God and His Torah, not against Samuel, as it is written (Exodus 16:8): 'Your complaints are not against us, but against the Lord.'" (Malbim, I Samuel, 8:6).

123. Rabbi Yigal Ariel, *Oz Melech* (2008), 38.

124. Rabbi Shlomo Aviner, *Nesichei Adam*, 213.

125. "The Sages taught: King Hezekiah performed six actions. With regard to three of them, the Sages of his generation conceded to him; and with regard to three of them, the Sages did not concede to him... He intercalated the year, delaying the advent of the month of Nissan during Nissan, and they did not concede to him" (Babylonian Talmud, Pesachim 56a). The Talmud explains that he declared the first day of the Hebrew month of Nissan to be the thirtieth of Adar and only then intercalated the year (see II Chronicles 30:2).

126. Jeroboam instituted a festival "in the eighth month, on the fifteenth day of the month ... the month which he had devised of his own heart," deliberately altering the Torah calendar in imitation of Judah's festivals (1 Kings 12:32–33), an act condemned throughout the Hebrew Bible as the paradigmatic sin that "made Israel sin" (e.g., 2 Kings 10:31; 13:6; 14:24) and later summarized by rabbinic writers as effectively "uprooting the Torah" by changing its divinely mandated times of worship (*Yalkut Shimoni*, I Kings 12 §184).

127. Rabbi Jonathan Eibuschitz, *Ahavat Yonatan* (1760), Parshat Balak.

128. Jeremiah 29:10.

A Civil War for the Jewish Soul

129. The Cyrus Cylinder, now housed in the British Museum, is a clay barrel inscription dating to around 539 BCE. Discovered in Babylon in 1879, it records Cyrus's policy of restoring displaced peoples to their homelands and returning their sacred objects. Some scholars have cited it as evidence that the biblical account of Cyrus's decree (Ezra 1:1–4) is merely an expression of standard Persian imperial policy. But the text of the decree is notably different from the Cylinder's general

language. It names the God of Israel specifically, charges the Jewish people with a particular mission, and frames Cyrus' own authority as a gift from Israel's God. See Edwin Yamauchi, *Persia and the Bible* (1990).

130. Ezra 10.

131. Rabbi Yitzchak Nissenbaum, *Masoret V'Cherut* (1939).

132. Noam Levavi and Elisaf Ofen, Between Judaism and Jews, Between 'My Judaism' and a Covenant with God, *Olam Katan* #1018, 2 Cheshvan 5786.

133. Dara Horn, interview by Haviv Rettig Gur, *Ask Haviv Anything*, podcast audio, Episode 52, Why Do People Hate Jews, October 12, 2025, https://podcasts.apple.com/us/podcast/ask-haviv-anything/id1794590850?i=1000732282556.

134. Gersonides, Esther 3:8.

135. 2 Maccabees 4:7–15, 20. Jason "wrote to the king, permitting the Jews to follow the Greek way of life... he set up a gymnasium right below the citadel... many even of the priests... neglected the altar and... went to the gymnasium and stripped and acted lawlessly there, disdaining what was holy" (11–14).

136. Maimonides, *Mishneh Torah*, Hilchot Megillah veChanukah, chapter 3.

137. Louis Casiano, VP Harris' husband botches Hanukkah story on social media during celebration of major Jewish holiday, *Fox News*, December 11, 2023, www.foxnews.com/politics/vp-harris-husband-botches-hanukkah-story-social-media-celebration-jewish-holiday.

138. 1 Maccabees 3:59.

139. Elie Mischel, Maccabees in MAGA Country: Ben Shapiro's AmFest Moment, December 23, 2024, *The Israel Bible*, www.theisraelbible.com/maccabees-in-maga-country-ben-shapiros-amfest-moment/.

140. Purim and Chanukah commemorate separate historical events occurring roughly two centuries apart. According to modern historical scholarship, Purim likely took place in the mid-fifth century BCE during the later period of Persian rule, closer in time to Chanukah than the earlier rabbinic tradition suggests. Chanukah, by contrast, marks the Hasmonean revolt and rededication of the Second Temple in Jerusalem in 165 BCE. Purim celebrates Jewish survival in exile without national sovereignty, while Chanukah commemorates the restoration of political independence and religious independence in the land of Israel.

141. Babylonian Talmud, Megillah 14a.

142. Babylonian Talmud, Moed Katan 26a.

143. Rabbi Israel Meir Kagan, *Mishnah Berurah*, 561:1.

The Self-Induced Death of Jewish Sovereignty

144. Nachmanides, in his commentary on Genesis 49:10, explains the necessity of keeping Jewish political leadership within the line of Judah: "In my opinion, the kings from other tribes, who ruled over Israel after David, went against the wish of their father Jacob by diverting the inheritance of Judah to another tribe... This was also the reason for the punishment of the Hasmoneans, who reigned during the Second Temple... It is also possible that [in addition to the Hasmoneans having sinned for assuming royalty when they were not

from the tribe of Judah,] they sinned in ruling on account of their being priests... it was not for them to rule, but only to perform the service of God." Nachmanides highlights two violations: usurping the throne from the line of Judah and exercising priestly authority, when priests were intended only for the service of God.

145. Josephus, *Antiquities of the Jews* XIII.301–323, XIV.1–6; *The Jewish War* I.89–98.

146. Josephus, *Antiquities* XIV.16–74; *The Jewish War* I.123–157.

147. Barry Strauss, *Jews vs. Rome: Two Centuries of Rebellion Against the World's Mightiest Empire* (2025).

148. Flavius Josephus, between Rome and Jerusalem, www.morasha.com.br/en/biographies/flavio-josefo-between-rome-and-jerusalem.html.

149. Menahem Mor, *The Second Jewish Revolt: The Bar Kokhba War, 132–136 CE* (2016).

150. The classic Christian caricature of Pharisees as cold-hearted legalists is both historically inaccurate and tragically antisemitic. Far from rigid enforcers, Pharisees were often lenient popular teachers who democratized Torah study through synagogues and oral tradition, emphasizing mercy (Hillel: "What is hateful to you, do not do to another" as the whole Torah [Shabbat 31a]). Paul never abandoned his identity as a proud Pharisee (Philippians 3:5). This caricature, which developed in later Christian interpretation and preaching, fueled two millennia of Christian antisemitism by conflating Gospel villains with all Jews, birthing "Pharisee = hypocrite" in Western consciousness—a

slur scholars today universally reject as polemical distortion turned genocidal libel.

151. Joan E. Taylor, *The Essenes, the Scrolls, and the Dead Sea* (2012), 55–67, 291–313.

152. Rabbi Yehuda Leon Ashkenazi, *Sod Midrash HaToldot* 6:243.

153. Rabbi Yehuda Leon Ashkenazi, *Sod Midrash HaToldot* 7:316.

154. Babylonian Talmud, Yoma 9b.

155. Babylonian Talmud, Gittin 55b–56a.

156. Babylonian Talmud, Nedarim 81a.

157. Rabbi Zvi Yehuda Kook, *Sichot Rav Tzvi Yehuda*, volume 8, "Talmud Torah," 3.

The Nation that Refused to Die

158. Shmuel Yosef Agnon, Nobel Banquet Speech, Stockholm City Hall, December 10, 1966, www.nobelprize.org/prizes/literature/1966/agnon/speech/.

159. Rabbi Yehuda Leon Ashkenazi, *Haggadah Ivrit* (2005), 17.

160. Mark Twain, Concerning the Jews, *Harper's New Monthly Magazine* 99, no. 592 (September 1899): 789–803.

161. Heinrich Graetz, *The Structure of Jewish History, and Other Essays* (1975) [originally delivered as a lecture in 1874 and first published in *Monatsschrift für Geschichte und Wissenschaft des Judentums* 23: 1–16, 49–64], 84.

162. Rabbi Reuven Sasson, *Kumi Ori*, 30–31.

163. Babylonian Talmud, Berachot 8a.

164. Rabbi Jonathan Eibuschitz, *Ya'arot Devash* (1783), 2:10.

165. Rashi, Ezekiel 36:20. "And they profaned My Holy Name: They lowered My honor. And what is the profanation? In that their enemies said of them, 'These are the people of the Lord, and they have come out of His land, and He had no power to save His people and His land.'"

166. Rashi, Numbers 31:3.

167. Jerusalem Talmud, Berachot 2:4.

168. Rabbi Shlomo Aviner, *Commentary on Lamentations*, 126.

169. *Pesikta d'Rav Kahana*, Vayishlach 32:25.

170. *Midrash Shochar Tov* 8:3.

171. Rabbi Judah HaLevi, *Kuzari* 2:23–24.

172. A later medieval legend claims that Rabbi Judah HaLevi was killed upon reaching Jerusalem, trampled by an Arab horseman while reciting his Ode to Zion at the Western Wall. This account appears only in much later sources, such as *Shalshelet Ha-Kabbalah*, and has no contemporary corroboration. The earliest reliable evidence regarding HaLevi's final journey comes from documents preserved in the Cairo Geniza. These include letters showing that he departed Alexandria by ship for the land of Israel in the late spring of 1141, including a letter written while awaiting favorable winds. A subsequent Geniza letter dated November 1141 refers to him as zichrono

livracha, indicating that he had died by that time. On the basis of these documents, modern scholars conclude that HaLevi did leave Egypt and may have reached the land of Israel, but died shortly thereafter; the precise circumstances and location of his death remain unknown. See S. D. Goitein, *Letters of Medieval Jewish Traders* (1973).

173. Rabbi Isaiah Horowitz, *Shenei Luchot HaBrit*, end of Commentary to Sukkah. The Torah records: "An Aramean sought to destroy my father, and he went down to Egypt and sojourned there" (Deuteronomy 26:5). From the word "sojourned," the Haggadah derives that "Our forefather Jacob did not descend to Egypt permanently but only to dwell there temporarily." Rabbi Aharon Lichtenstein points out that this cannot refer to Jacob's conscious intent at the time—it is hardly conceivable that a sick, half-blind old man, utterly dependent on his family and consumed with thoughts of his own death, harbored fantasies of eventually returning to Israel. Rather, the Sages are describing his mindset. Jacob knew full well that he would die in Egypt. What he insisted upon was that he would live there as an outsider—separated from Egyptian culture by an unbridgeable existential and spiritual chasm. He could not, physically, go home. But he refused, until his last breath, to feel at home. See Rabbi Aharon Lichtenstein, Diaspora Religious Zionism: Some Current Reflections, in *Religious Zionism and the Secular World*, Orthodox Forum Series (1998), 21–22.

174. Rabbi Abraham Isaac Kook, *Orot*, Eretz Yisrael 6.

175. In traditional Jewish thought, tikkun olam ("repairing the world") originates in the *Mishnah* (Gittin 4:3–9; Bava Metzia 5:7) as a rabbinic legal principle for specific enactments that preserve social order and prevent injustice within Jewish communities, such as limiting

debt collection or clarifying divorce procedures. It appears poetically in the Aleinu prayer (c. 2nd–3rd century CE), expressing hope for God's messianic reign where idolatry ends and all nations recognize the Creator. Progressive American Jews since the 1960s, particularly in Reform circles, redefined it as a vague mandate for humanitarian activism—like building houses for the poor in Central America—severing it from Jewish law and thought to create a feel-good "social justice" ethic that substitutes generic niceness for Torah observance and Jewish peoplehood.

176. Rabbi Ashkenazi saw this self-deception clearly: "The common excuse [for remaining in exile] today is that we have a mission among the nations. Perhaps there is still something left to do there, who can know? This is what some of the anti-Zionists claim. 'There is still work to do in the exile.' Have we not learned the lessons of history? This is what the Jews of Frankfurt in Germany said more than a hundred and fifty years ago. They saw themselves as fulfilling a messianic mission among the Germans. They saw themselves as the educators of these barbarians. There exists a very deep naiveté within the people of Israel, a vanity of innocence." *Sod Midrash HaToldot*, 2:162.

177. Rabbi Yehuda Leon Ashkenazi, *Sod Midrash HaToldot*, 7:133.

178. Rabbi Steven Pruzansky, American Rabbi 'Blessed' to Make Aliyah, July 30, 2020, unitedwithisrael.org/american-rabbi-blessed-to-make-aliyah/.

Faith Without a People: Christianity's Turn from Israel

179. James Kirchik, Tucker Carlson's Dark Turn, *National Review*, July 24, 2025, www.nationalreview.com/magazine/2025/09/tucker-carlsons-dark-turn/.

180. Rashi, Genesis 41:55. The verse states: "And when all the land of Egypt was famished, the people cried to Pharaoh for bread; and Pharaoh said to all the Egyptians: 'Go to Joseph; what he says to you, do.'" Rashi comments: "For Joseph was telling them to circumcise themselves. When they came to Pharaoh and said, 'This is what he tells us [to do],' Pharaoh replied: 'Why didn't you gather produce? Didn't he notify you that the years of famine were coming?' They said to Pharaoh, 'We indeed gathered, but it rotted!' He said to them, 'If that is the case, do whatever he tells you. You see that he decreed against your produce and it rotted; what if he should decree against us and we die?!'"

181. Menachem Kellner, *Must a Jew Believe Anything?* (2008), 24.

182. Raphael Jospe, *Jewish Philosophy in the Middle Ages* (2019), 15.

183. Joseph Klausner, *From Jesus to Paul* (1943), 591.

184. Pamela Eisenbaum, *Paul Was Not a Christian: The Original Message of a Misunderstood Apostle* (2009), 252.

185. Rashi, the greatest Jewish Bible commentator of the medieval period, who lived in France from 1040 to 1105, a full thousand years after Paul, believed that the moment Paul announced had not yet come. In his commentary on Deuteronomy 6:4, the verse that forms the Shema, Judaism's central declaration of faith ("Hear O Israel, the Lord is our God, the Lord is one"), Rashi reads the words "our God" carefully: if God is "our God"—Israel's God—then He is not yet the God of the other nations. That day is coming, but it has not arrived. As Rashi writes: "The Lord, who is now our God and not the God of the other nations—He will be declared in the future 'the one God,' as it is said: 'For then I will convert the peoples to a pure language

that all of them call in the name of the Lord' (Zephaniah 3:9), and it is also said: 'On that day will the Lord be one and His name one' (Zechariah 14:9)." Every observant Jew recites the Shema twice a day. According to Rashi, they are affirming each time that God is not yet universally recognized as the God of all humanity—that this remains a promise, not yet a reality. Paul believed the hour had struck. Rashi, a millennium later, saw no evidence that it had.

186. Rabbi Yehuda Leon Ashkenazi, *Sod Midrash HaToldot* 5:322–324.

187. Rabbi Yehuda Leon Ashkenazi, *Sod Midrash HaToldot* 5:325.

188. Yoram Hazony, *The Virtue of Nationalism*, 21.

189. Rabbi Elijah Benamozegh, *Israel and Humanity* (1995) [Original French title: *Israël et l'Humanité*, 1914].

190. Ruth Wisse, *Jews and Power* (2007), 14. See also Dr. Michael Wyschogrod, *Abraham's Promise: Judaism and Jewish-Christian Relations* (2004), 183–184: "Israel refuses to exchange its historical and national messianism for a doctrine of individual salvation. Israel refuses to invent the idea of a church which forces men to live in two jurisdictions and to assume two identities: a member of a nation and a member of a church."

191. Pontifical Biblical Commission, *The Jewish People and Their Sacred Scriptures in the Christian Bible* (Vatican City: Libreria Editrice Vaticana, 2002), no. 64.

192. *Extra ecclesiam nulla salus* ("Outside the Church there is no salvation") is a longstanding Catholic dogma originating with St. Cypri-

an of Carthage (Ep. 72.21), affirmed in councils like Lateran IV and Vatican II.

193. Cyprian of Carthage, *On the Unity of the Church* (*De ecclesiae catholicae unitate*), 6. See https://christianhistoryinstitute.org/incontext/article/cyprian.

194. The Seven Noahide Laws, derived from rabbinic tradition in the Talmud (Sanhedrin 56a–b), form a universal moral code given to all humanity via Noah after the Flood: (1) establish courts of justice; (2) prohibit idolatry; (3) prohibit blasphemy; (4) prohibit murder; (5) prohibit sexual immorality (adultery, incest); (6) prohibit theft; (7) prohibit eating flesh torn from a living animal. These basic ethical principles—prohibiting violence, immorality, injustice, and cruelty while affirming monotheism and social order—are intuitive moral truths endorsed by all God-fearing peoples across civilizations. Adhering to these laws lets each nation freely serve God in its own unique way, shaped by its culture and traditions, without needing to take on Jewish ritual law (Maimonides, *Mishneh Torah*, Kings 8:11; 9:1).

195. Amy-Jill Levine, *The Misunderstood Jew: The Church and the Scandal of the Jewish Jesus* (2006), 158.

196. Eric Levenson, Outrage spreads wide after federal agents kill man in Minneapolis, *Los Angeles Times*, January 24, 2026, www.latimes.com/world-nation/story/2026-01-25/protesters-demand-immigration-agents-leave-minneapolis-after-fatal-shooting.

197. See Yoram Hazony, *The Virtue of Nationalism*, 105: "Just as a family can feel pain, so too can it experience triumph and tragedy, desire and fear, interests and aspirations. A nation can suffer pain, for we have all experienced it. We have experienced it when the members

of our nation are cut down in our streets or held hostage in a foreign land... A heavy sense of hurt and humiliation fills the public spaces and clings to everything taking place throughout the land, so that even very young children, who do not understand what has happened, feel pained and ashamed. It is the nation that has been harmed. It is the nation that has been shamed."

198. Anders Runesson, The Question of Terminology: The Architecture of Contemporary Discussions on Paul, in *Paul within Judaism: Restoring the First-Century Context to the Apostle* (2015), 65.

199. Shmuel Feiner, *The Jewish Enlightenment* (2004), 51–60.

200. Maimonides, *Mishneh Torah*, Laws of Kings 11:4.

201. Historical data confirms rapid Jewish assimilation after conversion to Christianity. In 19th-century Germany, approximately 30,000 Jews converted between 1810–1871; by 1900, their descendants showed intermarriage rates approaching 90% in the second generation, leading to near-total absorption (Uriel Zimmer, *Torah-Judaism and the State of Israel* (1961), 143). In Tsarist Russia, 40,000 Jewish conversions (1880s–1914) resulted in complete cultural dissolution within 50 years (*Jewish Encyclopedia*, "Conversion"). Spain's conversos (1449–1492) exemplify this: first-generation marranos often practiced crypto-Judaism, but by the third generation, most had fully assimilated into Spanish Christian society.

202. Mrs. Meir Says Tension Marked Talk With Pope, January 20, 1973, *New York Times*,
www.nytimes.com/1973/01/20/archives/mrs-meir-says-tension-marked-talk-with-pope-mrs-meir-says-that.html.

203. Rabbi Yehuda Leon Ashkenazi, Le Mythe et le Midrach, *Maayanot* 8 (1970), 20.

Liberty, Equality... Oblivion

204. Berr Isaac Berr, Letter from a citizen, member of the former community of Jews of Lorraine to his fellow Jews, on the occasion of the right of active citizenship granted to Jews by the decree of September 28, 1791.

205. Count Stanislas de Clermont-Tonnerre, National Assembly debates, December 22–24, 1789.

206. Assembly of Jewish Notables and Grand Sanhedrin, Paris, May–March 1807, cited in Center for Jewish History, "France."

207. The same challenge to Jewish peoplehood arose in France a few generations later, though the ideology had changed. In the 1950s, French Jewish students faced pressure to abandon their Jewish identity not for French nationalism, but for Communist internationalism and loyalty to the proletariat. Rabbi Yehuda Leon Ashkenazi recalled: "I remember that during the 1950s we were able, within the framework of the UEJF (the Union of Jewish Students in France), to maintain a unified position regarding Jewish students who belonged to the Marxist movement—especially members of the Communist Party, which at the time was at the height of its power. We succeeded in preserving this unity for several years, despite the very wide range of opinions held by different members. But the issue became too sharp for us not to decide. After the war, we reached the conclusion that there is a limit to the diversity of opinions we are willing to tolerate. We adopted a clear position: anyone who denies our national dimension places himself outside the collective. Anyone who does not merely

think this way but actively denies our national foundations betrays his people. This is what happened with the early Christians—they were Jews who betrayed Judea and came to see themselves as Romans. The same thing happened here: instead of seeing themselves as part of Israel, those student members of the Communist Party saw themselves as part of a 'new Israel' and acted against their own brothers. I remember that one of them once told me: 'If the price of the world revolution is the murder of a hundred thousand Jews, I am willing to pay it.'" (Rabbi Yehuda Leon Ashkenazi, *Sod Midrash HaToldot*, 7:45). Whether the demand was to become French nationalists under Napoleon or Communist internationalists in the 1950s, the pattern remained constant: Jews were pressured to abandon their peoplehood for acceptance in the broader society.

208. Assembly of Jewish Notables and Grand Sanhedrin, Paris, May–March 1807, cited in Center for Jewish History, "France," American Jewish Archives.

209. Rabbi Lazare Isidore, cited in Simon Schwarzfuchs, *Les Juifs de France* (1992), 266.

210. Herman Cohen, a leading voice of liberal Judaism in early twentieth-century Germany, similarly argued that the absence of sovereignty and power allowed Jewish thought to focus on universal ethics and Messianic ideals, unburdened by the demands of government. Freed from political constraints and territorial claims, Jews in the diaspora could refine their moral vision and become exemplary citizens in their host nations. See Ruth Wisse, *Jews and Power*, 6. For Cohen and other intellectuals, "the Jewish people was in its essence an achievement of the 'spirit,' which would be degraded and corrupted the moment it was harnessed to tanks and explosives, politics and

intrigue, bureaucracy and capital—in short, to the massive worldly powers of the state." See Yoram Hazony, *The Jewish State: The Struggle for Israel's Soul*, XXIV.

211. Friedrich Schleiermacher, *On Religion* (1996), 22–23.

212. Leora Batnitzky, *How Judaism Became a Religion: An Introduction to Modern Jewish Thought* (2011), 26.

213. Leora Batnitzky, *How Judaism Became a Religion*, 37.

214. Michael Walzer, The Anomalies of Jewish Identity, quoting Gabriel Riesser in the Frankfurt Assembly (1848). In the same vein, the Jewish political economist, Franz Oppenheimer, said: "Germany is my fatherland, my homeland, the land of all my yearnings." Yoram Hazony, *The Jewish State: The Struggle for Israel's Soul* (2000), 181.

215. Rabbi Mordechai Benet, cited in Israel Bettan, Early Reform in Contemporaneous Responsa, *Jubilee Volume (1875–1925)* (1925), 278–280.

216. Rabbi Samson Raphael Hirsch, *Nineteen Letters* (1995) [Originally published in German, *Neunzehn Briefe über Judenthum*, 1836], 224.

217. Leora Batnitzky, *How Judaism Became a Religion*, 42–43.

218. Ambassador Yechiel Leiter, *Aloh Naaleh* [1982], 137–138.

219. Rabbi Yissachar Shlomo Teichtal, *Eim HaBanim Semeicha* (1943) Chapter 3, Part 8, The Exile Jew.

The Illusion of Acceptance

220. Ronald W. Clark, *Einstein: The Life and Times* (1971), 374.

221. Karl Lueger, speech at a meeting of the Christian Socialist Workers' Association, Vienna, 20 July 1899, cited in *Weiningers Nacht* (1989), and quoted in "Karl Lueger's rise to Mayor of Vienna," *Die Welt der Habsburger*.

222. Karl Lueger, cited in Richard S. Geehr, *"I Decide Who Is a Jew!": The Papers of Dr. Karl Lueger* (1982).

223. *Encyclopaedia Britannica*, J'accuse, last updated April 11, 2011.

224. Rabbi Meir Simcha of Dvinsk, *Meshech Chochmah*, Bechukotai.

225. Rabbi Yaakov Moshe Charlop, *MiMaayanei HaYeshua*, 186.

226. Rabbi Moshe Leiter, *Derash Darash Moshe*, Vayeshev.

227. Rabbi Yehuda Leon Ashkenazi, *Sod Midrash HaToldot* 5:247.

The Sickly Girl Awakens

228. Both Rabbi Abraham Isaac Kook and Theodor Herzl used the image of a critically ill young girl to symbolize the Jewish people after exile. Kook wrote of "the gentle and well-loved girl...after a long, desperate illness...opened her eyes...her spirit and body growing stronger, asking for medicine, food, learning, and work" (*Orot HaRe'iyah* 148:204). Herzl similarly evoked a people emerging from a long slumber, fragile but alive, ready to reclaim their destiny.

229. Maimonides, *Mishneh Torah*, Hilchot Teshuvah 7:5.

230. Babylonian Talmud, Ketubot 110b.

231. Rabbi Yehuda Alkalai, *Petach ke-Chudo shel Machat* (1868), 324.

232. Rabbi Yehuda Alkalai, *Petach ke-Chudo shel Machat*, commentary on Jeremiah 31:20–22.

233. Rabbi Zvi Hirsch Kalischer, *Derishat Tziyon* (1862), 179.

234. Aryeh Newman, "Rabbi Zvi Hirsch Kalischer: Father of the Third Return to Zion," *Tradition: A Journal of Orthodox Jewish Thought* 5, no. 1 (Fall 1962): 76–89, https://traditiononline.org/rabbi-zvi-hirsch-kalischer-father-of-the-third-return-to-zion/.

235. Moses Hess, *Rome and Jerusalem* (1862), Fourth Letter. The Latin phrase literally means, 'Where it goes well, there is my fatherland,' expressing the idea that one's homeland is simply wherever life is comfortable. Hess condemned this attitude as rootless assimilation that denied the historical and spiritual bond of the Jewish people to their own land.

236. Moses Hess, *Rome and Jerusalem*, Twelfth Letter.

237. Moses Hess, *Rome and Jerusalem*, Twelfth Letter.

The Man Who Ignited a Nation

238. Theodor Herzl, *The Complete Diaries of Theodor Herzl*, 2:607–08 (August 29, 1897).

239. *Encyclopaedia Britannica*, Dreyfus Affair, last updated September 3, 2025.

240. "The Jews today have no more burning aspiration than to be invisible among the nations... They are more English than the English, more French than the French, more German than the German. Only the Zionists, my friends, want to be Jewish Jews (jüdische Juden)." Theodor Herzl, Letter to anonymous correspondent, June 9, 1903, in *Theodor Herzl: Selected Letters* (1989), 287.

241. Theodor Herzl, A Solution of the Jewish Question, *Jewish Chronicle*, January 17, 1896, 10–12.

242. Theodor Herzl, *The Jewish State: An Attempt at a Modern Solution of the Jewish Question*, February 14, 1896.

243. Theodor Herzl, *Diary of Theodor Herzl*, January 26, 1904.

244. Chaim Weizman, Introduction to *Theodor Herzl: Medinat HaYehudim*.

245. Elie Mischel, When Herzl Refused to Kiss the Pope's Ring, *HaMizrachi*, Yom HaAtzmaut 2026, https://mizrachi.org/hamizrachi/when-herzl-refused-to-kiss-the-popes-ring/.

246. Theodor Herzl, *The Complete Diaries of Theodor Herzl*, September 3, 1897. In an 1899 speech in London, Herzl reflected on the first Congress: "At the time we began our movement we only believed there was a Jewish nation. Today we know it... We Jews shall yet live in the land of Israel as free men. Whether I shall be there or not is of little account to the cause, but should I be spared to be there, nothing will give me greater joy, no memory will afford me greater delight, than the recollection of the first Basel Congress of 1897. For it was then that this seemingly dead Jewish nation gave its first signs of life renewed; no matter with what trepidation and hope, we listened to the weak

breathing and the slow pulsation, we were convinced that our people as a nation yet lived." Theodor Herzl, Next Goal, Charter for Palestine, speech given in London, June 26, 1899; cited in *Jewish Chronicle*, June 30, 1899, 13.

247. Rabbi Abraham Eliyahu Kaplan, *B'Ikvot Hayirah* (1956), 85.

248. Theodor Herzl, *Zionist Writings*, Volume 1 (1960), 65.

249. Vladimir Jabotinsky, article in *Odesskaya Novosti*, 1 January 1908, cited in Hillel Halkin, *Jabotinsky: A Life* (2014), 68–69.

The Jews Who Could Not See

250. Edwin Montagu, Memorandum on the Anti-Semitism of the Present (British) Government, submitted to the British Cabinet, 23 August 1917, in Cabinet Paper 24/24, www.jewishvirtuallibrary.org/montagu-memo-on-british-government-s-anti-semitism.

251. Ibid.

252. Rabbi Shimon Glitzenstein, *Haketz HaDochek*, 86.

253. Cited in Georges Yitshak Weisz, *Theodor Herzl: A New Reading* (2013), 15, n.53.

254. Theodor Herzl, *Zionist Writings*, 16.

255. Babylonian Talmud, Sotah 48b.

256. Rabbi Zvi Yehudah Kook, Selected Teachings of HaRav Tzvi Yehuda HaKohen Kook, Adapted from the book, *Torat Eretz Yisrael*, by Rabbi David Samson, based on Rabbi Shlomo Aviner, *Sichot*

HaRav Tzvi Yehuda (1991), https://machonmeir.net/selected-teachings-of-harav-tzvi-yehuda/.

257. Rabbi Shmuel Mohilever, cited in *HaKetz HaDochak*, 54.

258. *Yalkut Shimoni*, Lamentations 3, #1038.

259. *Tanchuma*, Metzora 9.

260. Rabbenu Bahye ben Asher, *Kad HaKemach*, 117–118.

261. Rabbi David Kimchi, Isaiah 59:16.

Ashkenazic Amnesia, Sephardic Memory

262. Mia Amran, Yavnieli and the Yemenite Aliyah, https://blog.nli.org.il/en/yavnieli-yemenite-aliyah/.

263. Gavriela Ben Shmuel, *Min HaAyin el HaAni*, 354.

264. Martin Gilbert, *Israel: A History* (1998), 234–236.

Vindicated at Last

265. Mark Twain, *The Innocents Abroad, or The New Pilgrim's Progress* (1869), 349–350.

266. Sir John William Dawson, *Modern Science in Bible Lands: Their Scenery, Early Inhabitants, Geological Formation, Natural Resources, Monuments, and Antiquities, as Illustrating and Illustrated by Sacred History* (1889), 449–50.

267. Nachmanides, Leviticus 26:32.

268. Rabbi Elijah of Vilna, end of commentary to *Sifra DeTzni'uta*.

269. Rabbi David Altschuler of Prague, Psalm 102:19.

270. Rabbi Yehuda Leon Ashkenazi, *The Adventure in Orsay*, 9–28.

271. Gavriella Ben Shmuel, *Min HaAyin el HaAni*, Introduction.

272. Ibid, 39.

The Post-Zionist Revolt

273. Arnold J. Toynbee, cited in Toynbee Predicts Gains by Judaism; Historian Assails Zionism as Akin to Apartheid, *The New York Times*, May 7, 1961.

274. The Herzog-Toynbee Debate, McGill University, Montreal, January 31, 1961, in Yaacov Herzog, *A People that Dwells Alone: Speeches and Writings of Yaacov Herzog* (1975), 46.

275. Yair Rosenberg, When an Israeli Ambassador Debated a British Historian on Israel's Legitimacy—and Won, *Tablet*, January 31, 2014, www.tabletmag.com/sections/news/articles/herzog-toynbee-1961.

276. United Nations General Assembly Resolution 3379, November 10, 1975.

277. Rabbi Abraham Isaac Kook, *Iggrot HaRe'iyah*, Volume 1, #182.

278. Rabbi Meir Y. Soloveitchik, Moshe Dayan's Tragic Blunder, *Commentary*, February 2023, www.commentary.org/articles/meir-soloveichik/moshe-dayan-temple-mount/.

279. Babylonian Talmud, Sanhedrin 44a.

280. Yoram Hazony, *The Jewish State: The Struggle for Israel's Soul*, 10.

281. Baruch Kimmerling, Academic History Caught in the Crossfire: The Case of Israeli-Jewish Historiography, in *History and Memory* (Spring-Summer 1995), 42–43.

282. Israel's Law of Return, passed July 5, 1950, https://main.knesset.gov.il/EN/About/History/Documents/kns1_return_eng.pdf.

283. David Ben-Gurion, Knesset speech introducing the Law of Return, July 3, 1950 (paraphrased; see full debate at Knesset archives: main.knesset.gov.il).

284. Yoram Hazony, *The Jewish State: The Struggle for Israel's Soul*, 56–59.

285. Israel's State Education Law, 5713-1953, §2(a): "State education... is intended to base its curriculum on the values of Jewish culture and the achievements of science, on love of the homeland and loyalty to the State and the Jewish people..."

286. Elham Maree, *Reforms in Education System in Israel: A Journey Between Centralization and Decentralization* (2020), 396–401.

287. Adam Eliyahu Berkowitz, More Religious Education Necessary To Win the War, *Israel365 News*, February 15, 2024, https://israel365news.com/386420/more-religious-education-necessary-to-win-the-war/.

288. Zev Stub, Even as Western aliyah picks up, new arrivals replace fewer than half of Israeli emigrants, *Times of Israel*, September 14, 2025, www.timesofisrael.com/even-as-western-aliyah-picks-up-new-arrivals-replace-fewer-than-half-of-israeli-emigrants/.

289. Yoel Marcus, Ideology is Taking Off for Anatolia, *Ha'aretz*, July 4, 1995.

290. Tzvi Ben Gedalyahu, Olmert Slammed For Being 'Tired of Winning', *Israel National News*, August 22, 2006, www.israelnationalnews.com/news/110547s.

291. Rabbi Abraham Isaac Kook, *Iggrot HaRe'iyah*, Volume 1, #182.

292. Tefillin are small black leather boxes containing passages from the Torah, bound to the arm and head with straps during weekday morning prayers, in fulfillment of the biblical commandment to "bind them as a sign upon your hand and as frontlets between your eyes" (Deuteronomy 6:8).

293. Elie Mischel, Holy Rebellion: Israeli Youth Choose Tefillin and God in Defiance of their Parents, *Israel365 News*, July 7, 2025, https://israel365news.com/410308/holy-rebellion-israeli-youth-choose-tefillin-and-god-in-defiance-of-their-parents/.

294. Tzitzit are fringes attached to the four corners of a special four-cornered garment worn by Jewish men, in fulfillment of the biblical commandment to "look at it and remember all the commandments of the Lord" (Numbers 15:39). They serve as a physical reminder to live according to God's laws.

295. Elie Mischel, A religious revival? Mordecai, Esther and the lion within, March 21, 2024, *Israel365 News*, https://israel365news.com/388145/a-religious-revival-mordecai-esther-and-the-lion-within/.

296. Douglas Murray, A Time of War, *The Free Press*, October 2, 2024, www.thefp.com/p/douglas-murray-a-time-of-war.

Jews Who Won't Fight

297. WATCH: Haredi demonstrators clash with passersby, throw objects at reporters covering protest, *Jerusalem Post*, October 30, 2025, www.jpost.com/israel-news/article-872174.

298. A notable exception to the broader trend of limited Haredi enlistment is the Haredi Hashmonaim Brigade. This unit allows Haredi soldiers to maintain their religious lifestyle, including daily Torah study and strict observance of Jewish law within the military framework, addressing many of the concerns that have traditionally led to resistance against enlistment. Despite this accommodation, the number of Haredim serving in the brigade remains small—fewer than 300 after the third company began training—far below the IDF's target of tens of thousands from the estimated 80,000 eligible Haredi men. See Yonah Jeremy Bob, IDF to open third Haredi Hashmonaim Brigade Company, *Jerusalem Post*, August 31, 2025, www.jpost.com/israel-news/article-865981.

299. In Jewish law, a milchemet mitzvah ("commanded war") is a war that all members of the Jewish people are religiously obligated to participate in, such as a defensive war to protect the Jewish people or fulfill specific Torah commandments. Unlike a milchemet reshut (discretionary war), where participation may be optional, a milchemet mitzvah leaves no room for exemptions, emphasizing the collective duty to defend and preserve the community. Classic examples include wars to defend Israel from attack or to destroy Amalek.

300. Cited in Menachem Rahat, They Are Disconnected, *Israel National News*, November 6, 2025, www.inn.co.il/news/682442.

301. Menachem Rahat, They Are Disconnected, *Israel National News*, November 6, 2025, www.inn.co.il/news/682442.

302. A Haredi kollel is a Jewish institution where married men study Torah full-time, often receiving government or community support, rather than working a regular job.

303. Yehuda Yifrach, The alliance with the Haredim has become a national existential threat, *Makor Rishon*, October 24, 2025, www.makorrishon.co.il/news/politcal/article/207604.

304. Cited in Menachem Rahat, They Are Disconnected, *Israel National News*, November 6, 2025, www.inn.co.il/news/68244 2.

305. Attributed to Rabbi Avraham Mordechai Alter of Gur, author of the *Imrei Emes.*

306. Rivka Ravitz, in Rivka Ravitz Answers 18 Questions on Israeli Politics, the Draft, and Israel as a Religious State, *18Forty*, www.youtube.com/watch?v=IIinatfwZ60&t=427s.

307. Aharon Rose, "The Haredim: A Defense," *Azure* 25 (Summer 5766 / 2006): 87–119, https://azure.org.il/include/print.p hp?id=129.

308. Sam Sokol, Ex-chief rabbi: If Haredi draft dodgers arrested, ultra-Orthodox will leave Israel, *Times of Israel*, www.timesofisrael.com/ex-chief-rabbi-if-haredi-draft-dodg ers-arrested-ultra-orthodox-will-leave-israel/.

309. Ambassador Yechiel Leiter, *Aloh Na'aleh*, 14–15.

310. Cited in Sam Sokol, Extremist Haredi rabbi: Army service leads to secularization, is 'worse than death', *Times of Israel*, March 21, 2024, www.timesofisrael.com/extremist-haredi-rabbi-army-service-leads-to-secularization-is-worse-than-death/.

311. Cited in Rabbi Yehoshua Pfeffer, Charedi Army Service: A Matter of Jewish Belonging, in *Tzarich Iyun: Charedi Thoughts and Ideas*, March 2024, https://iyun.org.il/en/sedersheni/charedi-army-service-a-matter-of-jewish-belonging/.

312. Rabbi Yehoshua Pfeffer, Charedi Army Service: A Matter of Jewish Belonging, in *Tzarich Iyun: Charedi Thoughts and Ideas*, March 2024, https://iyun.org.il/en/sedersheni/charedi-army-service-a-matter-of-jewish-belonging/.

Self-Loathing, For an Honorarium

313. Alan Dershowitz, Temple Emanu-El Silences a Pro-Israel and Amplifies an Anti-Israel Voice, *Gatestone Institute*, December 7, 2021, www.gatestoneinstitute.org/18009/dershowitz-temple-emanu-el.

314. Peter Beinart, interview by Amy Goodman and Nermeen Shaikh, *Democracy Now!*, February 5, 2025, www.democracynow.org/2025/2/6/peter_beinart_being_jewish_gaza_book.

315. Alan Dershowitz, The Persistent Failure of American Jewish Leadership: A Case Study, in *Betrayal: The Failure of American Jewish Leadership* (2024), 150.

316. See Rabbi Pesach Wolicki, Mordechai and Schumer: A tale of two court Jews, March 20, 2024, *Jerusalem Post*, www.jpost.com/judaism/article-792778.

317. The estimated Jewish population in the United States in 2025 is between about 7.5 and 8 million people, including those who identify as Jewish by religion, culture, or family background. The figure of more than 6 million cited here refers specifically to individuals considered Jewish by traditional Jewish law—that is, born to Jewish mothers or formally converted. The larger number includes many people with Jewish grandparents who are not considered Jewish by this traditional standard.

Who Needs Jerusalem When You Have Pittsburgh?

318. MR. SCHIFF FINDS A FLAW IN ZIONISM; Doesn't See How a Jew Can Be a True American and a Good Zionist. NO LIEN ON CITIZENSHIP This Country Isn't a Mere Asylum for Jews—They Have Given Allegiance of Their Free Will, *New York Times*, August 23, 1907, Page 6.

319. Rev. Gustavus Poznanski, *Charleston Mercury*, March 20, 1841, cited in Solomon Breibart, "The Synagogues of Kahal Kadosh Beth Elohim," *South Carolina Historical Magazine* 80, no. 3 (July 1979), 224.

320. "The Pittsburgh Platform," adopted by the Central Conference of American Rabbis at the Pittsburgh Conference, November 1885, in Declaration of Principles of Reform Judaism (1885). Text available at www.ccarnet.org/rabbinic-voice/platforms/article-declaration-principles/.

321. *Yearbook of the Central Conference of American Rabbis*, 1897–1898, xli.

322. Rabbi Morris S. Lazaron, "Judaism's Message to the World," sermon delivered before the Council of the Union of American Hebrew Congregations, Baltimore, January 16, 1937, in *Year Book of the Central Conference of American Rabbis* 47 (1937): 189–203.

323. Thomas Kolsky, *Jews Against Zionism: The American Council for Judaism, 1942–1948* (1990), 54; Yoram Hazony, *The Jewish State: The Struggle for Israel's Soul*, 250.

324. Cited by Yakov Rabkin, Book Review, 14 November 2011, Reform Judaism and the Challenge of Zionism: Jack Ross, *Rabbi Outcast: Elmer Berger and American Jewish Anti-Zionism*, www.euppublishing.com/doi/10.3366/hls.2011.0020.

The Parlor Zionists Awaken

325. Jeffrey S. Sarna, Louis D. Brandeis: Zionist Leader, in American Jewish Culture and Scholarship, Brandeis University, www.brandeis.edu/hornstein/sarna/americanjewishcultureandscholarship/Archive4/LouisD.BrandeisZionistLeader.pdf.

326. Cited by Richard G. Pearce, How Jewish was Justice Louis Brandeis?, *Fordham Law Review* Vol. 85, 2017, 354.

327. Louis Brandeis, Letter to Regine Wehle, December 20, 1917, cited in Jeffrey D. Sarna and Gerald Sorin, The Jewish Legacy of Louis D. Brandeis, in *Studies in Zionism* Vol. 6, Autumn 1994, 28–45.

328. Anita Shapira, *Golda Meir: Vision and Leadership* (2013), 178–180.

329. Jonathan Sarna, Louis Brandeis: Zionist Leader, *Brandeis Review*, Winter 1992.

330. Rabbi Meir Bar Ilan, *From Volozhin to Jerusalem* (1939–1940), 562.

331. Jeffrey S. Gurock, *American Zionism: Mission and Politics*, vol. 8 of *American Jewish History* (1998).

332. Hillel Halkin, *Letters to an American Jewish Friend* (1977), Letter Two, 30.

333. Alex Grobman, Jewry's Response to the Balfour Declaration, *jewishlink.news.*

334. Ibid. Rabbi Wise, tragically, would soon be proven wrong. Within a few years after the Balfour Declaration, Britain reneged on its promises due to its desire to appease the Arab population in Palestine and other Arab nations. This shift was formalized through several White Papers issued by the British government, notably the 1939 White Paper, which severely restricted Jewish immigration to Palestine. These immigration limits tragically left many Jewish refugees unable to escape Nazi persecution, resulting in the slaughter of thousands of Jews during the Holocaust.

335. Central Conference of American Rabbis, The Columbus Platform (1937), in Union for Reform Judaism, https://reformjudaism.org/columbus-platform.

336. Despite detailed knowledge of the mass murder taking place at Auschwitz by mid-1944, the Roosevelt administration repeatedly rejected requests to bomb the gas chambers or the rail lines leading to the camp. See David S. Wyman, *The Abandonment of the Jews: America and the Holocaust, 1941–1945* (1984), 288–309.

337. Deborah Lipstadt writes that "the realization that American Jews had been powerless to save European Jewry profoundly shaped postwar Jewish identity and generated intense support for Jewish sovereignty in Palestine." Deborah E. Lipstadt, *Beyond Belief: The American Press and the Coming of the Holocaust, 1933–1945* (1986), 269–274. Melvin Urofsky concludes that after 1945, "Zionism came to be seen as the necessary answer to Jewish vulnerability and as a moral imperative born of the catastrophe." Melvin I. Urofsky, *American Zionism from Herzl to the Holocaust* (1975), 405–410.

338. Rabbi Abba Hillel Silver, "Speech to the United Nations General Assembly," November 1947, as chairman of the American Section of the Jewish Agency, www.jewishcleveland.org/news/blog/rabbi_abba_hillel_silver_speech_to_the_united_nations/.

339. Michael B. Oren, *Six Days of War: June 1967 and the Making of the Modern Middle East* (2002), 86.

340. Richard B. Parker, ed., *The Six-Day War: A Retrospective* (1996), 7–8.

341. Nadav Safran, *Israel: The Embattled Ally* (1978), 363.

342. Efraim Halevy, They Were Digging Graves in Parks, But I Was Not So Gloomy, *The Jewish Chronicle*, June 5, 2017.

343. Michael B. Oren, *Six Days of War: June 1967 and the Making of the Modern Middle East*, 158–160.

344. Ben Sales, How the Six Day War changed American Jews, May 11, 2017, *The Jewish News of Northern California*.

From Am Yisrael Chai to "My Judaism"

345. Joseph Schechtman, *Vladimir Jabotinsky: Fighter and Prophet* (1956), 320–321.

346. Louis Rosenblum, interview by Daniel Rosenblum, Involvement in the Soviet Jewry Movement: A Personal Account, 1961–1978 (Cleveland: Siegal Education Center/Cleveland Jewish History Initiative), 3.

347. Ibid, 16.

348. Gal Beckerman, *When They Come for Us, We'll Be Gone: The Epic Struggle to Save Soviet Jewry* (2010), 46–72.

349. Gary Rosenblatt, 'Am Yisrael Chai' has become an anthem for the Jewish people—but where did it come from?, November 3, 2023, *Forward*, https://forward.com/culture/568200/am-yisrael-chai-jewish-anthem/.

350. Cited in Tova Benjamin, Introduction: The Soviet Jewry Movement, Revisited, May 23, 2022, *Jewish Currents*, https://jewishcurrents.org/introduction-the-soviet-jewry-movement-revisited.

351. In the summer of 2023, a few weeks before October 7, I conducted an informal survey at a Modern Orthodox summer camp. I asked approximately one hundred teenage counselors—young people who had spent years in Jewish day schools and received far more Jewish education than the average American Jewish teenager—a simple question: had they ever heard of the Soviet Jewry Movement? Ninety-five percent of the teens had no idea what I was talking about. A handful said they thought they'd heard the words before, but none could say what the movement was or what it had accomplished. I was

astounded; the Soviet Jewry Movement is not ancient history. I was at the Freedom Sunday rally in 1987. Soviet Jews were still streaming into America and Israel in the early 1990s. Virtually every one of those counselors had grandparents—and many had parents—who stood at Soviet Jewry rallies, who sang Am Yisrael Chai outside the Soviet mission, and traveled to Washington for Freedom Sunday. Yet they never told their grandchildren about it. A people with no active struggle quickly loses its memory of the last one.

352. Charles S. Liebman, Post-War American Jewry: From Ethnic to Privatized Judaism, in *Secularism, Spirituality, and the Future of American Jewry*, ed. Elliott Abrams and David G. Dalin (1999), 7–18.

353. Ibid, 8.

354. David E. Campbell and Robert D. Putnam, *American Grace: How Religion Divides and Unites Us* (2010), 148.

355. Pew Research Center, "A Portrait of Jewish Americans" (2013), shows that most U.S. Jews today define being Jewish more by culture or moral values than by religious observance or peoplehood.

356. Jonathan Jaffe, The Erasure of Jewish Peoplehood, October 13, 2024, *Times of Israel*, https://blogs.timesofisrael.com/the-erasure-of-jewish-peoplehood/.

357. When God commanded Jacob to return to the land of Israel, He accompanied the command with an explicit promise of protection: "Return to the land of your fathers and to your birthplace, and I will be with you" (Genesis 31:1). Yet when Jacob finally approached the border and faced the prospect of confronting his brother Esau, he was terrified — and he split his people into two separate camps. The simple

reading is tactical: if Esau strikes one camp, the other will escape. But Rabbi Yehuda Leon Ashkenazi finds a deeper message hidden in Jacob's own prayer before the confrontation. Jacob cries out: "Save me from the hand of my brother, from the hand of Esau" — and then gives his reason: "I have become two camps." Read this way, the division is not Jacob's solution. It is his problem. He is telling God: I am afraid precisely because I am split in two. When Israel is united, no enemy can prevail against it. But internal division opens a crack through which enemies can enter. Rabbi Ashkenazi reads this as a parable for the Jewish people across history. The "two camps" represent the two dimensions of Jewish identity: Jacob, the exile dimension, and Israel, the national dimension rooted in the Land. As long as Jews are divided between Israel and the diaspora, that division itself empowers Israel's enemies. In his words: "This is what grants Esau his power — and not only him; also Ishmael, through the covenant made between them. As long as there are Jews outside, we are weakened. Our full identity cannot find expression, because Esau and his prince can always claim that we have no need for the Land — the fact is that there are Jews living abroad who observe the Torah! Why do you need a state? You are a religion!" Rabbi Yehuda Leon Ashkenazi, *Sod Midrash Ha Toldot* 7:290.

358. David Gedzelman, Teach the Idea of the Jewish People, April 11, 2024, *Jewish Priorities*, www.jewishpriorities.net/p/david-gedzelman-teach-the-idea-of.

Scarlett Johansson and the End of the Line

359. Scarlett Johansson quits Oxfam over SodaStream, January 30, 2014, *Globes*.

360. Joseph Dolsten, Natalie Portman slams Israel's nation-state law as 'racist', December 14, 2018, *Times of Israel*, www.timesofisrael.co m/natalie-portman-slams-israels-nation-state-law-as-racist/; See Portman Instagram statement, April 20, 2018: "The mistreatment of those suffering from today's atrocities [in Gaza] is simply not in line with my Jewish values," explaining why she declined the Genesis Prize.

361. Rashi, Deuteronomy 7:4.

362. National Jewish Population Survey (NJPS) 1990, Council of Jewish Federations, Summary Report of Key Findings.

363. Lawrence Goodman, Is Intermarriage Good For The Jews?, *Brandeis*, www.brandeis.edu/jewish-experience/jewish-america/20 22/june/intermarriage-interfaith-marriage.html.

364. According to the National Jewish Population Survey (NJPS) 1990, mixed-married households contained 770,000 children under 18, of whom only 28% were being raised as Jews, while 41% were raised in another religion and 31% with no religion at all. Will Your Grandchildren Be Jews? The Facts Don't Lie, *Aish*, https://aish.com /48910307/.

365. *Jewish Americans in 2020*, Pew Research Center, www.pewrese arch.org/religion/2021/05/11/marriage-families-and-children/.

366. Ira M. Sheskin and Arnold Dashefsky, United States Jewish Population, 2024, *American Jewish Year Book 2024*, estimating the U.S. Jewish population at about 7.7 million (broad definition including partial ancestry); and about 4.4–4.7 million per Jewish law (matrilineal descent criteria, excluding patrilineal-only), per Brandeis American Jewish Population Project adjustments to Pew 2020.

367. Rabbi Lord Jonathan Sacks, *Will We Have Jewish Grandchildren? Jewish Continuity and How to Achieve It* (1994).

Self-Hating, and Proud of It

368. *Jewish Americans in 2020*, Pew Research Center, www.pewresearch.org/religion/dataset/jewish-americans-in-2020/.

369. How U.S. Jews are experiencing the Israel-Hamas war, Pew Research Center, April 2, 2024.

370. Ben Harris, These Jews want to normalize not circumcising with their synagogue's help, December 28, 2021, *Jerusalem Post*, www.jpost.com/diaspora/these-jews-want-to-normalize-not-circumcising-with-their-synagogues-help-681430.

371. *Jewish Americans in 2020*, Pew Research Center, www.pewresearch.org/religion/dataset/jewish-americans-in-2020/.

372. Asaf Eliav-Shalem, Study finds 'shortage' of US rabbis is more about fit than numbers, November 12, 2025, *Times of Israel*.

373. Cited in Haley Cohen, Rabbi Ammiel Hirsch and the possible 'crisis' facing Reform Judaism, April 5, 2024, *eJewishPhilanthropy*, https://ejewishphilanthropy.com/rabbi-ammiel-hirsch-and-the-possible-crisis-facing-reform-judaism/.

374. Debra Miszak, Current and former members of the Union for Reform Judaism call for cease-fire, December 19, 2023, *Forward*, https://forward.com/fast-forward/574086/members-union-for-reform-judaism-call-for-cease-fire-war-gaza/.

375. The name "Conservative Judaism" is often misunderstood. It does not refer to political conservatism, and it does not signal religious conservatism. Historically, the movement defined itself as conservative relative to Reform Judaism (which rejected most ritual law) while always liberal compared to traditional Orthodox Judaism. It aimed to conserve core Jewish law and practice while embracing modern scholarship and social change, and the label remained even as its practical positions moved in a liberal direction. In contemporary terms, Conservative Judaism is religiously liberal relative to traditional Judaism and usually politically liberal as well. It endorses mixed seating during prayer, the ordination of women, and driving to synagogue on Shabbat. Its rabbis and organizations commonly align with progressive positions on American politics, social justice, and questions relating to Israel and the Palestinians. Today, the Conservative movement has become very similar to the Reform movement—the very movement it initially sought to separate from.

376. Stella Linson, Teaching hatred of Israel in Hebrew school, October 30, 2025, *JNS*, www.jns.org/teaching-hatred-of-israel-in-hebrew-school/.

377. Moving Traditions, "Funding Partners," www.movingtraditions.org/about/funding-partners/.

378. Moving Traditions, www.movingtraditions.org/.

379. Naya Lekht, Woke in content, Jewish in Firm: On the Failings of Jewish Education in America, in *Betrayal: The Failure of American Jewish Leadership*, 83–88.

380. Asaf Eliav-Shalem, Half of US's 25 most generous philanthropists are Jews. Few give to Jewish groups, January 26, 2023, *Times of Israel*.

381. Adam Eliyahu Berkowitz, NEW POLL: Over 70% of Israelis oppose "Two-State Solution", February 4, 2025, *Israel365 News*, https://israel365news.com/399982/new-poll-71-of-israelis-oppose-two-state-solution/.

382. Andrew Lapin, Countering Israel's far right, several US Jewish groups say they oppose resettling Gaza, December 10, 2024, *Times of Israel*.

383. Caroline Glick, The Two-State Solution and American Jewish Survival, in *Betrayal: The Failure of American Jewish Leadership*, 71–73.

384. Stuart Winer, Jewish Google employees call for tech giant to publicly support Palestinians, May 19, 2021, *Times of Israel*.

385. Hannah Einbinder, interview with Simone Zimmerman, Beyond Israelism with Simone Zimmerman, Tikkun Olam Productions, October 26, 2025, www.youtube.com/watch?v=X-eLWZLs8Q8.

386. Daniel Gordis, Are Young Rabbis Turning on Israel?, June 2011, *Commentary*, www.commentarymagazine.com/article/are-young-rabbis-turning-on-israel.

Vote Mamdani!

387. How Zohran Mamdani Came to Embrace the Palestinian Cause, *New York Times*, October 8, 2025; What has New York mayor-elect Zohran Mamdani said about Israel?, *Unpacked*, November 4, 2025;

NYC mayoral candidate Zohran Mamdani criticized for 'globalize the intifada' remarks, *NBC News*, June 19, 2025.

388. Luke Tress, Poll finds a third of NYC Jews voted for Mamdani, while Cuomo dominated Jewish neighborhoods, November 5, 2025, *Times of Israel*.

389. Jacob Kornbluh, post on X, October 9, 2025, https://x.com/jacobkornbluh/status/1976404004524720154?s=46.

390. Jennifer Bardi, Jewish Word | Askan: 'The Guy Who Knows a Guy', January 29, 2026, *Moment*, https://momentmag.com/jewish-word-askan/.

391. Motti Inbari, How Did the Satmar Rebbe Survive the Holocaust?, January 23, 2018, *Times of Israel*.

392. The Satmar Rebbe's anti-Zionist theology centers on the Talmudic concept known as the "Three Oaths," a teaching found in the Babylonian Talmud, Ketubot 111a, which interprets *Song of Solomon* as God imposing three oaths on the Jewish people and the nations: that Jews should not ascend to the land of Israel "as a wall" (i.e., en masse or by force), not rebel against the nations of the world during exile, and that the nations should not oppress Jews excessively. Satmar interprets these oaths as a divine prohibition against establishing Jewish sovereignty or a state before the coming of the Messiah, viewing any secular Zionist state-building as a rebellion against God delaying redemption. However, this interpretation is not accepted by most other Jewish authorities, who point out that the oaths are aggadic (non-legal) in nature, may be metaphorical or conditional, and that other sources command Jews to settle and actively conquer the land in every generation. Prominent medieval commentators, including

Nachmanides and Maimonides, have argued that Jews retain a positive, ongoing obligation to live in the land of Israel, and that the "Three Oaths" do not legally forbid Zionist endeavors. This divergence explains why Satmar's theological opposition remains a minority position in the broader Jewish world.

393. Kayla Greenfeld, Anti-Zionism Among Jews, *Jewish Virtual Library*, www.jewishvirtuallibrary.org/anti-zionism-among-jews.

394. Rabbi Yehuda Leon Ashkenazi, *Hesped L'Moshiach*, 65: "There is a debate in the Torah world about whether one must wait for the Messiah in order to return to the land of Israel, or whether one should instead return to Zion on the initiative of the people of Israel themselves, without waiting for heavenly indications. But what do those who say one must wait actually mean? Implicitly, there is here an expression of a kind of magical mindset—a tendency to expect miraculous, almost magical phenomena, different from the miracles found in the stories of the Bible."

395. Yitzchok Landa, The Kingmaker from Williamsburg, November 25, 2025, *Mishpacha*, https://mishpacha.com/the-kingmaker-from-williamsburg/.

Next Year in Jerusalem. Maybe.

396. Rabbi Abraham Isaac Kook goes further, arguing that living outside the land doesn't merely disconnect Jews from the Torah's national mission—it limits their very capacity to understand the Torah itself. In *Ein Aya* (Berachot 47a), he writes that while quantitative Torah knowledge and sharp analytical reasoning can be developed anywhere, "inner perception naturally grows in the land of Israel, because it is its true place." The full inner dimension of Torah understanding is

simply not accessible in exile—and the tragedy is that one who lacks it cannot even recognize what is missing.

397. See *Mishnah* Yoma 8:9 for the classic distinction between commandments governing the relationship between man and God and those between man and other people. At the same time, the Torah repeatedly commands a person to guard his inner life and refine his character (e.g., Deuteronomy 4:9; 10:16; Leviticus 19:2, as understood by Nachmanides). The Sages likewise emphasize personal growth and self-mastery as central religious obligations (*Ethics of the Fathers* 2:1; 4:1). Later works of Jewish ethical thought develop this into a third domain: a person's responsibility to cultivate and elevate himself.

398. Rabbi Shalom Rosner, Symposium: Diaspora Judaism at a Crossroads, *YU Torah To-Go*, Passover 5786, 17.

399. Ambassador Yechiel Leiter, *Alon Naaleh*, 213–214.

400. Maimonides, *Iggeret Kiddush Hashem.*

401. Rabbi Jacob Emden, *Siddur Shaarei Shamayim* (1748), Introduction, 13.

402. Rabbi Joseph B. Soloveitchik, *Kol Dodi Dofek* (1956), www.sefaria.org/Kol_Dodi_Dofek.

403. Hillel Halkin, *Letters to an American Jewish Friend*, 146.

404. Rabbi Yehuda Leon Ashkenazi, *Sod Midrash HaToldot*, 7:300.

405. Rabbi Josh Wander, Every Excuse in the Book — And the One Reason Behind Them All, November 19, 2025, https://geulamovement.substack.com/p/every-excuse-in-the-book-and-the.

406. Zechariah 8:4.

Professors of Powerlessness

407. My criticism of Rabbi Blau is directed solely at his public letter and the ideas it represents, and should not be construed as a personal attack on his character. During my years at Yeshiva University, I witnessed firsthand the genuine warmth and care Rabbi Blau extended to countless students. He has dedicated decades of his life to the welfare of young men and women at YU, and is by all accounts a kind and good man. I disagree sharply with his public statements on this matter, but that disagreement is entirely with his ideas—not with the man himself.

408. Rabbi Yosef Blau, A Call for Moral Clarity, Responsibility, and a Jewish Orthodox Response in the Face of the Gaza Humanitarian Crisis, cited in *Jewish Telegraphic Agency*, www.jta.org/2025/08/28/ideas/yosef-blau-author-of-an-orthodox-rabbis-letter-calling-out-israel-responds-to-his-critics.

409. Charlie Kirk, The Gaza Starvation LIE Exposed | Charlie Kirk Interview, YouTube video, July 31, 2025.

410. Did Charlie Kirk believe Israel starved Palestinians in Gaza?, The Israel Truth Network.

411. Amichai Stein, Israel's Ambassador Leiter rebukes US rabbis over Gaza claims, urges apology, September 12, 2025, *Jerusalem Post.*

412. Philisa Cramer, 80 Modern Orthodox rabbis call for 'moral clarity' in the face of Gaza humanitarian crisis, August 19, 2025, *Jewish Telegraphic Agency*.

413. Andrew Sillow-Carroll, Yosef Blau, author of an Orthodox rabbis' letter calling out Israel, responds to his critics, *Jewish Telegraphic Agency*, August 28, 2025.

414. Rabbi Dr. Shlomo Zuckier, post, Facebook, April 24, 2025.

415. Yoram Hazony, *The Jewish State: The Struggle for Israel's Soul*, 196.

416. Martin Buber, Concepts and Reality, in *Der Jude* 5 (August 1916), translated in Mendes-Flohr and Reinharz, A Debate on Zionism and Messianism: The Buber-Scholem Correspondence (1986), 449, 451–452.

417. Martin Buber, They and We, *Ha'aretz*, November 16, 1939, reprinted in Paul Mendes-Flohr, *A Land of Two Peoples: Martin Buber on Jews and Arabs* (2005), 138–143.

418. Judah L. Magnes, letter to Louis Brandeis, September 2, 1915, cited in Sarah Goren, *The Dissenter: Judah L. Magnes, American Zionist* (2023), 149–150.

419. The 1929 pogrom refers to a wave of anti-Jewish riots across British Mandatory Palestine in August 1929, sparked by incitement over false claims that Jews intended to seize or desecrate the Temple Mount. In Hebron, where Jews have lived for millennia, Arab mobs went from house to house with knives, clubs, and axes, murdering and mutilating Jewish men, women, and children, looting homes and synagogues, and in some cases burning victims alive. Between 65 and

70 Jews were slaughtered in Hebron in a single day; the British authorities evacuated the survivors, ending the ancient Jewish presence in the city until it was reestablished in the 1970s following the Six-Day War. Similar attacks took place in Safed and other localities, and in total 133 Jews were killed and hundreds wounded in the 1929 massacres.

420. Yoram Hazony, *The Jewish State: The Struggle for Israel's Soul*, 203.

421. The Yishuv (Hebrew for "settlement" or "community") refers to the organized Jewish population in the land of Israel during the late Ottoman and British Mandate periods, from the late nineteenth century until the establishment of the State of Israel in 1948. The term encompasses the network of Jewish towns, agricultural settlements, schools, political institutions, and defense organizations that together formed the social, economic, and political infrastructure of the future Jewish state.

422. Judah Magnes, Address opening the Hebrew University academic year, October 29, 1947. Magnes Papers, file P3/2114, Central Archives for the History of the Jewish People, Jerusalem.

423. Ronald W. Clark, *Einstein: The Life and Times* (1984), 378.

424. Ibid., 379.

425. Ibid., 402.

426. Ibid., 381.

427. Martin Buber, Zionism and 'Zionism', *Ba'ayot Hazman* (Problems of the Time), May 27, 1948, reprinted in Paul Mendes-Flohr, *A Land of Two Peoples: Martin Buber on Jews and Arabs*, 154–159.

428. Susan Lee Hattis, *The Binational Idea in Palestine during Mandatory Times* (1970), 216–219, 221, 223–224.

429. Yoram Hazony, *The Jewish State: The Struggle for Israel's Soul*, 218.

430. Rabbi Yaakov Zvi Mecklenberg, *Haketav Vehakabbalah* (1839), Genesis 27:12.

431. Rabbi Yehuda Leon Ashkenazi, *Sod Midrash HaToldot*, 6:250–251.

432. Vladimir Jabotinsky, cited in Hillel Halkin, *Jabotinsky: A Life*, 47.

Jerusalem on the Euphrates

433. Rabbi Binyamin Lau, *Shivat Zion* (2018), 33.

434. Ibid., 34.

435. Ezekiel 11:22–23: "The cherubim lifted up their wings and the wheels beside them; and the glory of the God of Israel hovered above them. The glory of the Lord rose up from the midst of the city and stood on the mountain which is east of the city." Rashi there explains: "this is the third stage of the Divine Presence's departure [to exile with the Jewish people]. The Sages teach: 'Every place to which they [Israel] were exiled, the Divine Presence went with them. They were exiled to Egypt and the Divine Presence was with them, as it is written: "Did I reveal Myself to the house of your father when they were in Egypt?" (I Samuel 2:27). They were exiled to Babylon, and the Divine Presence was with them, as it is written: "For your sake I have sent to Babylon" (Isaiah 43:14). And when they will be redeemed in the future, the Divine Presence will be with them, as it is written: "Then the Lord

your God will return [with] your captivity" (Deuteronomy 30:3).'" Babylonian Talmud, Megillah 29a.

What Do You Love More?

436. Address of the President of the United States, Donald J. Trump, to the Knesset Plenum, October 13, 2025, https://main.knesset.gov.il/EN/activity/Documents/SpeechPdf/trump.pdf.

437. Duff McDonald, Meet the Woman Behind Sheldon Adelson, February 8, 2012, *Fortune*, https://fortune.com/2012/02/08/meet-the-woman-behind-sheldon-adelson/.

438. Alex Griffing, 'She's An American Citizen': House Republican Sparks Fury On the Right By Questioning Patriotism of GOP Mega-Donor, November 10, 2025, *Mediaite*.

439. Senator Bernie Moreno (R-OH), New Moreno Bill to Outlaw Dual Citizenship, press release, December 1, 2025.

440. Dorothy Thompson, Israeli Ties and U.S. Citizenship: America Demands A Single Loyalty, *Commentary*, March 1950.

441. Gore Vidal, The Empire Lovers Strike Back, *The Nation*, March 22, 1986.

442. Bill Christison and Kathleen Christison, Bush's Dual Loyalties, *Counterpunch*, December 13, 2002.

443. John Mearsheimer and Stephen Walt, *The Israel Lobby and U.S. Foreign Policy* (2007).

444. Aaron Kligman, Ilhan Omar & the Line between Criticism of Israel and Anti-Semitism, *Aish*.

445. H.Res. 241, 116th Cong. (2019), Condemning the anti-Semitic comments of Representative Ilhan Omar from Minnesota.

446. Melissa Weiss, Tufts student alleges antisemitism and harassment at university, *Jewish Insider*, February 23, 2025.

447. infoLibre News, post, X (formerly Twitter), October 28, 2025.

448. Pennsylvania's Shapiro: Harris team asked if I'd ever been 'a double agent for Israel', January 19, 2025, *Times of Israel*.

449. Candace Owens, post, X, June 13, 2025.

450. Dr. Simon Goddek, post, X, June 16, 2025.

451. Tucker Carlson, host, and Darryl Cooper, guest, The True History of the Jonestown Cult, WWII, and How Winston Churchill Ruined Europe, *The Tucker Carlson Show*, podcast episode, September 2, 2024.

452. Darryl Cooper (MartyrMade), post, X, June 22, 2025.

453. Tucker Carlson Network (@TCNetwork), post, X, June 18, 2025.

454. Tucker Carlson, address at Turning Point USA Student Action Summit (SAS 2025), Tampa, Florida, July 11, 2025.

455. Megyn Kelly, Megyn Kelly Goes Off on Trump's Epstein Comments, *The Megyn Kelly Show* (SiriusXM), March 2, 2026.

456. Sarah Stern, The shaky state of American Jewry, December 9, 2025, *JNS*.

457. Gil Troy, Proud Americans, Good Jews: Embracing Dual Loyalty, April 3, 2025, *Jewish Journal*.

458. Gabriel Schonfeld, Dual Loyalty and the "Israel Lobby", *Commentary*, November 2006.

459. Rabbi Joseph B. Soloveitchik, shiur on Parashat Vayechi (1980), as transmitted by Baron Alain de Rothschild, in Rabbi Aaron Goldscheider, *Torah United: Teachings on the Weekly Parasha from Rav Avraham Yitzchak HaKohen Kook, Rabbi Joseph B. Soloveitchik, and the Chassidic Masters* (2023), https://oupress.org/excerpts/vayechi-going-home/.

460. Tucker Carlson conducted a softball interview with neo-Nazi Nick Fuentes (Oct. 26, 2025, Tucker Carlson Network), treating him as a credible voice rather than challenging his antisemitism—praising Fuentes' "brutal honesty" on "demographic replacement" and letting claims like "Zionist Jews control immigration policy" pass unchallenged, effectively normalizing him for 2.5M viewers. Jewish groups (ADL, AJC) condemned it as "legitimizing white supremacy." Cenk Uygur (*Young Turks*) called Orthodox Jews "inbred geniuses ruining the world" (2015 clip, resurfaced 2025); claimed "1% of the population [Jews] control media, banks, wars" (2024 broadcast); hosted Hamas' spokesman praising Oct. 7 (2023). These go beyond Israel—pure Jew-hatred tropes. Their pattern: Jews as disloyal schemers, Zionist or not.

461. *Ethics of the Fathers*, 3:2.

462. During the May 30, 2020 Los Angeles riots associated with Black Lives Matter protests, rioters vandalized synagogues with antisemitic graffiti and destroyed kosher restaurants and other Jewish-owned

businesses in the Fairfax District. Reports and city officials confirmed that Jewish institutions were targeted, with antisemitic messaging accompanying the attacks. Ariel Sobel, LA City Councilmember Condemns Targeting of Jewish Institutions During Protests, May 31, 2020, *Jewish Journal*.

463. Babylonian Talmud, Bava Batra 54b.

464. Rabbi Yehuda Leon Ashkenazi consistently emphasized that one must distinguish between the concept of nationhood (le'um) and the concept of citizenship. He noted that French political culture habitually rejects this distinction: "In its view, there is no place for a separate community; there is only one thing—the French people. There is a people—the French people—and no distinction is made between being part of that people and being a citizen. One cannot claim to be a French citizen of a different nationality" (*Sod Midrash HaToldot*, 7:32). This is precisely the problem. When a country refuses to distinguish between citizenship and nationhood, it forces Jews to choose between their identity as Jews and their status as citizens. A political system that cannot accommodate Jewish peoplehood alongside civic loyalty is fundamentally incompatible with Jewish life. America, at least in theory, has historically allowed for this distinction—permitting hyphenated identities and dual allegiances in a way that France does not. Whether that remains true today is increasingly uncertain.

465. *Genesis Rabbah* 42:8.

466. Nachmanides, Genesis 40:15.

467. Jonathan Sarna, *American Judaism: A History* (2004), 263.

468. Dr. Miriam Adelson, biographical profile, IAC 360, https://iac360.org/iac-rg/dr-miriam-adelson/; see also Dr. Miriam and Sheldon G. Adelson Medical Research Foundation, annual giving data (2023); Adelson Clinic for Drug Abuse Treatment and Research, services overview.

469. David Ben-Gurion, letter to Joseph M. Proskauer, July 18, 1960, quoted in Tom Segev, *The Seventh Million: The Israelis and the Holocaust* (1993), 330.

470. Ezra Mendelsohn, *The Jews of East Central Europe between the World Wars* (1983); Antony Polonsky, Jewish Political Life in Poland on the Eve of the Second World War, in *Polin: Studies in Polish Jewry*, vol. 13, Focusing on Poland: The Jews and the Poles, 1939–1945 (2000), 3–21.

471. Ambassador Yechiel Leiter, *Aloh Naaleh*, 106–107.

472. Rabbi Moshe Shmuel Glazner, *Zionism in the Light of Faith* (1921). Selected essays available in English translation at https://mg1329.github.io/dor4/zionism.html.

473. MAGA infighting erupts at Turning Point USA Conference, December 18, 2025, *Politico*.

474. Nick Fuentes, interview by Tucker Carlson, *The Tucker Carlson Show*, October 27, 2025.

Toasting Self-Destruction (With Kosher Catering)

475. The chronological setting of the Book of Esther has been debated among the Sages since antiquity. Two primary views emerged regarding when these events occurred: The Minimalist View: Rab-

bi Yose ben Halafta's second-century CE work *Seder Olam* presents what scholars call the "minimalist approach" to Persian history. According to this view, there were only four Persian kings mentioned in the Bible—Cyrus, Ahasuerus, Artaxerxes, and Darius—with some of these names referring to the same ruler at different times. This approach places the Purim story near the end of the 70-year Babylonian exile prophesied by Jeremiah, sometime before the Second Temple was rebuilt in 516 BCE. This is the majority opinion among traditional commentators. The Historical-Archaeological View: Beginning with 19th-century archaeological discoveries at Shushan (ancient Susa), historians reconstructed Persian chronology using multiple international sources. This approach identifies ten Persian kings in the Achaemenid dynasty and identifies Ahasuerus from the Esther story as Xerxes I (ruled 486–465 BCE), based on linguistic, historical, and textual evidence. The story of Esther would thus begin in Xerxes' third year (483 BCE)—nearly 40 years after the Second Temple was rebuilt and approximately 50 years after Cyrus's proclamation. This book follows the second view, accepted by most modern historians and many contemporary Jewish scholars including Shani Taragin (see Megillat Esther: Historical Context and Satirical Message, Bar Ilan University's Beit Morasha Audio-Visual Center). This chronology carries significant theological implications. If the Purim story occurred decades after the Temple was rebuilt, the Jews of Persia were not prevented from returning home—they chose to remain in exile. This transforms the Book of Esther from a simple story of salvation into a satirical critique of voluntary diaspora living, as Mordecai and Esther wrote to a community that had the opportunity to rebuild Jewish sovereignty in the land of Israel but preferred the comforts of Shushan and Persian society. I am grateful to Shani Taragin, one of the great

Bible scholars of our generation, for generously sharing her expertise on this topic with me.

476. See Ezra 1–2 (Cyrus's proclamation and the return of the exiles, alongside those who remained in Babylon and supported the rebuilding financially); Yoma 9b (the Talmud's diagnosis that only a minority ascended, thereby depriving the Second Temple of the full spiritual stature of the First); Esther 3:8 (Haman's description of the Jews as "a people scattered and dispersed"); and Megillah 12a–13b (the Talmud's account of Persian Jewry's spiritual slumber, linking their participation in Ahasuerus's feast to their alienation from the commandments).

477. Babylonian Talmud, Megillah 12a.

478. Ibid.

479. Babylonian Talmud, Megillah 11b. The Talmud understands the Purim story as taking place before the rebuilding of the Second Temple, in which case Ahasuerus was celebrating the destruction of a Temple that still lay in ruins. This book follows the view that the Temple had already been rebuilt by the time of the Purim story. Yet the Sages' insight loses none of its force. The Jews had their Temple—built by permission of their Persian masters—and they were still subjects of Persia. If anything, Ahasuerus had more reason to celebrate. The physical Temple had been restored, and the Jews were his subjects anyway. What clearer proof could there be that Jewish national redemption was dead and buried forever?

480. Rabbi Moses Schreiber (the Chatam Sofer), *Derashot Chatam Sofer* (published posthumously, 1929), Parashat Tetzaveh, Derashah 158.

481. The Men of the Great Assembly, known in Hebrew as Anshei Knesset HaGedolah, were a distinctive group of Jewish leaders who took charge of Jewish affairs between 410 BCE and 310 BCE. This era began after the destruction of the First Temple and extended into the early years of the Second Temple period, culminating with the invasion of the Greeks under the leadership of Alexander the Great.

482. See Rabbi Benjamin Lau, *Shivat Zion*, 153–155.

483. Rabbi Meir Leibush ben Yehiel Michel Wisser (Malbim), Esther 2:19.

484. Rabbi Abraham Ibn Ezra, Esther 2:9.

The Day the Music Stopped

485. The Achaemenid Persian Empire (539–330 BCE) was notably tolerant of subject peoples' religions and customs, as evidenced by Cyrus's decree allowing Jewish return to Jerusalem (Ezra 1:1–4) and the prominence of Jews like Nehemiah, cupbearer to King Artaxerxes (Nehemiah 1:11).

486. Esther 3:1 identifies Haman as "the Agagite," which rabbinic tradition understands as a descendant of Agag, king of Amalek (I Samuel 15:8). The Talmud (Megillah 13a) explicitly identifies Haman as an Amalekite: "Haman was from the descendants of Agag... as it is stated: 'Haman the son of Hammedatha the Agagite.'" *Targum Sheni* on Esther expands this genealogy, tracing Haman's lineage directly back through Agag to Amalek. This identification explains Haman's inexplicable hatred of the Jews as an inheritance of the eternal enmity between Amalek and Israel (Exodus 17:16, Deuteronomy 25:17–19).

487. Babylonian Talmud, Sanhedrin 105a.

488. *Esther Rabbah* 7:6.

489. Babylonian Talmud, Sanhedrin 74a.

490. Rabbi Yaakov Medan, But Mordechai Would Not Kneel or Bow—Why?, in *Hadassah is Esther: A Memorial Volume for Hadassah Esther (Dassi) Rabinowitz, of blessed memory, a collection of essays on the Book of Esther* (1997), 163–166.

491. *Yalkut Shimoni*, Esther 1054.

492. Amalek is the grandson of Esau. "Timna was a concubine of Eliphaz, Esau's son; and she bore to Eliphaz Amalek" (Genesis 36:12).

Found and Lost Again

493. Rabbi Yigal Ariel, *Mor V'Hadas: Iyunim B'Daniel V'Esther*, 420–421.

494. Babylonian Talmud, Shabbat 88a.

495. Martin Luther, *Table Talk*, No. 4192 (1566).

496. Erik Bundy, Esther: Not a Fairy Tale!, sermon, *Logos Sermons*, March 12, 2024.

497. Babylonian Talmud, Megillah 10b.

498. Rabbi Yehuda Leon Ashkenazi, *Kol HaMoed: Lessons on the Festivals*, 274.

The Price of Being American

499. Etan Nechin, Jon Ossoff Tells Haaretz How His Jewish Upbringing Taught Him to Fight for Justice, *Haaretz*, December 20, 2020.

500. Senate Majority Leader Chuck Schumer, Majority Leader Schumer Calls On Israeli Government To Hold Elections, press release, U.S. Senate Democratic Caucus, March 14, 2024.

Who Holds the Ring?

501. Ben Rhodes, *The World as It Is: A Memoir of the Obama White House* (2018), 303–305.

502. Michael Crowley, Obama vs. Bibi, *Politico*, January 29, 2015.

503. Netanyahu denounces Iran nuclear deal but faces criticism from within Israel, *The Guardian*, July 14, 2015.

504. US President Joe Biden repeats that he's a Zionist during White House Hanukkah event, December 12, 2023, www.youtube.com/watch?v=Jov9jxRecFc&t=5s.

505. Jennifer Shutt, U.S. House rebukes Biden administration over pause in heavy bomb shipments to Israel, *Colorado Newsline*, May 16, 2024.

506. Secretary of Defense Lloyd J. Austin III, Joint Press Conference with Defense Ministers of Australia, Japan, and the Philippines, May 8, 2024.

507. Bernie Sanders Calls on Congress to Block Funding to Israel, *The Guardian*, January 2, 2024.

508. Pelosi Joins Democrats Urging Biden to Rein In Arms to Israel, *Politico*, March 22, 2024.

509. Letter to President Biden and Secretary Blinken on U.S. Policy Toward Israel's War in Gaza, Project on Middle East Democracy (POMED), April 2024.

510. Alex Henderson, How Tucker Carlson Is Dragging J.D. Vance Down Into The Neo-Nazi Fever Swamp, *National Memo*, November 7, 2025.

511. On Vice President JD Vance's regular appearances on Tucker Carlson's program and their close political rapport, see, e.g., "Tucker Carlson Network: JD Vance on Israel and America First," October 2025 episode.

512. Ben Samuels, Trump's VP Pick JD Vance Defends Tucker Carlson for Platforming Holocaust Revisionism, *Haaretz*, September 7, 2024.

513. Andrew Lapin, JD Vance sidesteps college student's antisemitic question while defending Trump's Israel stance, *Jerusalem Post*, October 31, 2025.

514. Harrison Berger, Tucker Carlson Talks 'the West,' Collective Punishment, and Antisemitism, *The American Conservative*, December 27, 2025.

515. Tucker Carlson, "Tucker Carlson Interviews Nick Fuentes," *The Tucker Carlson Show*, October 27, 2025.

516. Lazar Berman, Israel, US envoy reject Tucker Carlson's claim he was detained and interrogated at airport, *Times of Israel*, February 19, 2026.

517. See, e.g., Tucker Carlson's November 2025 monologue targeting Jewish conservative commentators Mark Levin and Ben Shapiro: "Give us the money for our preferred little country... You're flirting with real backlash. Like a real one"—a remark implying that Jewish voices demand U.S. funds for Israel at America's expense (Micha Danzig, Tucker Carlson's Latest Attack on Jews Is His Worst Yet, *The Algemeiner*, November 26, 2025); his July 13, 2025 call to revoke the citizenship of American IDF volunteers over alleged "dual loyalty" (Nathan Guttman, Tucker Carlson Suggests Revoking Citizenship of American IDF Volunteers, *The Forward*, July 13, 2025); and his October 28, 2025 agreement with Nick Fuentes that Jewish neoconservatives prioritize Israel over U.S. interests (Raphael Ahren, Tucker Carlson Discusses 'These Zionist Jews' with Avowed Antisemite Nick Fuentes, *Times of Israel*, October 28, 2025).

Under the Vine and Fig Tree

518. Moses Seixas, Address of the Hebrew Congregation of Newport, Rhode Island, to George Washington, August 17, 1790, in Founders Online, National Archives.

519. George Washington, Letter to the Hebrew Congregation in Newport, Rhode Island, August 18, 1790.

520. Rabbi Meir Soloveitchik, A New World for Jews, *National Review*, January 22, 2026.

521. Micah 4:4. "And they shall dwell each man under his vine and under his fig tree, and no one shall make them move, for the mouth of the Lord of Hosts has spoken."

522. Don Isaac Abarbanel, Micah 4:4.

523. *Exodus Rabbah* 1.

524. Rabbi Meir Wisser explains God's dual method for keeping His people close to Him: "Behold, the means that God will choose so that Israel will stand firm in His Torah and fear Him are through two ways: Sometimes it will be through punishments or that He will hide His face from them, and many evils and troubles will find them until they recognize that this is because of their sins. And sometimes it will be through His watching over them with constant providence and showing them His signs and wonders, so that they may recognize that He is their God and that all their good comes from Him" (Malbim, I Kings 8:57). American Jews today are experiencing both simultaneously: rising antisemitism and accusations of dual loyalty alongside Israel's miraculous military victories over Hezbollah, Hamas, and Iran—divine messages through both hardship and providence.

The Day Michael Became Mordecai

525. Jewish actor Michael Rapaport: How I became spiritually stronger through wearing tefillin, *Israel National News*, October 26, 2025.

526. David Brinn, From 'Friends' actor to vocal defender of Israel: Michael Rapaport's New Yorker's guide to advocacy, *Jerusalem Post*, May 15, 2024.

527. i24NEWS, "Breaking News" post, X, April 7, 2025.

528. Jewish actor Michael Rapaport: How I became spiritually stronger through wearing tefillin, *Israel National News*, October 26, 2025.

529. Ben Shapiro, The Threats We're Facing, *The Ben Shapiro Show*, episode 1523, November 2023.

530. Nick Fuentes, Nick Fuentes BLASTS Ben Shapiro On Israel, segment on *The Young Turks*, October 30, 2025.

531. Andrew Howard, MAGA infighting erupts at Turning Point USA Conference, *Politico*, December 18, 2025.

The Coming Decree

532. Hillel Halkin, *Letters to an American Jewish Friend: A Zionist's Polemic.*

533. Rabbi Yehuda Leon Ashkenazi, *Sod Midrash HaToldot*, 2:139.

534. Babylonian Talmud, Sanhedrin 97b.

535. Rabbi Abraham Isaac Kook, *Shemoneh Kevatzim*, 1:70.

Written In, or Written Out?

536. Babylonian Talmud, Yoma 9b.

537. "We inquire into and expound upon the laws of Passover thirty days before Passover" (Babylonian Talmud, Pesachim 6a). Since Passover begins on the 15th of the Hebrew month of Nissan, counting back thirty days brings us to the 14th of Adar—the date of Purim. This requirement means that Jews must begin their Passover study

the moment Purim ends, creating an immediate transition from one festival of salvation to the other.

538. Babylonian Talmud, Shabbat 88a. The Sages teach that after the salvation from Haman, the Jews willingly reaccepted the Torah that had originally been given under coercion at Mount Sinai. The Purim miracle inspired them to accept it again, this time out of love rather than fear.

The Countdown has Begun

539. Romain Chauvet, 'I'm afraid every day for my children': As antisemitism soars, French Jews flee to Israel, *Times of Israel*, January 6, 2024.

540. Australia's government failed its Jews in the long runup to Bondi Beach attack, *New York Post*, December 14, 2025.

541. *Midrash Tanchuma*, Ki Tavo 7. Rabbi Ashkenazi writes: "The presence of the Children of Israel in the Diaspora when the Master of the Universe has decided to put an end to His mourning is not only a terrible desecration of God's name; it is dangerous, because from that moment, the nature of Divine providence over the Jews of the Diaspora changes." *Sod Midrash HaToldot* 8:334. To describe that change, Rabbi Ashkenazi invoked the language of Rashi, who used the Hebrew word hefker: ownerless, abandoned (Rashi, Matir et Besarchem, Ketubot 111a). In Jewish law, hefker describes property that has been relinquished by its owner, left without protection or legal claim. When Rabbi Ashkenazi applies this word to the Jewish people in exile during the era of redemption, he is not saying that God has ceased to love His people, but rather that He has withdrawn the special protection He extended to them throughout the long centuries

of exile. They are no longer under His protective custody; they are hefker. Rabbi Ashkenazi elaborates on this principle with reference to the reunion between Jacob and Esau. "Esau ran to meet him, embraced him, fell upon his neck, kissed him, and they wept" (Genesis 33:4). "On the surface, this verse seems to reveal brotherly love, yet Rashi asks us to pay attention to the fact that Esau came to the meeting 'with four hundred men.' We must not be naïve. We must not imagine that Esau has become an angel who desires our good. Therefore Rashi immediately emphasizes: 'It is a fixed rule, well known, that Esau hates Jacob; it was only that at that moment his compassion was aroused and he kissed him with all his heart.' The principle remains valid, even if there are particular moments when Esau's mercy is stirred. One cannot rely on that over the long term." Rabbi Ashkenazi draws a parallel to Abel, who failed to recognize that his life was in danger from his brother Cain. Jacob, by contrast, understood the threat and fled when Rebecca warned him. "This is the immediate and straightforward meaning of the first part of the verse. It seems simple, perhaps even obvious, yet the history of our people proves, unfortunately, the opposite. When have we truly understood this? How many times did we fail to flee—and what happened as a result? We must not be naïve. We must not imagine that Esau is righteous or an angel. He is not." *Sod Midrash HaToldot* 7:108.

542. Babylonian Talmud, Megillah 29a.

543. Rabbi Aharon Lichtenstein, Diaspora Religious Zionism: Some Current Reflections, in *Religious Zionism and the Secular World*, Orthodox Forum Series (1998), 20.

544. Rabbi Yehuda Leon Ashkenazi, *Sod Midrash HaToldot* 7:22.

545. From Genesis to Malachi, God's commitment to the Jewish people and the Land of Israel is stated so clearly, so repeatedly, that misreading it requires herculean effort. Replacement theology—the belief that God rejected His people for failing to accept Jesus as Messiah and transferred His covenant to the Church—was perhaps understandable when Jews were suffering in exile. Today it is a desperate theology, and an embarrassing one. The restoration of Jewish sovereignty, the ingathering of millions of exiles, the rebuilding of Jerusalem—these are the specific fulfillments of specific biblical prophecies, unfolding in real time. Every honest Christian has seen this and drawn the obvious conclusion. Those who still insist that God rejected His people are not making an honest theological argument. They are willfully blind to the obvious truth. For a beautiful musical rendition of this verse, see Rabbi Shlomo Katz's cover of Michael Shapiro's Everlasting Love: www.youtube.com/watch?v=c4aszHzF61E.

546. Rabbi Yehuda Leon Ashkenazi, *Sod Midrash HaToldot* 7:120.

547. Babylonian Talmud, Sanhedrin 98a.

548. Ibid.

549. Rabbi Yehuda Leon Ashkenazi, *Sod Midrash HaToldot*, 7:286. "The power of Joseph is found in his declaration before his death... This is his true strength. He shows us the path of return, the way back to the land."

550. Rabbi Yehuda Leon Ashkenazi, *Sod Midrash HaToldot*, 7:169.

Afterword

551. Rabbi Yehuda Leon Ashkenazi, *HaSod HaIvri*, 1:95: "Another image the Torah uses to describe our history is the idea of betrothal.

The essential dynamic between two people who are engaged—especially felt by the woman—is that the end of the engagement is eagerly awaited, yet also approached with anxiety. Betrothal is a temporary stage of preparation and testing. The entire relationship points toward its conclusion, because the engagement has no real meaning unless it culminates in marriage. And yet, the couple also fears that moment, unsure if they are truly ready for the weight and responsibility that marriage brings. This was the challenge faced by the generation of the wilderness, and it is the challenge facing Jews in exile today. These Jews are in a state of eternal engagement with Jerusalem—but from afar. It is a passionate betrothal, yet they fear the marriage itself. A two-thousand-year engagement is, to say the least, quite long. The bride longs for the meeting to finally happen, but deep inside she fears the upheaval that such a moment would bring. She hopes the meeting will be delayed—just a little longer. Until when? As long as it's not today. 'Next year in Jerusalem...'"

552. Rabbi Joseph B. Soloveitchik, *Kol Dodi Dofek* (1956), www.sefaria.org/Kol_Dodi_Dofek.

553. *Ethics of the Fathers* 2:15.

IN HONOR OF

ELIE & REBECCA

We are so proud of your efforts to bring to the forefront the need for our brethren in the Diaspora to heed the signs that so clearly signal the light of redemption.

May your writing continue to be a ray of light and may Hashem bless you and strengthen you in all that you do.

Howie & Terry Mischel

Judah & Ora Mischel

Sara & Ari Goldberg

Ariel & Yosef Ginsberg

To the man who proves you can
actually survive on coffee, prayer,
and writing manuscripts.

We are so incredibly proud of the wonderful Rabbi, Father, Husband, and Jewish Leader you are—even if we still don't know how you find time to sleep between your dedication to the Nation of Israel and writing insightful books.

May your wisdom always be deep, your disposition always remain sunny, and your love for and from your family always be bountiful. Keep walking this wonderful path; we're behind you every step (and every page) of the way.

With all our love, admiration and
a permanent spot on our bookshelf,

Opa and Grandma

In loving memory of

Naava Malka Livne

Naava Malka bat Aharon Mordechai
Hakohen v'Chana

Who saw the prophecies of Tanach
unfolding in our time,
whose heart burned for the
redemption of Am Yisrael,
and whose love for Israel and
the Jewish people inspired
all who knew her.

Chaim Livne

Rabbi Mischel,

We wish you great success with your new book about redemption and the American Jewish community. May it be as enlightening as your first book, “The War Against The Bible”.

You are a Talmid Chacham who has focused on the Torah portions that help us understand the challenging and confusing times that we are living in.

May HaShem continue to protect our nation and may he open the hearts of our friends and family in North America to join us soon for his redemption.

With blessings to you and your family,

Jonathan and Tamar Miller

With love and support
for Rav Elie for his continued
meaningful and heroic work
on behalf of Klal Yisroel!

The Suss Family

Mazal Tov to R' Elie Mischel

On publishing his new book,
Countdown: American Jews and God's Plan for Redemption.

It is an honor to pay tribute to R' Judah and Ora Mischel.
A couple who is involved and accomplishes
so much for K'lal Yisrael!
May HKB"H give them the strength to continue
in their avodat hakodesh.

With much admiration,

Ephraim and Chaya Miller

Rick and Patricia Neel

To the scattered of Israel,
near and far—

*"At that time I will bring you in,
and at that time I will gather you"*
(Zefaniah 3:20).

May this book awaken the prayer of
Kibbutz Galuyot within every heart,
drawing us home in body and spirit.
And may it serve as a segulah for
remembrance, return, and redemption—
until we are gathered as one before Hashem.

Jeff Craig

In loving memory of Albert Allen A"H

L'ilui Nishmat Avraham ben Salcha A"H

Anthony Abma

Michael &Chani Chapman

Debbie & Tommy Cope

Barry & Donna Gordon

Bobby & Ruby Kaplan

Laura Davis

Lisa An'Ne Dumon-Watson

Donna Jollay

Shawn Raymond

Emilia Arrendondo

Donna Lauria

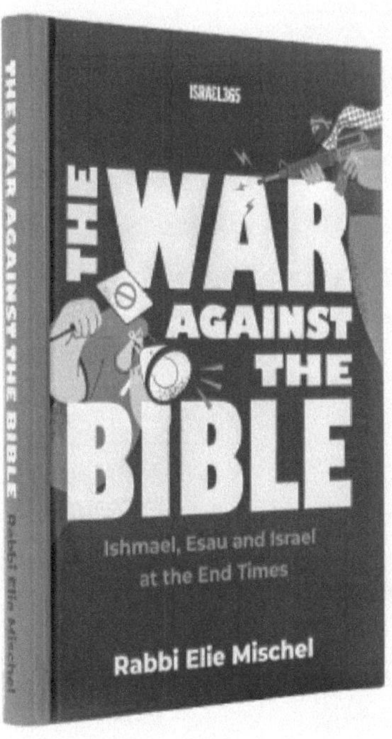

ISRAEL365
THE WAR AGAINST THE BIBLE
Ishmael, Esau and Israel at the End Times
Rabbi Elie Mischel
THE WAR AGAINST THE BIBLE Rabbi Elie Mischel

www.ingramcontent.com/pod-product-compliance
Ingram Content Group UK Ltd.
Pitfield, Milton Keynes, MK11 3LW, UK
UKHW041632190726
13854UKWH00006B/2453